Addicted to Christ

Addicted to Christ

*Remaking Men in Puerto Rican
Pentecostal Drug Ministries*

———

Helena Hansen

UNIVERSITY OF CALIFORNIA PRESS

University of California Press, one of the most distinguished university presses in the United States, enriches lives around the world by advancing scholarship in the humanities, social sciences, and natural sciences. Its activities are supported by the UC Press Foundation and by philanthropic contributions from individuals and institutions. For more information, visit www.ucpress.edu.

University of California Press
Oakland, California

Library of Congress Cataloging-in-Publication Data

Names: Hansen, Helena, 1969- author.
Title: Addicted to Christ : remaking men in Puerto Rican Pentecostal ministries / Helena Hansen.
Description: Oakland, California : University of California Press, [2018] | Includes bibliographical references and index. |
Identifiers: LCCN 2017045427 (print) | LCCN 2017050267 (ebook) | ISBN 9780520970168 () | ISBN 9780520298033 (cloth : alk. paper) | ISBN 9780520298040 (pbk. : alk. paper)
Subjects: LCSH: Recovery movement—Religious aspects—Christianity. | Recovery movement—Puerto Rico. | Masculinity—Religious aspects—Pentacostal churches. | Masculinity—Puerto Rico. | Substance abuse—Religious aspects—Pentacostal churches.
Classification: LCC BT732.45 (ebook) | LCC BT732.45 .H36 2018 (print) | DDC 289.9/40811097295—dc23
LC record available at https://lccn.loc.gov/2017045427
ClassifNumber   PubDate
DeweyNumber'—dc23   CatalogNumber

Manufactured in the United States of America

25   24   23   22   21   20   19   18
10   9   8   7   6   5   4   3   2   1

For Mark, Kirin, and Ananda, coauthors of this tale

CONTENTS

Between a Clinical and an Ethnographic Gaze

In the early 1990s I worked for the National AIDS Fund on assignment in the poorest city neighborhoods in New Jersey. My job was to walk street after street of public tenements and condemned buildings that sheltered people who were inject-ing heroin or smoking cocaine, looking for those living with HIV who could design peer interventions.

I found Leila recruiting for her storefront ministry in Newark. Before her Pen-tecostal conversion, she earned money for heroin through sex work and was infected with HIV. She also gave birth to ten children and had custody of her youngest child, a six-year-old boy with AIDS. In between clinic visits for her son, she ran her ministry's residential drug program and preached on corners where there was heavy drug traffic. Through Leila I met her pastor and his wife, ex-addicted migrants from Puerto Rico who had converted to Pentecostalism at Vic-tory Outreach Ministries and then opened a drug program of their own.

The program was something that Leila, her pastor, and his wife had created from the institutional models they knew—storefront churches. In a city with the nation's highest HIV infection rates among women and children, within a state that served as world headquarters for many pharmaceutical and health insurance companies and that had the country's wealthiest suburbs and poorest cities, there was little public investment in HIV prevention or addiction treatment. Leila worked sleeplessly to save the souls and lives around her.

After meeting Leila, I began to notice Pentecostal ministries in the low-income Latino and Black neighborhoods of every American inner city that I visited, including San Antonio, New York, Providence, Worchester, Chicago, Oakland, Hartford, and New Haven. Ex-addicts in these ministries held evangelist rallies in front of crack houses and shooting galleries,[1] performed youth theater in urban schools, and ran outreach programs in the prisons (Leland 2004). I asked myself if addiction ministries were a form of working-class, grassroots health activism.

My fascination with grassroots health activism led me to study medicine and anthropology in an MD-PhD program. In the early years of the HIV epidemic, anthropologists entered shooting galleries and crack houses to observe the social hierarchies of drugs and sex that fueled HIV transmission (Ratner 1992, Epele 2002) and the ways in which interlocking "syndemics" of substance abuse, violence, and HIV (Singer 1996) were killing an entire generation. I reasoned that if clinical medicine would take field research on the social causes of disease to the bedside—just as it takes research on the molecular causes of disease from the laboratory bench to the bedside—it could have an impact on health outcomes.

Five years later I was a medical student in an urban Connecticut hospital, admitting a nearly unconscious homeless man for abdominal pain. He had injected drugs for years and the staff called him a frequent flyer: a regular in the emergency room. His legs buckled under him, his belly poked through the folds of his hospital gown. After an ultrasound and an enema, his colon released twenty pounds of feces. As he cleared fecal toxins from his bloodstream he became more alert. The hospital staff could not have been less pleased. He demanded morphine for his pain, and when he did not get it, he grabbed a syringe and needle from his nurse and threatened to stick her with his HIV-positive blood.

The staff responded by dimming his lights, closing his door, and ignoring his calls for help on the intercom. They slipped in meal trays while he slept but did not linger to clear old dishes or to clean his bed. After two days of frantic intercom calls, the patient made good on a threat to smear feces on the walls of his room.

"He's disgusting!" grumbled the most seasoned nurse. The other nurses and a resident physician nodded. I asked the resident what had caused the patient's severe constipation, he told me noncompliance. Unaware that the patient had been on medication, I asked, "Noncompliance with what?" The resident snorted. "Noncompliance with our advice to stop using heroin because it paralyzes his intestines."

I clenched my jaw. If *only* he could just stop.

Until then I had not realized that my interest in addicted people started in childhood. My mother was a single parent working full time, so I spent much of my time with my grandparents in Oakland, California. The first floor of their house was a haven of plastic-covered easy chairs, Motown records, televisions in every room—including my grandparents' bedroom—and an enormous barbecue grill enshrined on the back porch. The second floor had three bedrooms that housed my mother, my brother, and myself along with a rotating collection of uncles in need of a place to stay.

My grandmother Mildred was the daughter of a successful Black female entrepreneur who opened her own beauty parlor in Oklahoma City in 1911. Mildred was a sharp dresser and an equally sharp money manager: in her mind, her investment funds neutralized her white supervisors' assumptions of her inferiority. My grandfather Johnnie—whose father had been a railroad Pullman porter in Shawnee, Oklahoma—told stories about walking uphill both ways in the snow to attend segregated schools during the Great Depression.

Mildred and Johnnie were proud and upwardly mobile, but there was also shame and rage in the air. They moved West during World War II because my grandfather had heard that in the Port of Oakland, a Black man could own his own company. And eventually he did. As a child I rode with him to his construction jobs, sitting next to the toolbox in the back of his shiny green 1952 Chevy pickup. He kept its engine, by then three decades old, purring by his constant attention. Oakland was indeed a place where, unlike Oklahoma, some White people would hire Black contractors.

But there was a hitch. More than once I heard the story of my grandfather's first bout of pneumonia, which he caught working in the rain from Christmas Eve until Christmas Day on the roof of a White family's home. His workers refused to work in the storm, so he did the job by himself. The White family did not pay him, pointing out that he had promised to finish before the holidays. My grandfather had no recourse in the all-White courts. A string of other failed contracts followed. In the long run, his business was not solvent, but he refused to fold it. Mildred worked in the Oakland schools and, tight lipped, she paid the bills.

Johnnie brought his rage home. He demanded perfection from his sons at school and at home. They foundered under the racist gazes of their teachers, and when they could not deliver, Johnnie beat them. Perhaps as a result, three out of four of my uncles—Bubsie, Billy, and James—struggled with alcohol and drugs. James had left home at sixteen and was heard from once every few years, drunk and cursing at my grandfather. Billy quietly nursed forty-ounce cans in his room upstairs in my grandparents' house, unable to hold a job or keep his driver's license due to multiple DUI arrests.

The uncle that was most painful for me to watch was my uncle Bubsie. Bubsie had been a football star in high school, and he was an avid reader who cited the Bhagavad Gita and Abraham Maslow in the same breath. When I reached high school and my mother refused to teach me to drive, he showed up in my room dangling the key to his VW bug from his fingers, prepared to risk his transmission for my freedom. I did not know then that his escalating binges on marijuana and cocaine would precipitate psychotic episodes that left him wandering the streets, muttering to himself and dodging the cars that he thought were following him. Unable to maintain his apartment, he moved back in with my grandparents, but they would not keep him. They were afraid of his outbursts, one of which landed him in handcuffs after he bit off the earlobe of a passerby on Telegraph Avenue. Another attempt at independent living—made while he was still in the throes of cocaine and marijuana use—ended with half his face burned by the bottle of Draino he used to threaten his roommate. Eight years later, in a state mental hospital, Bubsie died of heart failure likely caused by his psychiatric medications.

The irony was that my uncles had come of age during the Civil Rights Movement and were taught to aim high. James joined the military, Bubsie worked toward an engineering degree before dropping out of college, and Billy held a journalism degree. But their thwarted aspirations and substance use formed a vicious circle—shattering my grandparents' hopes for their sons. My grandmother blamed my grandfather for breaking their sons, and my grandfather blamed my grandmother for emasculating him by controlling their bank accounts. Their angry silence led them to divorce just before their fiftieth wedding anniversary.

Church had been the center of Mildred and Johnnie's lives; they and many of their childhood friends from Oklahoma attended the Methodist church two blocks from our home. Mildred and the churchwomen planned fundraising fashion shows, and heard financial advisors for their investment club. Johnnie and his church brothers set off from church on Saturdays in pickup trucks to go catfishing at Clearlake, ninety miles north, bringing the catch back to church for fish fries. My brother and I went to Sunday school, and church pageants at Christmas and Easter were occasions for Mildred and my mother to sew me lace-collared dresses and to buy me matching gloves and handbags. When my uncles decompensated, Mildred and Johnnie went to the pastor's house for counseling. Before their divorce, they went to the pastor in an attempt to stay together.

After their divorce, I alternated between going to the Methodist church with Johnnie, and to Mildred's newly adopted Black Baptist church half a mile away. My mother, Jackie, was not churchgoing; she was turned off by authoritarian preachers. But as the only one of her siblings who came out of the Civil Rights era with good health and a job, she was a moral standard bearer in the family. She was the child who achieved "perfection." She went to Stanford on a scholarship, one of three Black students to arrive in 1962. She traveled to Norway on an Eisenhower International Fellowship where she met my father then returned to America, where in two months she married and in three years divorced my father. My mother then earned a degree in social work. As a social worker, she was horrified by the racial patterns of foster care placement, which was often state-imposed on African American and Latina women living in poverty who tested positive for drugs. When I was in elementary school, my mother became the first Black Ph.D. student in U.C. Berkeley's developmental psychology program. Her mission was to correct racial bias in theories of child attachment that led to harmful foster care placements. Unfortunately, she was in the same department with Arthur Jensen and other proponents of racial-genetic determinants of intelligence. She got her degree, but she also challenged the claims of key faculty members, who saw to it that she did not get a viable academic job. Shut out of a research career, my mother returned as a social worker to a child protective service department where county guidelines forced her to place children in foster care against her will and against her knowledge of child development.

As pressures mounted, my mother's perfectionism became puritanical. Almost no processed sugar or caffeine passed her lips. She never used profanity, always kept our house meticulously clean, and monitored my every excursion. Later in life I realized that my grandmother's aunts and cousins—recent arrivals to California from Texas and Arkansas who my mother avoided because they had "strange ways" (they would not dance or show their legs)—were Holiness Pentecostals. My mother had more in common with them than she would admit. She embodied the ascetic personal morality characteristic of African American Holiness Pentecostal movements (Sanders 1996).

My uncles must have resented her. Uncle Bubsie once showed up at our door intoxicated, cursing and banging on the door hard enough to break its hinges while I hid behind the couch. Uncle James only came by to see my grandparents when my mother was not there, detonating his own drunken explosions. By the time I reached Puerto Rican street ministries, much about the strict daily discipline of ministry routines and the chaos of family life that the routines were supposed to guard against seemed familiar. Bubsie's death was followed by James' death from cocaine-related kidney failure. Billy drifted in and out of unemployment, but after my grandfather died, he joined Alcoholics Anonymous and my grandmother's church. He got credentialed and eventually taught English in the same middle school in which my grandmother had worked.

My family's frustrated aspiration, tenuous class background, and ethnic marginality guided my ethnographic curiosities. Although I had to check my tendency to project my family's concerns onto my island Puerto Rican informants, identifying with my informants might have enhanced my patience regarding our differences, as well as my interest in their self-image as members of families and communities rather than as deviants.[2] I noticed that my practice of inviting ex-cocaine and heroin users to my home was not matched my professional colleagues. As a public health researcher in Puerto Rico asked me in disbelief, "You mean, you let your daughter meet the addicts?"

Like most biomedical practitioners in Puerto Rico and the United States, I was taught the Biopsychosocial Model (Engel 1977) in medical school. In contrast to evangelists—who relate all forms of suffering to the state of one's relationship with God—the Biopsychosocial Model defines three discrete levels of influence on the health of an organism: biological, psychological, and social. The clinical diagnosis of substance dependence links physiological symptoms (such as tolerance and withdrawal symptoms) and psychological symptoms (such as the compulsion to use drugs) with social symptoms (such as avoidance of important occupational or recreational activities due to substance use). George Engel intended to call attention to neglected social factors with his Biopsychosocial Model, but in practice physicians often consider biology to be primary: physiological changes effect psychological changes, which in turn influence social adaptation. For these physicians, biomedicine enhances social functioning by improving physical functioning; social problems are caused by physical infirmities.

Because ex-addicted evangelists think of volition not in terms of biological vulnerability but in terms of spiritual power, they reject the central criterion for the diagnosis of substance dependence as described in the *American Psychiatric Association's Diagnostic and Statistical Manual* (DSM): loss of control. The idea of loss of control, in the biomedical frame, implies that an individual no longer is able to choose whether to use substances in a logical manner—he is the victim of his pathophysiology, psychopathology, or genetic inheritance. Many addiction specialists believe that framing addiction as disease reduces stigma and helps patients to accept and treat their conditions (McLellan et al. 2000).

The diagnosis of substance dependence offered in the DSM is seamlessly biomedical. Making the diagnosis requires a clinician to check off three or more items from a list of seven symptoms that the patient reports having had in the previous twelve months (*see* Appendix I DSMIV-TR). But moving from diagnosis to treatment in a doctor's office is not a straight path. Pharmacological treatments for narcotics dependence often yield suboptimal results and have side effects; and in the case of opioid maintenance for heroin dependence (such as the prescription drugs methadone and buprenorphine), they are so highly regulated that most physicians are not licensed to prescribe them (Greenfield 2005). Medical school and residency training in treating addiction is minimal. One study found that less than 1 percent of U.S. medical school curriculum hours are devoted to addictions (Miller et al. 2001), and only half of all U.S. residency programs offer any training in substance abuse intervention (Isaacson et al. 2000), despite the fact that substance abuse directly accounts for more than 10 percent of U.S. health expenditures (CASA 2009). As a result, many clinicians feel powerless when confronted with their most difficult patients: the addicted ones. Biomedical training does not provide clinicians with psychosocial tools; they resent their addicted patients as manipulators and, in turn, addicted patients suspect physicians' malice (Merrill, Rhodes, Deyo et al. 2002).

This thinning of social and cultural understandings of patients is acute in psychiatry—the biomedical specialty charged with treating addiction. In its effort to standardize diagnosis and treatment through biological models, psychiatry largely has become biopsychiatry and the strength of its doctor-patient communication has atrophied. Academic psychiatrists—with notable exceptions (e.g., Kleinman 1988, Kleinman 2007, Galanter 2005, Lewis 2011, Fullilove 2013)—focus on the neuroscience of mental disease and remain silent on spirituality and social connection. Psychiatrists understand and diagnose patients on their own biomedical terms rather than the patients' terms. Built on the authority of practitioners and the scientific expertise ensconced in pharmaceutical markets (Lakoff 2005, Martin 2006, Rose 2003, Healy 2006) that delimit pharmaceutical selves (Jenkins 2010, Martin 2006, Rose 2003, contemporary psychiatry does not recognize that many patients have their own theories of disorder and treatment. Neither does it recognize systemic ethnic and racial bias in health care (Roberts 2011, Metzl 2010), nor the criminalization of addiction through disproportionate drug-law enforcement in non-White neighborhoods (Alexander 2012). The outcome is that a great number of addicted people arrive at clinics desperate for help, but leave facilities alienated from their doctors.

Although biopsychiatry promises practitioners universal truths and power, its reductionism costs them; I repeatedly have seen that the patients who the hospital staff fear the most are the working-class Latino and black addicts.

This book represents my efforts to understand addiction from a vantage point as radically outside of biomedicine as I can imagine. Yet, in the end, I found commonalities between the biomedical and evangelical understandings of addiction, and recognized overlap in the practices of addicted people who move from biomedical to evangelical institutions and back again. Addiction ministries are autonomous from the clinic, but also are a reaction to the clinic. At times they are combined with biomedicine. Well-meaning people on both sides of the issue benefit from a nuanced understanding of the other position, and of the elements common to biomedicine and evangelism that ultimately move people beyond addiction. After all, addiction often leads to severe distress during which the meanings that people attach to their acts—and the openings that they find for hope and change—are matters of life or death.

ACKNOWLEDGMENTS

This book already has had a long life. Its early germination and cultivation began with its first official readers, Linda-Anne Rebhun, Kate Dudley, Philippe Bourgois, and the late Patricia Pessar, along with Tony George who helped me to cross-fertilize my ethnography with clinical investigations, even inside of the ministries. My first writing group partners had a profound early influence on my thinking: Ping-Ann Addo, Lyneise Williams, Judith Casselberry, Jennifer Tilton, and Gilbert Mireles.

I thank Roy Thomas, Robert and Mindy Fullilove, Robert Levine, Woody Lee, Kai Erikson, Nancy Angoff, Curtis Patton, Nora Groce, and my brother—Ben Hansen—for the inspiration and enduring support during my field research and beyond. My brother and sister—Martin Damhaug and Sara Brinch—and my stepmother, Kari Damhaug, also inspired me.

The financial and moral support in those early years of the NIH Medical Scientist Training Program, the Social Science Research Council, Yale's Williams Fund, John Perry Miller Fund, Council on Latin American Studies, and also my husband Mark Turner (who contributed multiple insightful readings of fieldnotes and drafts), my mother Jacquelyne Faye Jackson; my grandparents, John and Mildred Jackson, and Conrad and Eva Hansen (posthumously); my parents-in-law, Joyce and Al Dixon; my grandparents-in-law, Violet and Lewis Jackson and Millie Brown; and my father, Arne Bjerring Hansen, made this project possible.

I thank those who generously opened the doors to my study of addiction treatment, Christian life, and mental health policy in Puerto Rico, including those informants who I cannot thank by name, as well as Margarita Alegria, Carmen Albizu, Salvador Santiago, Irene Melendez, Ann Finlinson, Hector Colon, Tomas

Matos, Rafaela Robles, Maria del Mar Garcia, Gisela Negron, Midred Vera, Nemesio Moreno, Victor Vargas, and many others.

Jessica Rodriguez, Raul Medina, and Maria Teresa Botello gave me tremendous emotional and practical support during my field research. Juliana Herrera and the staff of Little Angels Daycare Center in Ponce, Alba Gomez, Theresa Rosenplanter, the staff of Creating Kids and Calvin Hill Daycare Centers, Sarah Bratchell, Ashley and Sharde Morris, Mrs. Smith, Mrs. Guo, Magda Ramos, and Neeraja Sankaran for providing childcare during my many hours of researching and writing this project in the early years. I thank my son and daughter, Ananda and Kirin Turner, for accompanying me in my field research and for the insights they have given me about family life.

In the years that followed that early period, my analysis and writing slowly blossomed through the loving care of editor Adi Hadad (thanks to a Columbia University Press book fellowship); my addiction psychiatry mentor, Marc Galanter; my second writing group including Mindy Fullilove, Ann Burack-Weiss, Jack Saul, Lourdes Rodriguez, and Maura Spiegel. As I trained in addiction medicine, Annatina Miescher, founder of the Sobriety Garden, as well as art therapist Lena Friedman and horticultural therapist Caren Bowers tutored me in art and gardening as spiritual techniques of transformation.

Lucy Anderton, Arlene Davila, Kim Hopper, Bruce Link, Caroline Parker, Bruce Grant, Arthur Kleinman, Alondra Nelson, Faye Ginsburg, and Sally Merry also gave timely and insightful suggestions. Bringing this book to the point of completion were the devoted editors and creatives Rayna Rapp, Emily Martin, and Peter Bearman.

Introduction

BAPTISM

Pastor Mendoza[1] stood in waist-high water. His face radiated sunlight, as did the pool that the ministry brothers had cleaned and filled that morning. The sun also warmed the pastel-painted walls of the ministry's residence for ex-addicts. Together the pastor and the home director caught each of the newly born Christians as they crossed their arms on their chests, closed their eyes, and fell backward into the water (fig. 1). Brothers and sisters in Christ sank into the pool one after another, and onlookers clapped as they emerged. The cheering got a few decibels louder when the grandfather of the group—a thin, stooped man in his seventies—bent his arthritic knees to immerse himself in water. As he left the pool two young sisters wrapped him in a towel. His alcoholic tremor shook a drop of water from the tip of his nose.

I fumbled with my camera as Eli and Wanda chattered in the festive mood of the morning. They were discussing whether to get in line; neither wanted to be left out. Eli was dressed for the occasion in shorts, a loose T-shirt, and rubber sandals—clothes that she would not be permitted to wear at the Victory Academy on any other day, when exposed knees and toes were taboo. Wanda was less certain about baptism, as it would require her to change out of her long rayon dress. Meanwhile, Yeyo, the assistant director of the home, found a microphone and urged candidates to line up.

The pastor's sons, playing synthesizer and drums, began singing "*Libre, yo soy libre—¡Las cadenas del pecado han sido rota!*" (Free, I am free—the chains of sin have been broken!)[2] in an upbeat *alabanza*, a song of praise. Men gathered arm in arm, and started to *brincar para Cristo* ("jump for Jesus") to the rhythm. Even the

1

FIGURE 1. A baptism at Victory Academy. Photo by Helena Hansen.

normally reserved wife of the pastor got carried away and began to hop in place. The band wound down with an *adoración*, a slow song of thanks. Tears streamed from the faces of a few brothers. A newly baptized man embraced the pastor, the tattoos on his muscular shoulders heaving with each silent sob.

Water baptism is a ritual of purification and consecration dating to pre-Christian Judaism. First-century Christians saw it as a reenactment of the death and resurrection of Christ. At this ministry, being reborn meant not only that the individual was no longer a marginal drug addict, but also that he or she joined the ranks of the privileged; the chosen. And that the chosen had an alternative addiction; one that—like drugs—altered their consciousness, heightened their senses, and provided moments of ecstasy, but—also like drugs—required total absorption and vigilance: an addiction to Christ.

Rings of onlookers surrounded the baptismal pool. Rebirth attendants stood knee deep in water preparing for delivery, lifting the heads and shoulders of the baptized from the water, one by one. Their vision was that those at the periphery of the pool would someday work their way toward the center, preaching, baptizing, and making room for new converts at the circle's edge.

Even the building that housed converted ex-addicts embodied renewal. An abandoned motel destroyed in hurricane Hugo, ministry recruits had patched its walls, rewired its electrical system, and landscaped its grounds with flowers. In the ministry office, a photo of the motel's crumbling entrance just after hurricane Hugo hung next to the current entrance, smoothed over with fresh plaster. On the motel's exterior wall was a mural of a man, syringes littering the ground at his feet, his arms reaching up to a great cross.

THINKING AT THE MARGIN

Watching the baptism, it seemed that a natural experiment was unfolding in front of me. Working-class addicted people were attempting to take matters into their own hands, to create and invest in a form of life outside of narcotraffic. Some of them had converted days before, and were now only blocks away from the crack houses and heroin shooting galleries they had known. Yet, in the buoyant mood of the baptism, they seemed to be in another world.

This effort to create another world is the focus of this book. Clinical approaches to addiction presume an intrapersonal imbalance or deficit that must be corrected to return individuals to "normal" social functioning. In contrast, Victory Academy presumes that "normal" social functioning is itself corrupt, that it must be transcended through a transformation of the relationship between self and society and, ultimately, a transformation of society itself. My research for this book took me from society—recognizing street ministries as social movements that resist the logic of narcotraffic; to self—examining the individual spiritual practices of converts that enable them to resist; and back to society—the ways that self-making creates collectivities that redefine what is "normal."

How do people with nothing make something? How do these people gain a sense of purpose, self-respect, and, ultimately, power?

The baptism at Victory Academy began to offer answers to questions that I had asked as an anthropologist and as a doctor who specialized in addiction; I was interested in the ways that people coped in the face of great odds. I knew that Puerto Rico's narcotraffic was the result of a crisis of capital, just as it was in the decimated cities of the mainland United States. It was a crisis of post-industrial ways of life, of waning personal security, of lack of trust in the future, and of uncertain social reproduction. Lack of capital—not just economic, but also social, cultural, and symbolic capital (Bourdieu 1986)—leads to destabilization, displacement, and disengagement that further drains capital. This is the vicious cycle faced by Puerto Rican workers when manufacturing disappears, faced in U.S. inner cities when urban renewal and planned shrinkage policies dislocate residents, and faced globally by non-dominant religious and ethnic groups in the wake of war and disaster. In this vortex, homes are lost, neighborhood social networks are shredded, and disconnected individuals turn to addictive substances for momentary relief (Fullilove 2004, Saul 2013, Erikson 1976). Victory Academy attempted not only to heal individuals from loss, but also to create new collective capital.

In 2000, by the time I moved to Puerto Rico to begin field research street ministries like Victory Academy made up three-fourths of all substance-abuse treatment centers registered with the Puerto Rican state (Melendez et al. 1998). Rather than "treatment," however, they offered a millenarian vision of redemption and transcendence of a corrupt world. Unlike clinics that identify biological or psychological predispositions to addiction, or that try to help patients to come to terms with traumatic memories, street ministries trained converts to fix their gaze forward and not dwell on the past. The only space they allotted for retrospection was in evangelical testimony, which contrasted past with present to narratively enact transformation and renewal. Converts were trained to cast old wounds aside, to shed them along with their pre-conversion selves.

My informants did not dwell on memories, but they were haunted by the lives they tried to leave behind. From my backroom conversations with Eli, at eighteen the youngest convert at Victory Academy, I learned of her childhood rape at the hands of her foster father. Each night Samaria, the leader of the women's home, cradled Eli through violent nightmares. I knew that, the year before, Wanda had left her sleeping toddlers at home alone in search of heroin, and that she now traveled two hours to San Juan for court hearings to get them back from foster care. Yeyo, who had lost his job as a mechanic because of crack addiction, later opened an auto shop at the Academy to train young male converts in repairs. Yeyo's ex-wife, skeptical of his conversion, disappeared with their sons. At the baptism, Yeyo was torn between his spiritual progeny in the ministry, and his compulsion to search for his sons. Additionally, despite Victory Academy's promise to free women from abusive men, Eli and Wanda would find little room for themselves in the reinvented patriarchy of Victory Academy, where men were spiritual heads of home, and unmarried, willful women were a threat. Yeyo, Eli, and Wanda saw in the ministry a chance to renew themselves, to plaster over old wounds and build on firm ground. Unlike the motel that housed the ministry, however, the transformation of their identities and domestic lives was never complete.[3]

Incomplete transformations of social hierarchies are common in grassroots religious movements; examples include Muslim women's attempt to forge their own leadership within the gendered structure of Islam, in places ranging from Egypt to African America (Rouse 2004, Mahmood 2004); and black Christian women's church-based political activism and influence on male preachers (Frederick 2003, Casselberry 2017), and the blend of progressive and conservative politics reflected in African American televangelism (Walton 2009). Pentecostalism in particular historically has housed an array of gender and racial politics, ranging from Aimee Semple McPherson, single mother and preacher who founded Four Square Gospel, one of the largest Pentecostal ministries of the early twentieth century; and William

Seymour, African American self-ordained pastor whose interracial 1906 Azusa Street revival was the progenitor of contemporary Pentecostalism; to televangelists Jimmy Swaggart and Jim Bakker, leaders of the anti-feminist and anti-integrationist U.S. Religious Right in the latter twentieth century.

Pentecostalism serves as an adaptable framework for social organization and cultural innovation, rather than being a stable set of practices, beliefs, or politics. To see its many valences, I provide foreground on the interpretations that converts make of themselves. I try to be cautious in applying theoretical frameworks that would give me narrative control, and am mindful of the words of social theorist bell hooks:

> No need to hear your voice. Only tell me about your pain. I want to know your story. And then I will tell it back to you in a new way. Tell it back to you in such a way that it has become mine, my own. Re-writing you, I write myself anew. I am still author, authority. I am still [the] colonizer, the speaking subject, and you are now at the center of my talk (Hooks 1990, 241).

Narrative control can lead to colonization akin to that which contemporary anthropologists critique; it also can lead anthropologists to miss innovations occurring at social margins.

In medical anthropology, much of the contemporary ethnography of social margins builds on concepts of social suffering, in which an individual's suffering is "taken as a manifestation of social structural oppression/or collective experience of cultural trauma" (Wilkinson 2005, Wilkinson and Kleinman 2016), as well as structural violence: the everyday violence of exclusion, deprivation, and vulnerability caused by institutional structures and policies that create inequalities (c.f. Scheper-Hughes and Bourgois 2004, Farmer 2005). These studies illuminate how power inequalities exact tolls on the bodies and minds of people on the margins. Global capitalist extremes of accumulation, deprivation, and war rob marginal people of their humanity. In post-industrial society, taken-for-granted bodily routines and popular discourses in themselves serve as technologies of control, theorized by Michel Foucault (1976) as biopower, in which people unwittingly reinforce their own domination as they manage and discipline themselves.

These bodies of work illustrate that individuals do not engineer their own marginality, but they leave open the question of how marginalized people can deliberately influence their own lives. Staying experience near to those at the bottom of social hierarchies, moral economy uses ethnography and popular history to theorize actions that appear self-destructive instead as acts of survival and resistance. Marxist historian E. P. Thompson (1971), who first elaborated the term "moral economy" in his study of the peasant bread riots of eighteenth-century Britain, and anarchist political scientist James Scott (1977), who popularized moral economy in his studies of Malaysian rice farmers, were both interested in peasant resistance to the encroachment of free market capitalism on the older systems of patronage and reciprocity that had ensured peasants' subsistence. In the United States, urban ethnographers also contrasted the moral systems of the industrial poor with the dominant structures that threaten their survival. In the 1970s, anthropologist Carol Stack's 1974 study of reciprocity among extended kin networks of African American women as a survival strategy challenged U.S. Secretary of Labor Daniel Patrick Moynihan's report depicting black single mothers as the pathological producers of a culture of poverty.

In the decades that followed, urban ethnographers adopted moral economy as a framework to understand how some inner-city blacks and Latinos came to see the drug trade as honorable, and to analyze drug-use practices as based on reciprocity and solidarity (Reinarman 1979, Murphy 1987, Bourgois 1995). These studies highlighted their logics of survival, but concluded that these logics locked them into short-term strategies that ultimately maintained their oppression rather than changing the institutions that constrained them. This analytical approach has been enriched by post-structural ethnographers such as Cheryl Mattingly, who describes hope among the families of poor, severely ill African American children as an active *practice* rather than an emotion or attitude. For her, hope is "the practice of creating, or trying to create, lives worth living even in the midst of suffering . . . to forge new communities of care" (Mattingly 2010, 6). She considers "larger macrostructures as powerful cultural resources . . . that inform life on the ground, not as containers that enclose it" (Mattingly 2010, 47).

The view that marginalized people have developed specific practices of hope, or—in the case of the street ministries described here—technologies of transformation, challenges the idea that social suffering is passive. It raises the question of how marginalized people imagine other ways of living; how they enter the state of openness to new relations and directions described by philosopher Gilles Deleuze as "becoming" (Biehl and Locke 2010), and how they work "to construct a livable world on the other side of their experiences of contact and colonialism" (Robbins 2013, 459). Imagining other ways of living requires vision and action; it calls for moral entrepreneurs who can name, interpret, and dramatize the areas where social hierarchies are contested (Becker 1963), and for moral pioneers who can creatively draw on "prior social relations and cultural understandings [to] condition the uses . . . [of new] technologies" (Rapp 2011, 12).

The details of how people imagine and interpret their alternatives matter. In the United States (including Puerto Rico), the figure of the inner city black or Latino addict sits in the center of debates about whether poverty is culturally or structurally determined, and about the merits of "bootstrapping" and mutual aid as opposed to a systemic political-economic overhaul. Some call on the addicted poor to discipline themselves, to earn societal inclusion and respect. Others call for a reordering of the State to address unemployment and basic needs as fundamental causes of addiction. Few ask if and how addicted poor people already are positioning themselves for change. Within a U.S. political discourse that casts evangelical politics as a product of the conservative white middle and lower classes, the complex practices and motives of evangelists from non-dominant ethnic and racial groups rarely are examined.

Puerto Rican street ministries address the social and political marginalization of ex-addicted converts with a narrative of collective redemption and ascendance. Pentecostal ex-addicts cast themselves as the nidus for worldwide re-enchantment, as reflected in their written and oral histories of themselves. In these histories, addicts are the unlikely instruments through which the Holy Spirit redeems an apocalyptic reality, placing addicts at the center, rather than the margins, of world events. Ironically, Puerto Rico itself is both marginal and central to global political economies. It sits at the geographical and political margin between the United States and Latin America, its burgeoning narcotraffic is the product of the Puerto Rico's rapid social transformation to meet the needs of U.S. national corporations, originally for low-cost labor and more recently as a primary corporate tax shelter. Puerto Ricans have U.S. citizenship and aspire to the living standards of the U.S. mainland, but do not control local capital. This creates the conditions for consumption of imports and for profound debt, and creates the political conditions to blame drug trade as the cause—rather than the result—of island-wide disinvestment. In this milieu, by 2000, the island's transition to managed healthcare emerged as the flagship of Puerto Rico's modernity and compatibility with U.S. mainland economy. Yet the governor—a physician—declared addiction a "spiritual-social" problem better addressed by faith- and community-based organizations than by biomedicine.

Street ministries raise questions about whether techniques of spiritual transformation are ultimately liberatory, whether they are complicit with domination, and whether liberation and domination are mutually exclusive. Here I track these questions through the attempts of a group of addicted, economically displaced Puerto Ricans to build spiritual power; to reinvent gender, family, and work in the alternate social order of self-fashioned ministries.

TRADING ON MORALITY

Ramón sat under the canvas awning that, with eight rows of rusted folding chairs and a makeshift altar of unfinished wood, marked the worship space at Victory Academy. As I studied the green tattoos that wound around his arms, his voice went up in pitch, he was silent for a moment. He was telling me about his daughters, born in the same year to two different women in a "crazy time" in his life, when he was injecting heroin.

His daughters, now nine years old, had shown up at his house wearing makeup. He made no comment. Instead, he grinned, "I played a trick on them." He made them a big breakfast, then asked them to clean after themselves. When they said "But Daddy, we're little, we don't know how . . . " he pointed to the Bible, "where it says 'Everything in its time.' I say 'If you're too little to clean, you're too little to wear lipstick.' "

Although Ramón was not formally employed—his tattoos and criminal record made it difficult for him to get jobs—he was being discipled, that is, trained in spiritual leadership. "Now that I'm assistant director of the Academy, their mothers come to me for advice."

Had Ramón made the transformation that people who are exhausted by addiction dream of? Was he—now an Academy director, trusted father and advisor—no longer an addict? Who is an "addict"?

In Puerto Rico, the people that I found in treatment for addiction did not mention withdrawal symptoms or the amounts of drugs they used when describing themselves as addicts. They described the moment that they lost their position in their families—of abandoning children and losing partners, or of being evicted from their parents' homes—as the turning point in their self-perception as an addict.

When the Puerto Rican popular press describes addicted people, it shows depraved behavior around gendered roles in families. In the period of Ramón's heroin use, daily newspapers ran articles with lines such as: "Addicts would even push their addicted sisters into prostitution to raise money for their fixes" (Suarez 1995). Such images were presaged by temperance-era discourses in which the voices of Puerto Rican feminist elites converged with those of local evangelists (as they did in Europe and North America), arguing that male Puerto Rican laborers caused their own poverty by drinking away their income and abandoning their families (Rosario Urrutia and Barcelo Miller 1989). A 1917 prohibitionist ad campaign in a Puerto Rican evangelical newsletter, for instance, featured a man on a barstool, chained to a bottle labeled "Slave to Rum," while in his home his crying daughter says to her mother "I'm hungry. Why hasn't Daddy come home?" (see fig. 2).

Addiction is gendered and laden with power inequalities. Davis (1994) observed that a Latin American man is labeled an addict if he is unable to fulfill his role as family provider, lowering his stature in his community; although heavy drinking is socially sanctioned, addiction (defined as alcohol or drug use that interferes with upholding social responsibilities) is associated with moral weakness. In U.S. cities, the narcotics trade has long generated its own social hierarchy. Those at the top who sell but do not use, or who use but keep their use under control, claim moral and psychological superiority (Hanson, Beschner, Walters et al. 1985). The type of drug used, the method of use, and the source of income to pay for drug supplies also figure into hierarchies. Drug users have described crack cocaine smoking as more stigmatized than cocaine sniffing, impersonal theft as more ethical than theft from friends or family, and sex-for-drug exchanges between acquaintances as more respectable than street prostitution (Inciardi, Lockwood

Stigma

PUERTO RICO EVANGÉLICO

"PRO CHRISTO"

REVISTA EVANGÉLICA QUINCENAL.
Sale a la luz los días 10 y 25 de cada mes.
Suscripción: En E. U. Cuba y México........75 ctvs. al año
En los demás países .... $1.00 al año
Las suscripciones se pagarán por adelantado.
Entered as second-class matter July 10, 1912, at the post office at Ponce, P. R., under the Act of March 3, 1879.

Juan Rodríguez Cepero, Director.
Redactores: Carlos Barrios Zapata, Ensenada; José Santana, Ponce; T. M. Corson, Humacao; Daniel Echavarría, Loíza; Srta. Nora E. Silel, Bayamón; José Espada Marrero, Ponce.
Philo W. Drury, Administrador.
Administración y Redacción: Calle del Jobo, —
Dirección Postal, apartado 537, Ponce, P. R.
Editado por la "Compañía Tipográfica Puerto Rico Evangélico."

AÑO 5   **PONCE, PUERTO RICO, ABRIL 10 DE 1917**   **NÚM. 19**

Mientras el padre está borracho,   la niña dice a su madre: "Tengo hambre, ¿por qué papá no viene?"

LA MALDICION DEL LICOR Y SU EFECTO EN EL HOGAR.

Nótese la apariencia del rostro del pobre hombre. El vicio del licor le aprisiona terriblemente a la botella, y él necesita ayuda para vencer su pasión por la bebida. Ud. puede ayudarle. Favorezca la causa de la prohibición, ayudando en la campaña a extirpar para siempre de esta isla el alcohol. Esto traerá gozo y felicidad a la esposa y niños, en cuyo hogar ahora es todo miseria, hambre y desesperación.

FIGURE 2. "I'm hungry. Why hasn't Daddy come home?" Cartoon from *Puerto Rico Evangélico*, 1917.

and Pottieger 1993, Rosenbaum 1981). Drug trade itself is structured around a motif of dominance and dependence, community respectability and stigma.

Domination and dependence also are recurrent motifs in Puerto Rico's political history. Puerto Rico has been a U.S. possession since 1898; its people are U.S. citizens and are eligible for most U.S. federal welfare benefits. In the last two decades of the twentieth century, Puerto Rico saw 60% of its population qualify for welfare benefits, and had unemployment rates as high as 20% (Cockburn 2003, Chavez 1998, Buckley 1998). Its employment patterns and federal subsidies also led to a gender reversal in family economics. Puerto Rican men saw higher unemployment rates than that of women due to preferential hiring of women by international industries. Industries noted lower absenteeism, reduced union membership, and the acceptance of lower wages among women workers. Additionally, Puerto Rican women with children qualified more easily for federally funded public assistance than did men (Safa 1995a). Excluded from both legal industries and government entitlements, men disproportionately look to the illicit drug economy with its violently enforced hierarchies of power—from cartel leaders down to the addicted consumers subject to the vagaries of daily street supplies. Many men turn to the drug economy in hopes of gaining autonomy, but find themselves violently dominated by drug suppliers and by law enforcement. The drugs on which their bodies depend thus become a medium for political control by drug cartels and by the State.

With its connotation of dependence and lack of self-determination, a gendered analysis of narcotics addiction among unemployed Puerto Rican men could frame it as the post-industrial phase of what Edward Said (1978) called the feminization of the colonized, Oriental male. Although popular images of Latin American and U.S. urban drug traders portray their hypermasculine excesses of aggression and accumulation, they portray addicted men living in those places as powerless victims.

Street ministries offer an alternative, austere masculinity. Most of the addiction ministries I surveyed in Puerto Rico used no medication for withdrawal, not even Tylenol.[4] Converts fast to build spiritual strength, putting the needs of the spirit before those of the body and relying on the Holy Spirit for sustenance. Where biomedicine works to eliminate pain, in Pentecostalism pain has spiritual value; it cleanses and strengthens. Within the Pentecostal logic, suffering is not a problem calling for relief. Suffering is a test of faith and a call to transcend the body.

These relationships with spirits, the way converts distinguish themselves through ascetic practice, and converts' growing biblical knowledge are elements of what I call spiritual capital. In tandem with religious studies scholar Verter (2003), I adapt the construct from social theorist Pierre Bourdieu,[5] who posited relationship-based *social capital*, as well as education and knowledge-based *cultural capital*, as forms of symbolic capital that are to some degree interchangeable with economic capital, and which enable the reproduction of social hierarchies from one

FIGURE 3. Evangelist with bullhorn in Ponce's Town Square. Photo by Helena Hansen.

generation to the next. Although Bourdieu's formulations of capital focus on the strategies of the upper strata to maintain its position, I examine an alternative capital located in moral economies of the poor seeking to change their position. Critics of Bourdieu's social capital theory question his assumption that the poor lack social capital (Lopez and Stack 2002). They broaden Bourdieu's formulation of social capital by including non-mainstream social networks—such as those of churches—arguing that these alternative social assets and strategies are key for black and Latino communities because "the social capital that works through states and markets is not race-neutral" (Lopez and Stack 2002, 11).

Anthropologist Elizabeth Brusco (1995), writing of evangelical converts in Colombia, cites the "reformation of machismo" by their clean-living doctrine, which curbs male spending on alcohol, gambling, and extramarital affairs as a source of their upward mobility. Sociologist David Martin builds on this idea of alternate sources of capital to explain why Pentecostalism has won over so many converts from Catholicism in Latin America, writing that "Analysts of the post-modern city have referred without much exaggeration to the 'impacted ghettoes' and 'ungovernable spaces' of megacities. . . . This is where the domestic order and cleanliness of the Protestant, the secure family, and the church support systems create social capital out of nothing" (Martin 2002) (fig. 3 and fig. 4).

FIGURE 4. Billboard near Ponce: "I don't question your existence.—God." Photo by Helena Hansen.

Street ministries are self-help organizations in which ex-addicted sufferers become experts in their own healing. As ministry members progress, they gain authority and spiritual power, propagating themselves through a pyramid scheme of sequential recruitment and leadership. This contrasts with patients in biomedicine, who progress by submitting themselves more fully to the authority of medical professionals, becoming "compliant" or "adherent" patients. Across the Americas, a growing number of evangelical ministries are running residential drug-rehabilitation centers and gang recovery programs that address addiction (Flores 2013, Brenneman 2011).

The distinguishing feature of these ministries is their attempt to rework relationships. Converts are told to call on the Holy Spirit for spiritual strength to suffer through withdrawal and cravings, sleeping on bare floors, and feeding themselves on sparse donations from local stores. They are told to look to fellow worshipers for new "families in Christ" when their families of origin have rejected them, and to seek help from community congregations in order to live "*por fe*" or by faith alone—relying on donations and the ministries' micro-industries (such as selling bottled water or chocolates on street corners). Although street ministries do not directly challenge the political systems and economic inequalities that produce narcotraffic, there are elements of the Pentecostalism of street ministries that serve as cultural critique. Ministries reject mass consumption and personal accumulation as a way to transcend the entrapments of popular culture.

Studies of Pentecostal rehabilitation in other parts of Latin America point to the influence of middle class white U.S. congregations and their neoliberal politics (O'Neill 2015), but many Puerto Rican street ministers see themselves as outside of worldly politics. Their discourse is otherworldly; converts renounce their bodily concerns to cultivate a connection to a dimension of spirits that gives them discernment—a way of perceiving and navigating the motivations and temptations of those around them. The less they rely on material comforts, the stronger their connection to spirits, the more elevated their consciousness and the more rewarding their emotional and sensory experience, as they become "addicted to Christ."

This image of transferred addiction adapts a broader motif of rupture in Charismatic Christianity. Pentecostals urge adherents to break completely with the mundane, and to pursue salvation through contact with the Holy Spirit, marking a "split between the transcendental and the mundane [that] is thus as extreme in Pentecostal and Charismatic Christianity as it is in any other form of Christianity or in any other world religion" (Robbins 2009, 62). This split contrasts with other religions, many of which "are not structured around a radical distinction between the transcendental and the mundane" (Robbins 2009, 59). Thomas Csordas builds on this idea of rupture when asking about the broader social significance of the global Charismatic Renewal; "whether we are witnessing an era of re-sacralization or re-enchantment" (Csordas 2009, 91). In using the term "re-enchantment," he alludes to Max Weber's classic work on the Protestant work ethic as the cultural foundation for a modern secular capitalism. Weber points to the Calvinist doctrine of predestination as producing a psychological need of followers to appear successful as a result of their material labor to signal that they were saved (although perversely hard work and success were no guarantee of having been predestined for salvation). This compulsion to labor and produce good works carried forward in the industrial era and shed its Calvinist roots in contemporary, bureaucratic forms of life that are "disenchanted" in their reduction of human activity to a calculus of maximization (Weber 1958). Csordas argues that the popularity of Charismatic and Pentecostal Christianity can be explained, in part, by the ways that Charismatic worship is "imbued with an aura of enchantment;" by a sense of alterity that is heightened through practices such as speaking in tongues, and by the "sensuous immediacy" of revelatory visions and spirit possession (Csordas 2009). Tanya Luhrmann further illuminates this dynamic in her description of middle-class American evangelicals who walk and "talk with God," who see their worship as a way to cultivate a personal relationship with God, a relationship that infuses the everyday with the mystical (Luhrmann 2012, Luhrmann 2004). The worshipers in her study therefore describe their enchantment as relational.

Despite the received wisdom that charismatic Christianity is centered on personal, inward transformation, rupture and re-enchantment are social processes. As Courtney Handman points out, Protestant missions have been associated with a "modernist refusal of sociality" with the ethos of individualism and private property of John Locke's social contract. Yet, ethnographies of charismatic Christianity reveal a rich social matrix of worshippers attempting to enact authentic Christianity with and against each other (Handman 2015). Thomas Csordas' (1994) classic ethnography of charismatic faith healing describes healers' manipulations of memory and sensory phenomena to craft a "sacred self." Although the goal is to transform selves, transformation requires carefully choreographed communication between supplicants and healers. The charisma, or gifts, of participants in these rituals are manifest due to the skills of healers and the concerted participation of other converts. Thus, the rupture and re-enchantment of Charismatic Christians are produced by collective practices (see also Comaroff 1985). But how complete is this rupture? Who ultimately benefits, and how?

This book examines the ways ex-addicted Pentecostals work toward rupture. One strategy for rupture is the performance of alternative masculinities. Having lost credibility with their families in the course of their addiction, converted men present themselves to their parents and spouses as spiritual heads of home. They draw on images of Christ to convert mainstream masculinity into an evangelical manhood that is based on domesticity, emotional responsiveness, self-sacrifice, and spiritual knowledge. This contrasts with the rise and fall of one of the only street ministries in Puerto Rico to cater to women. In their bid to cultivate the respectability and upward mobility of its male recruits, the ministries adopt a middle-class, patriarchal model of the family, over the working-class, female-headed extended families from which most of its membership comes, ultimately limiting the possibilities for women in the ministries.

I revisited several converted men and the outcome of their strategies of gender and domesticity two years after my original field research. Through these individuals we see that Pentecostalism—premised on the ultimate authority of personal, mystical experience—often is billed as an individualist replacement for extended family networks of the poor. In practice, however, Pentecostalism builds on these networks and its success is contingent on them. Together these chapters flesh out the promise and the limitations of Pentecostal strategies to rework gender and family as social technologies of transformation.

CHRONICITY AND CHANGE

Is addiction a disease?

Eight years after my research in Puerto Rican street ministries, in my last month of an addiction psychiatry fellowship, I was assigned to the inpatient addictions unit of a large New York City hospital. The staff hastily passed patients' rooms, hovering two feet from the door. Thick glass insulated the nursing station from patients who frantically knocked on its window to ask for phone calls—and for sedatives.

I made a point of greeting a Puerto Rican woman who the medical assistants warned me was "unpredictable." She was admitted the night before, had been sleeping all morning, but sat upright when I approached. Her hospital gown slipped off of her shoulder, showing skin as grey as the roots of her brassy hair. "Where is my methadone?!" she barked. Explaining that we hadn't started morning medications, I caught her fist squarely in my chest, all she could muster from her withered arm. I froze, leaning toward her bed. Within seconds someone pulled me into the hall as medical assistants and nurses formed a circle around her. The crisis team appeared: African American former high school football stars hired from local housing projects. They told her she was going to get some rest, and held her to the bed as she screamed for methadone. A Filipino nurse injected her with tranquilizers.

Six hours later, nodding from the medications, she called me in to apologize. "I'm sorry about that—it's just, you know, I need my methadone."

My supervisor scolded me for walking so far into the patient's room. "You see how the drug hijacks their brains." In our classroom he had stood at the chalkboard, drawing dopamine receptors in the nucleus accumbens of the brain and its pathways to the forebrain, the seat of conscious decision making. He cited experiments derived from the behaviorist conditioning models of B. F. Skinner, describing the pleasurable reward of cocaine and heroin as "focusing us exclusively on pursuit of the drug, and making future oriented, cost-benefit analysis impossible." It was an updated rendition of "Diseases of the Will" that historian Marianna Valverde (1998) had traced to Victorian doctors trying to account for addiction as a condition that took away self-control. Self-control, Valverde pointed out, was the distinguishing trait of humanity (as opposed to animal life) according to Enlightenment philosophy.   *human v. animal*

Biomedicine blames not only the substances, as Victorian temperance campaigns had, but also blames the individual's genetic predisposition to addiction, and blames irreversible damage to the brain from long-term drug use. For instance, biomedicine's "opiate receptor depletion hypothesis" proposes that chronic opiate use leads neurons to stop producing opiate receptors, to dampen the effect of high levels of opiates on neurons. This change explains why tolerance develops—that is, as the brain stops producing opiate receptors, higher doses of opiates are needed to achieve the same experiences of pain relief and pleasure. According to this theory, taking high doses of opiates daily over a period of years makes this downregulation of opiate receptors irreversible: the brain permanently requires higher doses of opiates to control pain and feel pleasure. The brain stops responding to its own physiological opiates, such as endorphins, and without doses of external opiates such people live in a state of pain and anhedonia, unable to experience everyday pleasures. This is the principal neurophysiological argument for opioid medication maintenance with methadone or buprenorphine as a clinical treatment for opiate addiction.

My supervisor's biological hijacking lecture came on the heels of President George H. W. Bush's "Decade of the Brain" (1990–2000), a decade during which Congress allocated billions of dollars to the National Institute of Drug Abuse (NIDA) for neuroscientific studies of addiction as a "chronic, relapsing brain disease." Addiction researchers and clinicians believed that conceptualizing addiction as a disease would reduce the stigma of addiction by mainstreaming addiction treatment into general medicine. The end of the decade was marked by a lead article in the *Journal of the American Medical Association*—authored by four prominent addictions researchers and entitled, "Drug Dependence: A Chronic Medical Illness" (McLellan et al. 2000). It argued that the heritability, etiology, and treatment adherence of addicted patients were similar to those of patients with diabetes, hypertension, and asthma, and that addiction should be treated in the same way (with medications) and in the same settings (in general clinics) as chronic physical illnesses. Addictions researchers hoped it would leave sufferers less stigmatized and with the more realistic goal of stabilization (instead of cure), than would a moral-deficiency concept of addiction.

In Puerto Rico—a U.S. territory that receives federal public-health funding—this biomedical view of addiction was making inroads. Two major universities near the capital city of San Juan had substantial NIDA funding for addiction research. State-funded biomedical detoxification and rehabilitation programs were firmly established and were being privatized in Puerto Rico's move toward managed care. Most of the converts I met in Puerto Rican street ministries had tried biomedical addiction treatment, and many of the patients that I interviewed in biomedical programs had been in street ministries; biomedical and Pentecostal approaches thus were intertwined in their biographies.

Yet, biomedicine and Pentecostalism are rooted in different views of the self. In biomedicine, the addicted self is damaged, cannot regulate itself, and therefore cannot protect itself from further harm. Its closed loop of physiology and behavior is captured in biomedicine's foundational "self-medication hypothesis," the hypothesis that addiction is a faulty attempt to treat oneself with substances that relieve symptoms, but that simultaneously weaken one's capacity for self-care (Khantzian 1985). The idea of self-medication infuses biomedicine's primary addiction-treatment strategies to this day—from maintenance medications such as methadone that relieve the discomfort of withdrawal and mimic the action of illegal opiates, to cognitive behavioral therapy and dialectical behavioral therapy, designed to give patients non-pharmacological strategies to regulate their own distressing emotions. A more recent addition to this framework is the "Stages of Change" theory (Prochaska and DeClemente 2005) that identifies deficits in patients' recognition of, and motivation to change, self-harming behavior such as addictive behavior. This theory has been combined with communicative strategies called "Motivational Enhancement" and "Motivational Interviewing" (Miller and

Rollnick 1992). Physicians and therapists use these strategies to change harmful behavior by providing verbal reinforcements that are tailored to the patient's stage of change, and are adjusted as the patient's motivation and insight progress. In this way, willpower is directly bolstered by the clinician. To interrupt the addictive loop of physiology and behavior, therefore, biomedicine provides either pharmaceutical or psychotherapeutic prosthesis that enables addicted people to care for themselves. Prosthesis is the technology of hope offered by biomedicine: the hope of targeting neuroreceptors and psychological deficits that drive addictive responses by using precise molecular and psychotherapeutic techniques—techniques that, by the scientific master-narrative of progress, continuously improve with new breakthroughs over time, restoring self-dominion. According to biomedicine, however, the addicted self always will require psychosomatic technologies to adapt to the world. This cultural model calls on our investment in the pastoral care of individuals as a requirement for their everyday survival. *versus* ...

For their part, street ministries turn the biomedical view on its head. In the ministries' frame, rather than helping addicted people to adapt to their environment, they call on people to remake their environment with spiritual techniques. Rather than accepting their powerlessness against their biology as "drug dependent," ministries attempt to tap the power of a spiritual movement. Rather than asserting that addiction is a disease of the individual, ministries see it as a sign of societal disease. The goal is not to adapt to the world, but to create a new one. By this logic, prosthesis (such as medications or psychotherapy) only delay the liberation awaiting addicted people when they reject the world. The self is not permanently damaged; rather, the self is an embryonic seed, stunted by addiction, whose capacities must be cultivated with spiritual practice. This is in contrast to an inward-looking biomedical concern with inherited or historically shaped individual flaws; Pentecostal discourses of addiction are future oriented, calling on communities of worship and spirits as agents of change. The street ministry pastors that I knew had their own critique of biomedical addiction clinics, saying "You can't cure drug addiction with drugs."

As a prescriber of methadone and other medications used to treat addiction, I agreed with them. Drugs do not cure addiction. Yet, clinicians do not claim to cure, they only claim to manage a chronic disease (of addiction) with their medications. The most committed and skilled addiction doctors do help people to transform their lives, in part with medications that make withdrawal and cravings tolerable, medications that enable addicted people to face the complexities of family and work with less distraction.

Apart from a small, committed group of addiction specialists, however, most doctors are not eager to treat addicted patients. The chronic disease concept of addiction has only penetrated biomedicine so far. In both Puerto Rican and U.S. mainland medical schools, students and clinical residents run from patients who

Why docu don't want to work z addicted patients

have "drug dependence" on their charts, delaying their admission exams for the next shift, or scanning their medical histories for reasons to refer them to a specialist. Addicted patients are non-compliant, have hidden motives, and are comorbid: sick with many diseases at once, including infections, liver disease, vascular disease, psychosis, and depression. They are the nemesis of overworked clinicians. Also, like many North and Latin Americans, clinicians often doubt that addicts deserve care. *harsh!*

pattern z people z addiction

In my own medical training, I was drawn to addicted patients. I pored over their social histories, convinced that they held the key to patients' compulsions. I did find a pattern: almost all of these patients grew up neglected; were sexually, physically, or emotionally traumatized; or lived in violent neighborhoods, with unstable housing, pervasive unemployment, truncated schooling, and other deprivations. Population studies show that drug-use rates increase when industries leave local towns, or when people are forcibly relocated to reservations (Shkilnyk 1985) or to new housing projects under Urban Renewal (Fullilove 2004) or planned shrinkage (Wallace 1999) when extended family systems are broken apart by welfare eligibility policies (Pessaro 1993) or forced migration (Borges et al. 2007, Alaniz 2002), or when organized crime targets fragile neighborhoods for narcotics retail (Agar and Schacht Reisinger 2002). The flooding of inner-city drug markets by drug cartels selling cheap Columbian and Mexican cocaine and heroin, and the disproportionate incarceration of blacks and Latinos from the War on Drugs have converged with unparalleled toxic effects on city neighborhoods (Singer et al. 1992, Bourgois 1995, Hamid et al. 1997, Agar 2003, Singer 2008), visible in "million dollar blocks": geomaps showing the low-income, black, and Latino census tracts whose residents cost the state the most due to high rates of incarceration (Badger

addiction as individual issue

2015). Yet, nothing in my clinical training prepared me to treat addiction as anything other than an individual biological and behavioral problem.

In fact, some ethnographers argue that biomedical treatment that lacks a social perspective actually perpetuates addiction. Philippe Bourgois (2000) describes methadone programs as tools of neurochemical discipline that consign patients to long-term opioid maintenance upon pain of withdrawal. Angela Garcia (2010) followed heroin-using New Mexican Hispanos in addiction programs that, she discovered, are structured around the expectation of relapse—assuring the chronicity of addiction that they claim to treat. Summerson Carr (2010), in her linguistic analysis of group therapies, found that clients are forced to learn a "script" of sobriety to meet the expectations of their therapists, deepening the gap between their goals and those of their treaters.

As Wanda at Victory Academy told me, she preferred Christian treatment because "In the ministry they don't say once an addict always an addict." In this way, ministries diverge from another well-known spiritual approach to addiction, that of Twelve-Step programs such as Alcoholics Anonymous. In both evangelism and Twelve-Step programs, uncontrollable drug use is the consequence of a lack of humility and the need to submit to a higher power. Both require personal reformation based on principles of the Bible (among charismatic Christians) or of the "Big Book" (among Twelve-Step followers). This similarity is not coincidental. In the 1930s, Alcoholics Anonymous co-founders Bill W. and Dr. Bob were members of the Oxford Group, a Protestant evangelical organization. Early on, Dr. Bob told hospitalized alcoholics to give their lives to Jesus (Dick B. 2005). The founders later expanded their membership by making the twelve steps non-denominational, and referencing a Higher Power rather than God (Valverde 1998). Yet, the Twelve Steps remain classic Protestant liturgy: admitting one's shortcomings, turning one's life over to a Higher Power, making reparations, and carrying the message to others (Alcoholics Anonymous 2004). The language has been secularized, but the steps refer to confession, salvation, penance, and evangelization. *popular?*

At the same time, Twelve-Step programs identify addictions as incurable diseases that require sufferers to attend meetings indefinitely for sobriety, with the lifelong threat of relapse. This discourse of addiction as a disease of the individual was the product of a cultural compromise struck in post–World War II United States, in which Alcoholics Anonymous and the medical profession appeased public resistance to alcohol prohibition by attributing alcoholism to individual vulnerabilities, rather than the properties of alcohol itself (Peele 1989).

Although Pentecostal street ministries recruit and convert on the basis of problem drug use, addiction is not the primary issue to be addressed through conversion. As one convert told me, "The problem isn't drugs or alcohol. The problem is sin." Street ministry sermons give equal time to adultery, promiscuity, jealousy, and egoism; they place addicted people on the same plane as all unconverted people who need to align themselves with the Holy Spirit. For them, sobriety is not a goal in itself, it is the result of conversion.

The Book of Acts mentions faith healing as a gift bequeathed to early Christians during the Pentecost, along with speaking in tongues and prophecy, so faith healing—including prayer and laying hands on the ill with the expectation of their recovery—is widely practiced in Pentecostal ministries. Yet, I never heard street ministers speak of healing addiction. They measure their success not by the number of converts who return to their lives as they were before substance use, but by the number who devote their lives to the ministry, who live on the ministry grounds, who complete missions to other parts of the island or to other countries, and eventually open new ministry homes. Unlike Twelve-Step programs, whose twelve traditions forbid them to own property in the name of the organization, street ministries own, rent, or squat on properties that are full-time residences. In street ministries, conversion means gaining a new address, a new vocation, and a new identity.

Despite my biomedical training and my religious agnosticism, my own concept of addiction resonated with that of street ministers in unexpected ways. Where street ministers rallied to locate spirits, I saw a movement of people striving to relocate themselves. Where ministries made addicts into prophets, I saw social technologies of transformation. With the ministers, I wondered if the disease concept of addiction constrained the possibility of recovery. This paradox is highlighted by studies finding that defining addiction as a disease, rather than de-stigmatizing addiction as intended, can increase stigma against addicted people because the concept of disease casts them as irreversibly flawed (Pescosolido et al. 2010, Link and Phelan 2010).

 My travels in street ministries required multiple ways of seeing addiction, and required holding the tension between a clinical gaze and ethnographic engagement. In a world where clinical medicine is dominant, where allopathic health care industries and pharmaceuticals represent the largest single sector of global industry (IMS 2012), I strove to understand strategies and ways of knowing that lay outside of biomedicine. How did conceiving of addiction as a spiritual disorder affect the possibilities for personal and social change?

PORTALS OF PENTECOSTALISM

By the end of the twentieth century, Pentecostalism was the fastest-growing religious movement in Latin America (Cleary and Stewart-Gambino 1997), having increased from 4% to 28% of the population between 1970 and 2005 (Pew 2006). In the early 2000s, Pentecostals were also the fastest growing Protestant denomination in the United States (Warner 2004). Pentecostals are characterized by the doctrine that any worshiper can establish direct contact with the Holy Spirit and receive its gifts as described in the biblical Book of Acts, including speaking in tongues, prophecy, and healing by faith. Pentecostalism gives ultimate authority to personal experience: to a communion with the Spirit that is available to all regardless of literacy, income, or previous knowledge of the Bible. As one worshiper in a Puerto Rican addiction ministry told me, "Pentecostals believe in personal sanctity, in long skirts and long sleeves. The experience of being saved is very clear, there is no doubt about the presence of God."

Pentecostalism is not one denomination, it is a multi-denominational movement characterized by charismatic worship and a theology of gifts. Although many of the ministries I studied referred to themselves simply as Christian or evangelical rather than Pentecostal, I use the term Pentecostal because it describes a worship style that unites most of the street ministries in Puerto Rico.

Street ministries target beleaguered neighborhoods much like those of the early twentieth-century American cities from which Pentecostalism first emerged. Like the Azusa Street Mission of 1906 inner city Los Angeles, that unified African American, Mexican, and white American worshipers in what many historians identify as the first Pentecostal revival, contemporary Puerto Rican street ministries blend a clean-living doctrine of abstinence from substances and from sex outside of marriage, with an expressive worship style drawing on African and Latin American music and oratory, that is designed to elevate worshipers to a state of contact with the Holy Spirit.

The Pentecostal movement has deep roots in Puerto Rico, where Pentecostalism was well established by 1920, and produced several generations of Puerto Rican leaders and missionaries (Moore 1998). Notably, anthropologist Sidney Mintz's classic 1950s biography of a Puerto Rican sugar-cane worker ends with the worker's conversion to Pentecostalism (Mintz 1960).

Upon U.S. occupation of the island in 1898, the Catholic Church—which had been intertwined with the Spanish colonial government—no longer could exclude Protestant sects from missionary work on the island. North American Protestants rushed to missionize Puerto Rico, envisioning it as their portal to the rest of Latin America. Puerto Rico became a training ground for a Puerto Rican clergy who went on to found missions in the rest of Latin America (Milham 1951). Puerto Rico thus was evangelized earlier than its Latin American counterparts, due to its political and geographical proximity to the United States.

Early Protestant evangelists strove to solve problems of poverty and respectability in Puerto Rico. They opened hospitals and schools, and gained converts as a result (Sprinkle et al. 1964). Protestants supported temperance and prohibition; they identified widespread drinking among the rural poor as signs of moral depravity. The Protestant clean-living program—including abstinence from substances, legal marriage, and fidelity—appealed to Puerto Ricans looking for upward mobility (Martinez-Fernandez 2000). As in other parts of Latin America, Protestant conversion promised to affect male consumption and behavior—for instance, to reduce money spent on alcohol and mistresses—to elevate the image and income of their families (see Brusco 1995). Male abstention through Christian temperance therefore has been a recurring theme in Puerto Rican society for longer than it has throughout the rest of Latin America—where the Catholic Church was enmeshed with the state (Clark 1995).

In fact, in Puerto Rico (as in other former Spanish colonies) Pentecostals see themselves in opposition to Catholics, as an anti-establishment movement that challenges the rigid social hierarchy of Catholicism, and that challenges what they see as Catholicism's empty moral pronouncements—the hypocrisy of lax personal practices among Catholic laypeople and clergy, who are said to drink alcohol and to be motivated by personal gain rather than spiritual connection. For Pentecostals, substances and material consumption detract from the spiritual authority of Catholics, whereas personal discipline builds the authority of Pentecostals.

Ironically, until the 1960s, many of these ascetic Pentecostal men worked in sugarcane fields, and thus helped to make Puerto Rico a major producer of rum for local consumption and for export to the United States. Beginning in the 1960s, however, Puerto Rico rapidly urbanized, becoming a manufacturing center for U.S. corporations seeking a lower-wage workforce and an import tax shelter. Later, as manufacturing plants sought even cheaper labor in Asia, Puerto Rico became a center of narcotraffic. As a U.S. possession, Puerto Rico's customs procedures were minimal compared to those of other nations bordering the United States. By the 1980s—when the U.S. heightened narcotics surveillance at the Mexican border—Puerto Rico became the main Caribbean transfer site of Colombian cocaine and heroin to the United States (Abel 1998). Soon after, Puerto Rico saw a rate of injection drug use–related AIDS greater than that of New York City (CDC 2001), and a drug-related homicide rate greater than that of the mainland United States (Booth and Drummond 1996, Abel 1998, Goodnough 2003).

The baptism that I observed at Victory Academy took place in 2001, the dawn of the new millennium. The last quarter of the twentieth century had been punishing for families like Eli's, Wanda's and Yeyo's. Lyndon B. Johnson's War on Poverty had become what many called the War on the Poor. A key element in this shift was the War on Drugs, declared by Richard Nixon in 1971 to appease middle-class white voters shaken by black inner-city riots in Watts, Newark, Harlem, Detroit, Chicago, and Washington: voters anxious about alienated Vietnam veterans who had returned to an economy bankrupted by the war. The War on Drugs was intensified by Ronald Reagan starting in 1981 as he signed into law mandatory minimum sentencing for drug convictions, abolished parole for those convicted, and instituted the death penalty for "drug kingpins." Since Reagan's presidency, progressively more punitive drug-control legislation has been proposed every election year, leading, for instance, to disqualification of those convicted of a drug charge from receiving federal welfare or food stamps, even if disabled (Baum 1997). These laws coincided with structural adjustment in international economic policy, and national austerity in the United States: historic cuts in social welfare programs, industrial deregulation, growth in income inequalities, and growth in narcotics trade between Latin American and North America.

By the time I reached Puerto Rico, the effects of mandatory minimum sentencing for crack cocaine possession and targeted searches in poor neighborhoods across the U.S. mainland and territories were clear, with one in three black men and one in six Latino men in the United States serving time at some point in their lives (Maurer and King 2007). In the 1980s through the 2000s, U.S. Congress spent more than $600 billion total on supply-side drug control, including narcotics interdiction in the Caribbean, at the Mexican border, and through U.S. street-level arrests in the War on Drugs (Chalk 2011). In response, narcotraffic between Latin America and the United States grew more organized, technologically sophisticated, and murderous—becoming an industry of an estimated $100 billion per year in the United States alone (Kilmer et al. 2014). In the ten years since 2001, the War on Drugs led to more homicides in the United States than deaths in the wars in Iraq and Afghanistan (Conroy 2012). By 2011, Puerto Rico had almost twice the per-capita murder rate of Mexico (Latin American Herald Tribune 2012), and six times that of the mainland United States (Connor 2013), with more than 70% of homicides directly attributable to drug trade (Shoichet 2012).

Ethnographies of U.S. urban drug use and trade at the end of the twentieth century depicted them as alternative routes to income and respect among Latinos and African Americans excluded from capitalist mobility in the formal economy (*cf.* Williams 1989, Anderson 1990, Duneier 1999, Dei 2002). Instead, the excluded cultivate "oppositional identities" which reflect the skills and knowledge that are valued and rewarded in narcotraffic (Bourgois 1995). In those ethnographies, addiction was not seen as a problem of depleted opiate and dopamine neuroreceptors—what I had been taught in medical school—but as a problem of capital. In fact, in Puerto Rico, it might be more precise to describe widespread addiction as the result of, and a necessary condition for, shifts in the island's economic base from agriculture and manufacturing to narcotraffic.

At the time of Victory Academy's baptism, addiction also had other economic implications, accounting for more than 10% of U.S. health expenditures and 60% of prison sentences—to a total cost of $468 billion per year in the United States and Puerto Rico (CASA 2009, U.S. Department of Justice 2005). Both U.S. President George W. Bush and the Puerto Rican Governor Pedro Roselló ushered in the twenty-first century by espousing evangelism as a primary answer to drug abuse in the Americas, while many grassroots ministries resisted governmental support, seeing it as an encroachment on their practice of faith (Hansen 2005). The politics of addiction and evangelism were publicly debated, yet there was little sociocultural analysis of addiction ministries and the symbolic, relational, and political work they did for converts. Historically and to the present, we can see Puerto Rico—"Rich Port" in English—as a port of entry for Latin American narcotics and rum to the United States, and simultaneously as a port of entry for North American ascetic Protestantism to Latin America. In the crosshairs, the impact of street ministries' efforts to reconfigure bodily practices, identities, relationships, and society has yet to be determined.

Puerto Rican street ministries strive to overcome addiction by re-imagining relations of power. This book begins by asking how spiritual transcendence, self-transformation, and enchantment of the world are cultivated in street ministries: that is, *how* Pentecostal healing of addiction "works" as a social technology. It ends by asking how these techniques ultimately influence a convert's marginality—that is, *if* they "work." I take up Pentecostal technologies of transformation that street ministries adapt to addiction: mysticism, ascetic practice, and the alternative power structure of ministries as "in the world but not of the world." I then track converts' gender-based attempts to establish moral authority in their ministries, their families, and communities. I end with elements of spiritual renewal and alternative community building that I recognized in the creative arts therapies and community gardening of a biomedical addiction clinic years after my research in Puerto Rico, elements that challenge the narrow pharmaceuticalization of addiction and mental health treatment. Pentecostal practices of identity change and re-valuation begin to answer the question to which I return at the end this book, of what clinical practitioners can learn and adapt from the other-worldly ministries encamped in Puerto Rico's abandoned storefronts and motels.

1

The Cosmology of Conversion

Pentecostal knowledge is experiential. It is based on a sensory theology, a theology of emotional and tactile encounter—some call it possession—that is all-encompassing. The encounter heightens awareness of the motives of others, and of one's own interior state. Street ministers describe the encounter as intimate contact with the Holy Spirit, marked by the sensation of being filled or embraced. They use the encounter to retrain desire, by giving personal testimony, by reinterpreting sensory experiences as signals from an occult spiritual realm, and by reframing setbacks as spiritual tests. The ultimate goal of the encounter is to achieve a complete break with pre-conversion ways of seeing the world, and to re-people the world with enchanted experiences, beings, and passions. Christian knowledge, then, only is gained through radical rupture with everyday perception.

This concept of knowledge presented me, a non-Pentecostal, with a dilemma of understanding. As Pentecostals are fond of saying, to know it, you have to live it. I could have dismissed their point as a ploy to convert me, but I sensed that it was also correct. The core of what sustained them and shaped their view of the world was not available through books, charts, or scientific instruments; not in the way that I'd acquired biomedical knowledge. To appreciate Pentecostal knowledge, I had to travel new ground.

. . .

The road to Restoration House is lined by wild grasses and mango trees, crossed by chickens and thin, balding dogs. The route passes old Spanish colonials of the town plaza—their boarded windows covered with graffiti, rows of tin shacks with peeling paint—over bridges, through fallow fields, and past shirtless men sipping beers in the heat on the porch. After a half mile on a dirt road up a mountain, I came upon a tall white gate attached to a twelve-foot iron fence. A young man sat in the guard's booth. He greeted me with "*Te bendiga*" ("God bless you"). I explained that I was there to see the director, and the gates slowly drew open.

Inside the gate, trimmed hedges, planted flowers, and rocks painted with biblical quotations contrasted with the wild grasses outside. The asphalt driveway from the gate implored those exiting the program in white and blue paint: "*Detente, Piensa: Cristo te Ama*" ("Stop, Think: Christ Loves You") (fig. 5). The muraled stucco buildings encircling the grounds read "*Cafetería*," (Cafeteria), "*Capilla*" (Chapel), "*Barbería la Fe*" (Faith Barbershop) (fig. 6), "*Biblioteca*" (Library), "*Dispensario*" (Dispensary). The quiet of midday siesta penetrated the banana grove and the basketball court (fig. 7), as well as the dormitories, each named for a book of the Bible, including "*Corintios*" (Corinthians) and "*Romanos*" (Romans). I noted how much the Christian programs resembled each other physically: on a mountain, with carefully groomed grounds and open space for games and gardens. The grit of condemned buildings and abandoned cars in the urban neighborhoods from which converts came was washed away in this bucolic rendition of a home for addicts. No more than five miles from the town center, the small compound nonetheless evoked the pilgrimage of prophets into the wilderness, its

FIGURE 5. Gate to exit Restoration House. The sign reads, "Stop, think: Christ loves you." Photo by Helena Hansen.

FIGURE 6. Faith Barber Shop at Restoration House. Photo by Helena Hansen.

FIGURE 7. The basketball court at Restoration House. Photo by Helena Hansen.

elevation conjured Moses on the mountain. The gates might have referenced New Jerusalem had the twelve-foot iron fence that enclosed it not been topped with barbed wire, as much to keep residents in as unwanted visitors out.

The guard led me through a glass door to Director Menocal's desk. Stocky and gray-haired, Menocal was flanked by plaques from the city recognizing his service to the community, and from a seminary in San Juan for his scholarly achievements. His curriculum, he explained, involved three basic steps: Detoxification in the dormitories for six months, recuperation while living on program grounds for up to twelve months, and spiritual growth in the community after that. As residents reached the recuperation stage they got weekend passes to leave the compound. They attended *culto,* or religious services, Bible classes, and were assigned tasks such as cleaning or cooking. They also learned potential occupations such as frame making, lamination, and barbering.

In the last phase, that of spiritual growth, some took university courses or got married to the women with whom they'd been living before treatment. Menocal pointed to wedding photos of program graduates on his desk. Success, he told me, is that the residents work, attend school, have a family and children, and that they are a Christian presence in their community.

Twenty-eight years prior, Menocal himself was a heroin user, living on the streets of San Juan. He went to prison and was rehabilitated in Silo, one of the original evangelical addiction treatment programs in Puerto Rico. He found the Lord there, and his calling in life; he graduated from seminary in Bayamón, then came to the South side of the island to found Restoration House with the help of local Pentecostal and Baptist churches, as well as a grant from the mayor. He was now a professional administrator, and some on his staff had state certification in counseling, social work, and nursing. For him, though, it was significant that he had been addicted.

> There are so many churches in the South of Puerto Rico, but few rehabilitation programs. It's hard work. You have to have had the experience (of addiction) and feel it in your heart.[1]

Menocal pulled over a staff member, Juan, a round man with a round face and a closely cut greying afro. "This one is a university student," Menocal said with a grin. "You have a lot in common." Juan led me across the compound to a room with plastic flowers framing the doorway and a metal desk in the center. The moist air weighed down on us.

He launched into *testimonio* (testimony) with no further prompting: this was his third time at Restoration House. The first time he came from jail. His mother was Catholic, and the Catholics let you smoke and drink, they don't teach that God is against that. Then he heard who Jesus was. Holding up a cup, Juan explained "I was like an empty glass. If you want to change, you have to do it inside," pointing inside the cup. "When I came, I cried for three days, I didn't know why. I heard 'Who wants Jesus? He'll change your life.' I said 'Me!'"

Juan saw the events of his conversion as auspicious.   *3 days*

> Why three days the first time? Because Jesus rose in three days! . . . I was in the program three days, closed my eyes, woke up on the floor. I wanted [Jesus] from the bottom of my heart. I wanted to talk with God. I read the Bible two times in three years. I learn so much.

Juan explained that what he and the other men who come to the program need is love. When he converted, he asked for God's love, but did not know he had it until he physically felt God's presence: "One day I asked Him to raise me. [He] took me by hand and (lifted) me, like a drug, then I said God is real."

God began to use Juan, to grant him powers to see and talk with spirits. When he first came to the program, someone was selling drugs inside the program. He prayed in a chain with a group of men through the night, each man taking a one-hour shift to lead prayer. With his eyes closed, he saw demons inside the program's walls. Channeling the Holy Spirit, he called them out and exorcised them.

Since then, Juan had been working with new recruits who were *en frio* (quitting "cold turkey"), and suffering through withdrawal with chills, aching bone pain, and insomnia. He saw how God was using him with them; when he laid his hand on their foreheads their withdrawal symptoms disappeared.

The first time he graduated from the program, Juan initially did well. "I went home, went to church every day. [I said] 'God, I want to study.'" God answered this prayer, and Juan enrolled in the Inter-American University. "I had [high grades] in the University, I had money. Why? Because I was praying every day. If not I'd lose everything."

Juan continued to guide others as he had in Restoration House: "I worked as a tutor for the handicapped. I liked it so much. I had to explain the sky and constellations to a *ciega* (blind person) using a pen."

He pointed to ridges on a pen, to indicate spatial relationships: "Here is to here as there is to there." Those times still inspired Juan. "I want to be a missionary, go to Africa, help the people. I can do that through the Pentecostal church."

Despite the possibilities he saw for himself in the church, however, after graduating from the first time Juan still struggled with temptation and disillusionment.

"When I had a relapse it was like God had one hand and [the Devil] the other. 'He's mine—no he's mine.' I felt like that."

Back to using cocaine after accepting Christ, Juan's faith was tested like never before.

"Jesus says 'It's much better not to know me than to know me and leave me.' In my church, they tell me pray, pray. They knew I was relapsing."

After a few months of crack use, Juan came back to Restoration House and begged for re-admission. "God is never late."

Juan found Restoration House to be a quiet place where the voice of God could be heard.

> I like to pray at 4 a.m. You'll have a wonderful day if you pray at 4 a.m. God says, "they'll find me when they wake up early in the morning." When you feel the bed shaking, it's God. He's waking you to pray.

Surviving the spiritual war that tested Juan required him to sharpen new senses.

> God gave you spiritual eyes and ears . . . [you] have to know Satan [was once] an angel. To know the difference, who is lying. If you want to do this work you have to know when a person wants to change.

I left Restoration House that day knowing that Juan would be an important guide. He was connected to a spiritual dimension not visible to outsiders leading secular, everyday lives. For fleeting moments, he was possessed by the Holy Spirit, and the memory of those moments kept him seeking more, moving him from a singular focus on drugs to a singular focus on the Spirit. Juan had offered me an astronomy lesson; I was to be his *ciega* ("blind person"), to whom he would describe the constellations using ridges on a pen.

SPIRITUAL EYES AND EARS

One night, after two months of attending evening *culto*, the worship service, at Restoration House, I found myself listening to testimony after a round of "You Are Sacred," a salsa-inspired hymn—complete with conga drums and timbales. The chapel pulsated with men's voices and percussion on drums, cowbells, and hands slapping the backs of metal folding chairs. Bright light spilled out into heavy night air, blanketed by nothing but the calls of tree frogs and crickets for miles. The music ended, and the men leafed restlessly through their Bibles. They looked over their shoulders for signs of the usual Wednesday night preacher, a graduate of Restoration House who was now a pastor in Guayama several miles away.

While they waited for the preacher, a program leader introduced the young man who was to give testimony to relapse as part of recuperation. The young man began with a shy smile, joking about Menocal's discipline. After three months at Restoration House, because he used drugs again, he was held for eighteen days alone in a room. He praised the Lord for waking him up during those eighteen days of isolation.

Juan plopped down next to me. His face was grey and drawn; he had been up around the clock with a new recruit who was "*rompiendo en frio*" ("going cold turkey"). As the pastor's car pulled up to the chapel, Juan explained that the young man giving testimony was sent by the drug court, and that if he had one more relapse he would spend twenty years in prison.

The pastor from Guayama entered, flanked by guests from his church. A trim, middle-aged man professionally dressed in wire-frame glasses, a pressed white shirt, and a bright yellow tie setting off his dark skin, he called on guests from his church to speak. A man in his thirties in shirt and tie gave his personal testimony. He had grown up in the church, but when he married he wanted to know the world and he forgot the church. It was the Devil saying the world is better. He began to drink a little, and then more, eventually he lost his job and his wife moved to the United States with their three children. He was watching a Christian program on TV one day and felt tear tracks on his face.

> I knew the message was for me. God was saying "I still love you." I went to the U.S. to find my wife and kids. ¡Gloria a Dios! ["Glory to God!"] I returned with them to Puerto Rico and my old job took me back. [But then] I found a blank check at work, I signed it and cashed it. . . . I went to prison, and my father signed away his house to bail me out. On the street corner, someone said "There is an answer for your problem." [Making motion of man handing him a pamphlet]. I reconciled with *El Señor* (the Lord), and he cleaned my legal record of all my cases!

Fidgeting in his seat, Juan whispered an offer to show me the grounds. We exited onto a grove of banana trees. "Have you ever seen this?" Juan asked. He moved the petals of a fist-sized purple blossom to uncover miniature green bananas inside.

We continued on a dirt path behind the chapel, passing a hardwood tree. The tree was missing most of its leaves, and shadow covered its cracked bark. Suddenly, a chill took me over. I stood on the path, speechless; I had a visceral urge to avoid the tree. Juan broke the silence in a harsh tone.

> See this tree? So dry. This is an ugly tree. The other tree next to it, it gets the same water, when it rains both of them get rain, and it looks beautiful. Why this one look like that? I'm gonna tell you a story. When I first got here I was passing this tree late at night with two people and all of a sudden I felt like God was hugging me and pulling me down. I fell on the floor. The guy ahead of me called for help. As he was helping me up we both saw demons in the tree. He started to pray, to pray. He said "God casts you out of here!" I used to be scared of things like that, but now I'm not. I know God protects me . . . when you look at this tree, what do you see?

I looked up and hesitated. "I feel cold," I said. "And I don't know if I should mention this, but when we first walked up that vine looked like a noose."

"What's a noose?" Juan asked.

"A rope to hang someone." I answered. Juan shook his head and told me there was a lot I could not see because I was at a different spiritual level.

We walked past the laundry building and the basketball court where Juan said he often slept in order to see the stars. I looked up and caught sight of Orion and the Big Dipper.

I love it! I pray, I hear God. I think about the people on the streets that night, nothing to eat, nowhere to sleep. I say, please God, help the people, give them something to eat. I know he hears me.

We looked to the detoxification room adjacent to the court, where four men lay motionless on cots. Christian rock music piped in at high volume. Juan told me he had to bolt the speakers to the wall. "They don't know what they're doing when they're in detox," he said. "They just tear out the speakers."

As we walked back to the chapel, *culto* was letting out, and two men ran up to us: "Juan, Juan, they're calling you!" Juan entered the chapel and talked with the pastor and two assistants while I stayed outside. Though I couldn't see into the chapel, I heard the ebb and flow of loud group prayer for several minutes.

Suddenly Juan ran out of the chapel door with tear stains on his cheeks, his eyes round and bright. "I don't know how to explain to you what just happened. I had something in my heart that God didn't like, and he just took it out! I feel light as a—what you call what you see on birds?" He made a hand motion imitating a feather floating to the ground. Juan then explained further.

That man that came with the pastor, that preached, I never seen him before. Last night he had a dream about me, he knew my name. In the dream I came to his house, I asked him for clothes, for shelter, to feed me. He gave me these things but I ran away. He said that meant I had something in my heart God didn't like. When they prayed for me [just now in the chapel] I felt this heat all through my body, it went up to my head, I felt like it would explode! But when I woke up I felt great. I had had a headache all night long and it was gone. *¡Gloria a Dios!*

I told him how glad I was that God helped him, because I'd noticed that he was not as happy as usual. He interrupted me, pointing to the sky behind me, "See that? There, again!" He was seeing flashes of light from his guardian angel.

Juan had been sullen that week. The pastor and guest preacher must have sensed his need for renewal. In Juan's words, it was the Holy Spirit working through them, reminding Juan of his privileged relationship with the Spirit.

Juan looked at me standing next to my car and said:

Okay, go home, because otherwise you'll be here all night. But you'll be safe. It will be as if the car was driving itself, and you'll end up right at home without knowing how you got there. And don't worry, your family will be safe, God has you all in his hands.

I seated myself in my station wagon and indeed, floated around the pitch-black bends of the roads leading to my house. Putting a cassette of Christian music that Juan had given me into the tape deck, I exhaled into my seat, and tried to hear the beauty that Juan found in the music. What was my spiritual ear and eye, and how did I know when I was using them? Was it as simple as noticing a banana blossom or catching a view of Orion and the Big Dipper? I knew that Juan would answer, "No."

back to the tree

He would point me toward the two trees we saw behind the chapel, to the forces that kept one tree green and thriving, and the other dried and cracked on the brink of death, despite that to my eyes they shared the same soil and water. He would remind me of the gray-shirted man who gave testimony that night, to whom God spoke through the television, and of the young man who gave testimony that he was shaken from his spiritual slumber while in solitary confinement, from the brink of a twenty-year prison term. He would cite the new recruits that he had shown me in the withdrawal room, whose heads were so full of malignant craving that they tore the speakers from their wall-mounts to silence the word of Christ.

IMMERSION

Evangelists had been a welcome sight in the decaying neighborhoods where I worked on HIV projects just after college. Evangelists exuded privileged knowledge, and their gaze was fixed above the decay, on an alternate reality. But I did not get to learn more about them until I was in my last year of medical school. With referrals from street ministries in Newark and Hartford to their branches on the island, I left for Puerto Rico—the epicenter of Pentecostal street ministries—for what stretched into a year, and then two additional years of follow-up visits.

From the beginning, I faced a methodological dilemma. Street ministries were gender segregated and the majority were for men. As a married woman with an infant, I could not live at a facility long term to get an intimate view of their cultural logics and practices. Reasoning that I needed to survey local ministries before taking root in one for participant observation, I rented a unit in the shadow of the Ponce cement factory with my husband and one-year-old daughter, next to a friend who worked for the Puerto Rican mental health worker's union. Ponce was a center of both drug trade and addiction ministries, and the cement factory was a reminder of Ponce's thriving industrial past, just one mile north of the abandoned Schering-Plough pharmaceutical plant that had anchored its once thriving manufacturing industry.

I enrolled my daughter in the local daycare, bought an aging Ford Escort, and (between its breakdowns) drove to every street ministry in Southwest Puerto Rico—from Añasco to Ponce—that I could identify by asking health administrators, addiction programs, and the programs' clients for referrals.

In the end, I visited thirteen ministries and interviewed their directors about their history, structure, treatment philosophy, curriculum, and clientele. The directors of Restoration House and Victory Academy[2] were especially welcoming and invited me to participate with, observe, and interview their residents for the year. The two ministries provided contrasts: one accepted government funds and hired state-licensed professionals; the other more radically evangelical ministry did not. These represented two poles of evangelical addiction treatment: one radically evangelical, which rejected the pre-conversion world in favor of a lifelong

two poles of evangelical addiction treatment

mission, the other a hybrid of clinical and evangelical techniques designed to produce Christian citizens that could re-enter everyday Puerto Rican society.

Neither program referred to its residents as "clients" or "patients." As the pastor's wife at Victory Academy explained it, "We don't call them clients, because that implies they're paying for something. Here we say brother, or sister, because we are like a family, or students, because it is an Academy." Long-term residents got the titles of program leaders or co-directors. Program directors did not see addiction as the primary reason that residents needed help. Instead they saw addiction as a symptom of moral weakness. At times, people who had never used drugs came to the ministry; one woman asked to live at Victory Academy to pray about the fact that her husband physically abused her, and another was there to earn custody of children that were in foster care because of alleged neglect.

In this atmosphere of open admission, the program leadership accepted that I was studying evangelism as a treatment for addiction, but told me that God led me to them, whether I knew it or not. They called me the student or, jesting about my broken Spanish, la Gringa ("the North American"). They were convinced that my writing would help the Holy Spirit to reach readers on the mainland. I was invited to baptisms, weddings, and family homes. I took my daughter with me. With their pronatalist ethos, my daughter's presence made me easier to place. Coincidentally, or not, family relations emerged as central themes in the stories they told about themselves.

I participated daily in *culto* (worship services), Bible study, training sessions for program leaders in discipleship, and the everyday life of the ministry. Helping to prepare meals in the kitchen and listening to conversation while cleaning the dormitories gave me a window onto the backstage performance (Goffman 1973) of ministry residents and staff. I was privy to gossip, conflict, and anxieties that people concerned about setting a Christian example did not make public. Taking part in the daily routine of ministry residents also taught me about the physical, embodied aspects of evangelism. Indoctrination was not only a matter of the spoken and written biblical Word, but was also a matter of upright posture, seating that was segregated by gender and seniority in the ministry, sleep deprivation, and emotional release while dancing to music at *culto*.

Ministry leaders reminded me that I could only truly understand Christian treatment for addiction by accepting Christ myself. And I was often mistaken for a convert: instead of the tight shorts and halter tops worn by unconverted young Puerto Rican women, I wore loose shirts that covered my shoulders, long skirts, and no makeup. On one occasion, Pagan, a former prison guard–turned–ministry program leader at Restoration House, stopped midsentence in our conversation to eye my ankle-length navy dress. "But you *look* so Christian!" he said plaintively. "Maybe you will find God this year."

I also tended to pass for "nuyorican" (New York Puerto Rican); with my curly hair and brown complexion, I was called "*trigueña*" ("wheat colored") in the rich

Puerto Rican vocabulary for describing skin tone.[3] It was easy for me and my informants to begin talking as if I were a convert. I reflexively greeted familiar faces with "*Que le bendiga*" ("May God bless you"), and carried a Bible. At times, I wondered if God was asking me to go native. I knew that, for Pentecostals, there could be no fence sitting, and there was no true knowledge external to faith. To keep his job, my husband spent much of his time on the mainland, so I often was with my daughter in the ministries, and it was there that I felt most connected and a part of a community. This immersion planted a seed of doubt in my agnostic worldview.

Although I was disturbed by this doubt, I also saw it as a source of insight.[4] I, too, was affected by their evangelist techniques, and I felt the same need to belong that my informants did. I saw that the boundary between believer and non-believer was permeable, that crossing over and back again was common, and that conversion could be tenuous. Sermon after sermon in *culto* was about doubt, and the need for Christians to be vigilant of their faith. I suspected that the drama of conversion and evangelical performance reflected converts' anxiety about this tenuousness.

COSAS OCULTAS ("THE OCCULT")

A few weeks passed at Restoration House before Juan introduced me to Octavio. Like Juan, Octavio was a program leader. Dark half-moons under his eyes accentuated his pale face and bony frame. Octavio was in a constant state of prayer; he was said to have given up sleep to talk with God without interruption. I had noticed Octavio in the front of the pulpit during *culto*. With a dimpled smile, he chanted ¡*Santo*! ¡*Santo*! ¡*Gloria a Dios*! ("Holy! Holy! Glory to God!") into the microphone and sang the opening lyrics to a salsa-inflected hymn. The congregation picked up the tune, and he kneeled to the far left of the altar and remained there, head down, for the duration of the two-hour *culto*.

Interviewing Octavio was no easy task. I had trouble maintaining the thread of our conversation. Octavio received messages from God every few minutes, and excused himself from our conversation to listen and answer out loud. A mysterious force also seemed to keep me from arriving for our interviews at the appointed time and place. This time I could not get my daughter down to sleep at the usual hour. By the time I arrived at Restoration House, *culto* had long since ended and Octavio was settled into evening prayer. His eyes were bloodshot. He and the other leaders had been praying around the clock on a difficult case.   *dedication to prayer*

The Bible says: "call on me; I will answer and show you grand and occult things that you have never known," in that order. There is a young man here because of his behavior, strange behavior. It is [due to] more than a trauma. In the name of Jesus we will get it out. It's something spiritual. Psychologists talk about multiple personalities, [but these spirits], in order to destroy, they have to be human, they enter the body. . . . The Bible talks about our struggle not being against blood, or flesh, but against spirits of evil in the celestial regions. We fight something that we can't see.

He warned me that these forces were operating even as he and I spoke about them: "In the name of Jesus. . . . Maybe you'll listen to this tape [that is recording the interview] and hear voices that aren't human."

Octavio told me that just as the Holy Spirit enter the body when called, demonic spirits can enter human bodies. The wounded heart is particularly vulnerable.

> It is a mystery how a God so large can enter our hearts, [which are] so wounded, so small, having suffered . . . the young man last night, somewhere [in his past] there is a trauma. Something happened, someone abandoned him . . . science studies only what can be seen. We're talking about something which can't be seen.

The spirits also work externally, driving events in ways that appear coincidental. Talking about my daughter's cries at bedtime, which had kept me from attending *culto*, Octavio was clear that more was at work than met the eye: "It was something occult." *beautiful!* ✗

As I listened to him, I sensed intention in the winds. Was it Octavio's scanning of the spaces behind me as we talked that was so contagious? Or was it his rhythmic incantation of the hidden? Was it the fact that he drew my story into his, weaving in my own struggles and superstitions? *divine intervention?* I found myself taking the mystical realm seriously in my own life. Starting my car that night, I wondered if its stalling was a sign that I should stay at the ministry. Once it started, I thought the car's quick acceleration was a sign that I needed to get home.[5] I drove away from the scene, attempting to pass from Octavio's world, crowded with spirits, back to the innocence of the mundane. But this was in vain. His narrative had altered mine.

Of all the men I met at Restoration House, Octavio was the one that lived most immersed in the dimension of spirits. He told me that God had cured him of the HIV and hepatitis that he'd gotten while injecting cocaine, and that he had not had any AIDS-related opportunistic infections since he accepted Christ. Octavio's communion with the Holy Spirit was his lifeline, a type of existential intravenous drip. This communion gained him the respect of his colleagues in the church; as they said, "Octavio is a man of God. He knows the Bible very well." They named him a medium. His communion with the Spirit sustained him in both the spiritual realm and in the everyday world.

Juan's teachings on spiritual eyes and ears helped me to understand why ministry converts did not see Octavio as mentally ill, but instead celebrated him as a beacon of spiritual health. Had I met Octavio in a medical clinic, without an understanding of Pentecostal cosmology, I would have diagnosed him with a psychotic disorder or with HIV dementia based on his limited attention to my questions, and his communication with beings that others could not see or hear. In the

God works through those we may deem "unqualified"

ministry, his unending dialogue with spirits was a coveted state that required focused self-discipline and skill.

And it was Octavio and Juan's testimony that allowed me to imagine, if not experience, the spiritual eyes and ears with which they perceived the occult realm and channeled spiritual power. Testimony was the narrative tool bridging the everyday world to the enchanted world of spiritual knowing that opened up to converts, a world in which hidden meaning was revealed, in which the apparent disorder of addicted pasts became part of a grander design, and which portended a victorious future. Juan and Octavio's testimony inserted glimpses of the occult into my own perceptions; they gave me experiential clues to the world they inhabited. Their testimony worked on me in a less cognitive, in a more visceral, somatic way than that described by Susan Harding (2000). Her classic linguistic analysis of witness—the testimony of fundamentalist Christians to the power and reality of their salvation—identified it as a narrative technique that moves listeners from unbelief to the gap between unbelief and belief (Harding 2000). What I observed at Restoration House was not the inculcation of sheer belief but, rather, of experiential proof, through Juan and Octavio's testimony: the occult perceptions and sensations that listening to testimony generated in naïve listeners stoked a curiosity and desire for more. At the same time, it was a practice that reinforced the single-minded commitment of those giving testimony, allowing them to experience and re-experience their own inhabitation by spirits in the intimate folds of their story.

Through testimony, moments of insight, spirit possession, and Christian passion could be relived again and again in a timeless space of memory and sensation that gave converts a sense of what eternal salvation might be like. As George Saunders (1995) wrote of Pentecostal conversion stories, "The 'eternalness' of Pentecostal time horizons . . . also allows them to live in the present moment, as 'inner-worldly' activists" (Saunders 1995, 335). In other words, converts use testimony to till and seed their inner terrain with guided imagery and the renaming of sensory experience; to make the self the site of action and change. Testimony allows converts to treat their thoughts and internal signals as clay to be shaped through narrative and bodily practices. In testifying to their choice to follow the Lord, argues Saunders, "They are liberated from their passivity. They have recreated their own histories and, in the process, have regained a presence in history itself" (Saunders 1995, 336).

What this means is that testimony is as important for the faith of the person giving it as for the future faith of the person receiving it. Harding (2000) describes testimony as a tool for evangelism, for creating doubt in non-believers and moving them toward belief. I came to see testimony as an equally critical tool for believers to cultivate their own belief. Testimony shapes the self by narrating it into an archetype of trial, decision, and transformation. It injects everyday life with a sense of significance and forward motion, locating converts in mystical time and space that is both immediate and perpetual.

Ironically, these themes of immediacy and perpetuity, repetition and memory, are echoed by clinical and neuroscience researchers describing addiction itself. Their descriptions highlight the phenomena of "triggers"; memory cues in the environment that lead to cravings, to the compulsion to give one's full attention to the pursuit of drugs in a way that is as absorbing and anticipatory as it is repetitive and unchanging. As stated in a special issue of the *American Journal of Psychiatry* that reviewed biological models of addiction, "evidence at the molecular, cellular, systems, behavioral, and computational levels of analysis is converging to suggest the view that addiction represents a pathological usurpation of the neural mechanisms of learning and memory" (Hyman 2005: 1414).

[handwritten margin note: what does addiction require (originally)?]

If nothing else, evangelical testimony is a practice of memory creation, a practice that is both relational and internal, one that cues the testifier to re-experience spiritual encounters. Yet, when neuroscientists propose "treating addiction through manipulations of learning and memory" (Torregrossa, Corlett, and Taylor 2011, 609) they refer to pharmaceuticals that disrupt the chemical reactions at neuroreceptors that consolidate memories and facilitate learning of new cues. Their studies are based largely on mice that model human behavior. Missing from their inquiry are the ways that human subjects shape their own external and internal environments to create new cues.

TESTS

One day I pulled up to the gates at Restoration House to find Juan in an upbeat mood. It was mild, not humid; typical of January in Puerto Rico, and the yellow sunlight filtering through the mango trees matched Juan's energetic walk to meet me at the gates.

> I passed a test today, with an "A." I feel so happy. I realize it's my decision to do or no. . . . Last night I sang, when I sing I'm flying. When I'm not singing I have to put my feet on the floor again. I felt Jesus very special.

At *culto* Juan had been called to the altar to receive a healing prayer from the pastor.

> I had a vision. I saw big hands. The Holy Spirit said look at this: it's a fruit. On the outside it was not very clean, but when the hands peeled it, it was beautiful inside. Preacher said come here—he answered all the questions I had for God. He said feel my love, don't try to understand me because you can't. You know I need you, gonna use you. You'll live your life in my hands.

This feeling of forgiveness through God's grace was one that Juan found habit forming. "I wanna feel like I feel now every time. Bible says watch yourself—think of God all the time. God is going to put a piece of God inside of you."

Trying out a theory that Juan's words brought to mind, I asked, "So you were feeling fortified this afternoon when you were tested?" Juan replied,

> The Bible says free will: you have to learn to say yes or no. It's like a fight inside of you. God says "don't do it, if you wanna feel [good] like that." I say it's like that? I laugh I'm so happy. I feel like the first time I met Him. I failed Him, I have to start up again. I'm under construction.

agency & free will

Juan's explanation reflected the complexity of Pentecostal ideas about agency and free will. Although becoming saved meant giving one's life over to the will of God, this required actively listening and looking in order to know what God was asking, through prayer, Bible study, meditation, and fasting. That is, converts had to culti-vate their communion with God. They had to do so regularly, such that they became a habit, and replaced the old habits that had left them vulnerable to evil spirits in their addiction. In this logic, personal agency and its opposite, addiction, link habit—the product of a series of willful acts—to the forces of spirits, which originate outside of the person; an individual is responsible for cultivating the interior environment for good spirits to dominate. Tests were reminders to be vigilant of one's inner state, to maximize unity with God.

Juan elaborated on his tests during a life-history interview that he granted me in his "office," the small stucco building in which he did intake interviews with new clients. He picked up where he left off. His father had died when he was twelve, leaving him, his mother, and eleven siblings to fend for themselves.

> I was mostly away from the house, working various jobs. I wasn't using drugs at work, but Friday and Saturday—wow! I made friends with the dealers at drug-cop-ping spots. One of my hobbies was washing cars. I was meticulous—I used Q-tips to clean the air conditioning filter. The dealers liked that and hired me. I met a woman, 31 years old with three kids, when I was 21. I lived with her 7 years. [When] she met me [I was] smoking marijuana. I met the person selling marijuana, then through him the person selling heroin, then through him the person selling cocaine. . . . I had to leave her because of my problem. She's a beautiful woman, not a drug user.

Juan bit his lips in regret.

> God knows everything. I came back to my mother's house. When she learned I used crack she was so hurt. My clothes on the porch—"You have to go." I said I don't have no place to go. [I] dismantled the car of a friend. When I came home the police were waiting. The friend knew it was me and called the police. That night I wanted to die. One month in jail. My sister said "You're leaving here but going to this place [Resto-ration House]." When I left [Restoration House] I was very blessed—I studied at the University, worked. I went to church, I had rose-colored glasses. Didn't know that [people in the church] have defects too. On that test I got an "F." I left church and went 6 months without drugs, then used drugs 2 months and came back here. God didn't leave me alone.

I asked, "What happened when you turned away from the church?"

When I left here [for the first time] I practiced everything I learned here. But I believed everyone was good people. I met a girl, but I didn't talk with her. One day I say God that's the woman you have in mind for me? The preacher said [during *culto*] "I don't know why I say this, but she's not the one." He said it 3 times [while preaching], "No." One day she said she's in love with me. I said how you in love with me, I don't talk to you. She said "Because I see in inside you—have a beautiful heart." She said let's pray. I forgot that God had told me "No" before. Then her mother, her friends rejected me. I didn't understand people [who had been] in church 30 years acting like that. She is still a woman of God. The problem was obedience. When you meet God, have to do what He say.

I wanted clarification: "You stopped going to church because they rejected you?"

Satan is intelligent too. When I was praying he said look how they treat you. I felt hurt. Satan used a person, a good person, not drugs. I changed churches, but I felt bad there too, because I have to pass a test when I get it.

Concerned that I was dredging up painful memories, I said, "I imagine it feels bad to look back."

No—to the contrary. I learn from that. It's like taking a test about life. You know you'll have to pass a bigger one on the same theme later [drawing a staircase in my notebook], and again, an even bigger test. . . . When we pass any test we're closer to God. . . . God is a pottery maker, molding me.

Juan made hand motions of spinning a pottery wheel. He pointed to the fog surrounding the mountains. "Look how beautiful the mist, the water. Everybody needs it."

The tape recorder stopped because the cassette was full. Juan nodded knowingly. "See, God knows when story is stopped."

I came to see, though conversations with many converts, that tests were a continuous part of Christian practice. The tests were not only of Juan's resolve to follow God's commands, but also of his ability to reinterpret the world around him in a manner pleasing to God. They tested the acuity of his spiritual eyes and ears; that is, knowing to whom he should listen, whether they were acting as God's agents or Satan's agents, and when to see events as signs from God. Listening and interpretation were abilities cultivated in prayer, meditation, and Bible study.

To prepare for God's tests, Juan undertook small, everyday acts of faith. They developed his ability to discern God's will and to maintain a transcendent perspective, abilities that over time, he hoped, would free him from earthly desires.

CHOICE AND POWER

The tension between obedience, choice, and freedom implied by Juan's tests is common to both Pentecostalism and other Protestant-derived North American approaches to addiction such as Alcoholics Anonymous. As Valverde (1998) points out, they define freedom not as absence of external control but rather as the presence of internal controls; internal controls that are built by the exercise of will-power in small, everyday practices that (re)form habits. They are rooted in an ideal of ascetic self-sacrifice; as Margaret Mead said that she learned in childhood, "virtue was distinguished by pain followed by pleasure, vice was pleasure followed by pain" (Mead 1973: 178). They reflect an ambivalent Protestant view of willpower which tries to reconcile the tension between the Calvinist doctrine of human frailty, and the liberal belief in every individual's limitless capacity to empower him or herself (Valverde 1998: 34).

Pentecostal concepts of addiction center on power: addiction as due to the unconverted individual's vulnerability to malignant spiritual forces. Addicted people can align themselves with a more powerful force, through fusion with the Holy Spirit, in which the frail, human subject channels tremendous transcendental power. Individuals must continuously renew this fusion in order to rise above the toxic influences to which they are exposed.

This is a concept of addiction that acknowledges its social nature. It problematizes everyday social relations that trap individuals into cycles of consumption and debt or withdrawal, and it calls for a social realignment to transcend them. The realignment is prompted by moments of revelation. It then requires daily practices that, from a secular point of view, are inward and develop the self, but that, from a Pentecostal point of view, are relational and develop mutual recognition and emotional exchange between human hosts and their spiritual inhabitants.

Using this framework, Pentecostals make power relations accessible to intervention. Converts break open an apparently closed loop of personal desire, consumption, and depletion by channeling spiritual power. They see themselves as moral entrepreneurs, explorers and traders in a dimension outside of ordinary perception.

Cheryl Mattingly (2010), in her ethnography of African American families with seriously ill children, coins the term "the practice of hope" to make visible a space of possibility in which marginalized families resist defeat. As she points out, post-structural theory focuses on totalizing networks of power and the illusory nature of resistance (cf. Foucault 1976). It omits the experiential and phenomenological perspectives of subjugated actors whose tactics (à la De Certeau 1984) to counteract oppressive strategies of dominant groups often only are perceptible in everyday acts. In Puerto Rican street ministries, the discourse of addiction—despite its reference to sin—is not a discourse of blame. It is a discourse of vulnerability, requiring self-defense with spiritual cultivation and empowerment.

In this self-cultivation, bodily desires are washed clean in a spiritual rebirth, starting with baptism. Baptism marks the beginning of a lifelong commitment to self-perfection. Other addiction treatment approaches call for adherence to medications, or to meetings, to manage an incurable disease. Charismatic Christians promise a complete transformation of the self through rebirth in the Holy Spirit.

Juan's image of the beautiful fruit inside of its rough shell is a metaphor for converts' revelation of their inner sanctity. *Culto* features rhythmic *alabanza* (music of praise) and dance to create a celebratory mood. Saved ex-addicts give their testimony over loudspeakers in parks, schools, and shopping centers. They see their stories not as shameful but rather as testaments to the miracle of their rebirth.

Rather than the stoic inventory of past wrongs and present weakness required by Alcohol Anonymous' twelve steps, designed to break through denial of members' powerlessness over substances,[6] street ministries focus converts on "spiritual victory." For unemployed Puerto Rican men, the revelation of inner power, rather than the admission that they have no power, might be appealing.

ADDICTION TO CHRIST

The Pentecostalism of Restoration House cultivates a way of relating to the spiritual realm that is reminiscent of West African polytheistic traditions. Historian Ian Mac-Robert (1988) attributes ecstatic Pentecostal spirit possession, oral liturgy and witness, participatory prayer and sermons, and the extensive use of rhythm and dance in worship to early African American Pentecostals whose invocation of spirits derived from West Africa. Although other scholars of American Christianity argue that such African continuity theses might be oversimplified—African American religious practices that resemble West African oratory or musical practices also resemble Welsh and Irish bard traditions (Pitts 1993, Jacobs and Kaslow 1991, Raboteau 1978)—it is true that Pentecostalism emphasizes bodily enmeshment with spirits. Additionally, though Pentecostal theology is certainly monotheistic, in Puerto Rican street ministries the Holy Spirit is the ruling member of an unseen realm peopled with lesser spirits—both good and bad. This rich pneumatic universe resonates with other religious traditions with which Puerto Rican Pentecostal converts are familiar, including Catholic saints and angels, and the Orishas of Santería. Pentecostals call upon or exorcise lesser spirits with the help of the Holy Spirit.

In Restoration House, a good *culto* is one where the group really feels the Holy Spirit, where worshipers are moved to tears, to speak in tongues, and to rest in the Spirit, where they are held unconscious on the floor by a supernatural force. It is one where the preacher does not speak but lets the Spirit speak through him, pulling new converts to the altar to accept Christ even against their own volition.

Craving the Holy Spirit

analogy!

The most devoted converts talk about the Holy Spirit as dominating and obsessing them, as something they crave: once they have felt the Holy Spirit's presence, they cannot stop thinking of it. They talk about the touch and voice of the Holy Spirit in the way that heroin and cocaine users talk about the rush from an injection or inhalation: as a euphoric sensation spreading throughout their bodies, removing their earthly cares. They talk about looking for the Spirit as a way of life, the way that habitual drug users talk of their constant search for drugs. They talk about wanting to reach a state of constant communion with the Spirit, much in the way that drug users talk about their fantasy of a high that never ends. They are willing to endure hunger, physical pain, and public ridicule to make contact with the Spirit, just as they had endured to score drugs before their conversion.

Alternately, worshippers speak of their relationship with the Holy Spirit in romantic terms. They speak of always wanting to please the Spirit, of wanting to show the Spirit their love and wanting to feel love in return. They speak of their guilt when they betray the Spirit, of their efforts to win the trust of the Spirit again, to prove their devotion, to grow in their relationship with the Spirit over time, and to maintain their relationship with the Spirit in the long haul. As the director of an addiction ministry in Yauco told me, "Knowing Christ is like your first love." Bomann (1999) points out that this language of love is characteristic of Pentecostals in Latin America and elsewhere. Cox (1994) relates this ecstatic devotion among Pentecostals to ancient and medieval erotic mysticism in Europe, in which saints described their desire for physical union with Christ (*see also* Burrus 2004). It is notable that, in contemporary times, active drug users also talk about drugs as a romantic love object, describing their first experiences with drugs as falling in love, and joking about their drug of choice as if it were a demanding spouse (Courtwright, Joseph, and Des Jarlais 1989).

In street ministries, however, the Holy Spirit is idealized; it is not seen as the source of temptation, cruelty, and destruction as drugs are. In their view, the Holy Spirit in itself is perfect. It is the object of desire because it is never fully attained by mortals for more than fleeting moments. In fact, as Chapter Three illustrates, Christian historians write that such fleeting moments inspired the Pentecostal movement itself. The emotional pull of Pentecostal worship—its affective concentration on the Holy Spirit as the singular object of ecstatic devotion—resembles the self-conscious monotheism of early Christianity, in its language of saintly passion and desire for Christ.

Pentecostal cosmology holds that power is located not in people, but in spirits. In this cosmos, freedom is not human autonomy, it is liberation from evil spirits, enabling individuals to submit their will to the Holy Spirit. As an observer of Pentecostal treatment for alcoholism in Brazil noted, for Pentecostals,

> Being free means being free to reject evil. . . . According to this model, the individual is fragile and the force of his own will is not strong enough to escape evil. . . . For this

reason, accounts of conversion do not stress repentance of sins but deliverance from evil (Loret Mariz 1998, 205, 219).

In the eyes of its charismatic Christian leadership, the most successful graduates are those who learn to inhabit the dimension of spirits that discretely directs the events around them. In this dimension, converts weave a new web of relations with spirits that disrupt their over-determined relations with people and with drugs. Holy Spirit possession, for instance, channels supernatural forces through discarded addicts, disrupting not only the intrapersonal, but also the social, order.

Ethnographers of spirit possession in a wide range of contexts have analyzed it as a mode of resistance to hierarchies of power; Alexander's (1991) study of African American Pentecostal spirit possession identified it as ritualized social protest. In his analysis, the speaking in tongues and unpredictable body movements of possession contradict middle-class European American behavioral norms, simultaneously rejecting dominant definitions of the worshippers' social status as inferior and affirming their sense of personal worth through union with the Holy Ghost. Janice Boddy (1989), in her study of trance possession among women in a gender-stratified Muslim Sudanese society, found that possession allowed them to speak in the voice of powerful men. Aiwa Ong (1987), in her classic study of young women factory workers in Malaysia, highlighted the ways that their spirit possession disrupted factory routines, and thereby the dehumanizing conditions of neoliberal expansion.

In this vein, conversion dislodges everyday social and conceptual relations, and opens an altered state of consciousness in which "a new and richer dimension of the old reality is envisioned and embraced" (Whitehead 1987: 25).

To achieve this altered state, Pentecostal converts disrupt routines through sleep deprivation, fasting, prayer, and drone-like incantation. They induce a state in which mental activity becomes less structured, and the normal rules of hierarchy, class, and causality cease to apply.

Themes of rupture and the discontinuity of the Spirit from the worldly or profane predominate in Pentecostal discourse internationally (Robbins 2004), ruptures that alter the social coordinates of converts. Pastor Mendoza of New Faith Academy, who had served in the U.S. Army during the Vietnam War, put it to me this way:

> When you accept Christ, you see things differently. Your priorities change . . . if you know [about God] but haven't experienced Him, you are not saved. It is an *experience*. . . . I didn't understand what happened when I converted. I [went through it] first and explained later. Suddenly I read the Bible. I saw my wife and children differently. I didn't see myself as Puerto Rican. I didn't see Vietnam. I didn't see racism.

I understood him to be pointing out that death of his old, carnal self on conversion also meant the end of his subordination, as a Puerto Rican on the U.S. mainland,

and as a veteran of an unpopular war. His new self was sacred, above the reach of human oppressions. In Juan's words, "God is a pottery maker, molding me." In the words of Samaria, a former heroin user at Victory Academy, "God breaks you up and puts you back together again the way He wants you."

The pastor's reference to losing his perception of himself as Puerto Rican also alludes to what Arlene Sanchez-Walsh (2003) has described as a current within Latino Pentecostal movements to reject ethnic solidarity in favor of an idealized global, Pan-Pentecostal community membership. This re-imagining of community as expansive and inclusive is appealing to Latinos who have experienced ethnic and racial marginalization in the United States, and perhaps even more so to ex-addicted converts who struggle with rejection from their own families and neighbors.

Converts speak of this re-imagined Christian self as timeless, as unmarked by ethnicity or class. Among Puerto Ricans, this re-imagining contrasts with struggles over identity politics that contend with anti-Latino, nativist sentiments on the U.S. mainland, and with Puerto Rico's liminal status as a U.S. territory without statehood or U.S. voting rights, in the midst of economic crisis and pervasive drug trade. Pentecostals across Latin America espouse total liberation, beginning with inner transformation, collectively creating small oases of healing in this world, and preparing for the Kingdom of God (Westmeier 1999). They call for separation from the world, for living a holy life as a critique of society.

Here the word "critique" might capture the moral righteousness of Pentecostal asceticism, but it misses the Pentecostal ethos of exhilaration, fascination, and engagement with the spirit realm that some describe as enchantment. Contemporary Pentecostalism seems to contradict Max Weber's classical thesis that the Calvinist-derived Protestant Ethic would be carried to its secular logical extreme in modernizing society, to a hyper-rationalized, bureaucratized, and disenchanted "iron cage." (Weber 1958). Juan, Octavio, and Pastor Mendoza's narrative of addiction and salvation is full of enchantments, beginning with enchantment by narcotics and their illusion of human self-control, ending with recognition of that illusion, and a new perception of the spirits that guide human events.

On Discipline and Becoming a Disciple

A WORK DAY

Dawn cast pink hues on the mountain as I pulled my mud-spattered station wagon past roaming chickens and empty fruit stands on the road to Victory Academy. I parked, hoping that the men of the ministry did not clean my car while I attended Bible study, as they had the week before. This morning I already was embarrassed by arriving half an hour late, knowing how much Academy leaders valued punctuality.

Jessica greeted me with a young recruit named Nanci. We climbed the stairs to the outdoor chapel where two rows of people kneeled on the ground. Their backs were turned to the altar, and their elbows rested on metal folding chairs, hands clasped together in prayer. To the right of the aisle were the men, the hum of their thirty voices speaking in tongues punctuated by "¡Gloria! ¡Gloria a Dios, gracias, gracias, Jesus!" (Glory! Glory to God, thank you, thank you Jesus!). To the left of the aisle, six women wearing long, shapeless skirts, with their hair pulled back from their bare faces, kneeled with their heads bowed. I settled my knees onto the concrete floor with the women, and tried to pray in my own way. I marveled that the others could maintain this position for so long, given that they had already been praying for half an hour.

But kneeling in prayer was only one of many physical tests that the Academy used to entrain converts. Indeed, my moving into the women's home at the Academy was about to open a window onto practices of welcoming pain and of suffering well—practices that, according to ministry leaders, left practitioners less vulnerable to addiction. These practices were a way to sanctify the addicted body and embody spiritual power. They were techniques of bodily and emotional discipline

philosophy of pain

used to retool narratives of addiction, from those of descent and isolation to those of ascent and connection.

After twenty minutes of prayer, Carmen, an Academy leader, tapped me on the shoulder. As we walked to the outdoor kitchen for breakfast Carmen told us that the women were served fifteen minutes before the men, so we had exactly fifteen minutes to eat. Two men who had been assigned kitchen duty served each of us a piece of white bread with one slice of salami and half of a stale doughnut. We seated ourselves, and Carmen led us in a prayer for our food. We ate in silence, and then walked downstairs to the dormitories to do chores. I was assigned the toilet and the bathroom sink, which I cleaned with Tilex and a rag. Nanci and Dalia swept and mopped around the bunk-beds next door.

After an hour of cleaning we walked to the outdoor chapel for a 9 a.m. Bible lesson. Carmen directed us to arrange our chairs in a circle. Her bun was pinned tightly to the nape of her neck, her long-sleeve pullover and ankle-length skirt swung loosely on her bony frame. She asked us to turn to Romans 12:1 ("Present your bodies as a living sacrifice, holy and pleasing to God; this is your spiritual worship"). Dalia and Tata opened their dog-eared paperback Bibles, Nanci opened her Precious Moments children's Bible, and Carmen her leather-bound teaching edition. Carmen's eyes pierced each of us in turn, asking us to read aloud and interpret what we read. Tata, a thick woman in her forties with cropped, bleached-blond hair, repeated that we should sacrifice ourselves to Jesus. Carmen nodded and explained what was meant by a living sacrifice. *meaning*

> One prayer I often repeat is "guard my lips so that I don't use negative words." This helps me to see things in another way, it opens my mind. We see things in a negative way when we can't see a way out. If you are weighed down, change how you see things. . . ! [W]hen I came (to the program) I only wanted to be here two weeks, but then my husband came. The Lord was telling me that I wasn't just bringing me.

Carmen called on Nanci, "What do you understand of what you read?" Nanci, looking at the floor, said, "Nothing." Carmen prodded her: "They say that evangelicals aren't ashamed." But Nanci was silent. Carmen read Romans 12:4 ("For we have many parts in one body, but these parts do not all have the same function").

> [That we are] the body of Christ means everyone has a function. When we were in the street, people didn't see the gold inside of us. He sees it. [He knows] that we have gifts. When we put others first, God takes care of our needs.

Carmen read a verse on forgiveness, and described a man who threatened her life.

> He raped me. I was filled with hate, I thought about killing him all the time. I finally forgave him. I was liberated, and I liberated him too. But God gave him justice—now he has HIV.

Carmen's eyes narrowed.

> Before, I hung out with drug users because they listened, they cared about me and my pain. I didn't think I could answer God's call. But God wants you to pass on lessons. Since you know the vice of crack [turning to Tata], you can help someone else [with the vice of crack]. God wants you to see we're useful. It's not true that we're garbage. [He wants us to see] that we have a function.

Tears streamed from Tata's eyes. Carmen continued, "We woke up sensitive today. Let's pray with her." Carmen bent over Tata, placed her hands on Tata's shoulders, and prayed.

Carmen led us to the outdoor chapel, where we settled onto our knees across the aisle from the men and prayed for ten minutes. The pastor's soft-spoken twenty-year-old son Samuel asked us to open the book of Solomon. His theme for the day was "Why does Satan want to get you out of prayer?" He called on one of the men, "Adam—why?" Adam responded "Because in the beginning Satan didn't agree that we should adore God." Samuel chuckled and shook his head from side to side.

> That's good, but we are talking about *oración* [prayer], not *adoración* [adoration]. Why? Because prayer strengthens our relationship with God, we give him our soul. Because prayer is a powerful weapon against the enemy. Sometimes people say God didn't answer me, but are you praying in your way or His way?

Samuel told us that through prayer, God would liberate us from our fears, that we would no longer be ashamed of ourselves, and that God would send His angels to defend us. If we prayed, we would make our names honorable, we would be blessed:

> How are you going to be blessed? You are going to have physical health and inner holiness; you will be covered with the blood of Jesus; full of the Holy Spirit. You are going to be a new man, transformed ... *la oración es ganancia, donde quiera te investes.* [He repeated this in English] Prayer is profit where you invest it. [Back to Spanish:] If you use your money to buy a business, you're going to produce a profit. You'll grow spiritually.

Someone shouted "Spiritual Wall Street!" in English.

Samuel picked up his guitar and led the group into singing "*Compromiso con Santidad*" ("Commitment to Holiness").

I considered Samuel's analogy, reminiscent of Ben Franklin saying that eating, sleeping and socializing steal from time in labor, and that labor leads to profit. It was a reversal of Max Weber's famous thesis in *The Protestant Ethic and the Spirit of Capitalism*, in which Weber argued that the Protestant ethic was the cultural foundation for modern secular financial markets—an ethic that demanded that every moment and effort be devoted to achieving a larger goal. In the sixteenth to

change of goal

eighteenth centuries, after the Protestant Reformation, this goal was to please God, but with the rise of modern capitalism—of which Ben Franklin is emblematic—the goal became to foster industrial growth. In a twist, Samuel drew on secular market values of maximizing growth to promote Protestant piety.

In the months that followed, I returned to Samuel's logic of prayer as an investment. His analogy of spiritual growth with economic growth resonated with Carmen's sermon on seeing your own value through your service to others. Carmen and Samuel's language of growth and value echoed themes of upward mobility that were pervasive in mainstream Puerto Rican television, magazines, and radio, yet I suspected that this language of uplift did different cultural work in the street ministries than in financial markets and popular media.

On the surface, prayer as investment might have sounded like evangelical prosperity gospel—the gospel of post-War U.S. preachers such as Oral Roberts, and later of megachurches and televangelists that promised financial returns on prayer or donations (Bowler 2013). But I never heard street ministers promise personal financial gain from prayer. In fact, they embraced a life of self-imposed poverty and suffering, a life that gained value the more it was oriented to giving to others and sacrificing its own material needs. Spiritual gain was inversely proportional to material gain, because, in their words, denying the flesh strengthened the spirit. Ministers redefined suffering as voluntary, as giving oneself in service to others; a source of honor and of spiritual power, not of marginality or disempowerment.

on suffering & the material world

The street ministries' concept of discipline also inverted the meaning of pain: enduring pain was a spiritual practice that ministers promised would free addicted people from fear and from fixation on pleasure. Pain helped converts to integrate their past experiences with their present identities as Christians, to identify with other converts and with the Holy Spirit. Suffering through the pain of withdrawal, and remembering addicted pasts, gives converts compassion for others, allowing them to "suffer with" new converts who are experiencing withdrawal and traumatic memories. They make pain productive, a valuable instrument of Christian selfhood, one that binds them to other converts. This differs from descriptions by social theorists of pain who argue that severe pain ultimately is alienating; that it cannot be effectively conveyed or shared with others, that it creates a vacuum of language and communication, a state beyond words and beyond empathetic imagination (Scarry 1986; Kleinman 1988).

discipline

In the ministry, bearing pain also meant restoring the capacity for delay, to dampen the impulsivity and sense of desperation that many described as core problems of addiction. Ironically, converts used their bodies as a vehicle to spiritually transcend the limits of their corporeal, everyday worlds. The addicted and withdrawing body—from a biomedical point of view a liability, needing to be tranquilized and managed—was, in the ministries, a sensitive instrument for channeling the will of God. Discipline was not simply an act of determination and

FIGURE 8. Amplified music during worship (*culto*). Photo by Helena Hansen.

self-control. Discipline also was a matter of giving over control. In this logic, the body in pain was exceptionally receptive, making a convert into a medium for contact with spirits, like a lightning rod pointed into a storm.

Lunch was canned pasta eaten in fifteen minutes of silence. We weeded the gardens, then had the afternoon to prepare for *culto* and to write reports on Christian books assigned during Bible study. Nanci wrapped doll's brushes and combs as gifts for her four small daughters. Tata sat on the mattress of her bunk bed writing a letter to her grown daughter. Samaria, Alexis, and Jessica showed up with two new converts, Eli and Dora. They complained that they were exhausted from making *pasteles* (Puerto Rican meat pastries) for Christmas sales the night before, then getting up the next morning to sell chocolates on the streets for the ministry.[1]

At 6:30 we lined up for dinner. The brothers on kitchen duty served us each two scoops of rice and beans and a cup of reconstituted frozen guava juice. As a vegetarian I ate hungrily, but Dora and Tata's long faces reminded me how sparse the meal seemed in this land of fried meat patties, stewed chicken, and beefsteak. By seven we filed into the chapel's left row of folding chairs that were reserved for women. We settled onto our knees to pray for twenty minutes, our elbows on the chairs and our backs to the pulpit.

FIGURE 9. Dancing during *culto*. Photo by Helena Hansen.

The men spoke loudly in tongues, punctuated by "¡Gloria a Dios!" A male leader circled both aisles, his palms to the sky and his eyes closed in a prayer of thanks. A band assembled on stage with Samuel on drums and Jose, the pastor's teenaged son, on electric piano. Jessica and Carmen sang backup into microphones (fig. 8). Samuel's songs built in momentum; the first two were slow and transitioned us from prayer to standing. The next three songs were faster (fig. 9), reaching a peak when the men jumped for Jesus (fig. 10), their bodies straight and their hands to their sides as they bounced higher and higher with the music. The women swayed and clapped; Dora, turning a toothy grin my way, thrust her palms over her head to the rhythm. Finally, a slow song brought the men to the ground and focused attention on the guest preacher.

Rail thin with a wispy beard and overbite, the preacher was the director of a home for addicted men in Guayama. He preached on the story of David and Goliath, asking us:

> What is your giant? The giant that is keeping you from blessings? If Goliath fights David, who else does he fight? God. [There is] the giant of fear, who wants you to lose confidence in your power. As Christians we can heal, we can exorcise demons. Giants can't tolerate difficult things. What happens when you do difficult things? You grow.

FIGURE 10. Jumping for Jesus (*Brincar para Cristo*). Photo by
Helena Hansen.

Another giant: the pride of Lucifer, to think yourself better. Before I relapsed, I was
Assistant Director of Crea, overseeing 20 programs. When I first came here I said
you don't have anything to offer me! Another giant: jealousy. My wife is alone tonight
with eight men in Guayama. I've had to work on jealousy.

The group laughed.

How do I know that you have [giants]? Because I have them. Even though I'm a
preacher, I have to come here and break my attitude. If you want to kill a giant, you
need prayer, [which is] the stone of Jesus, the Bible, [which is] the sword, and discipline.

He called us forward to renounce our giants. "Come up and accept Him." Five men
came up and kneeled in front of the altar with their heads bowed; the preacher and
four male leaders placed their hands on the men's shoulders and bent over them in
prayer. As they left, two women came forward and kneeled where the men had
been. Jessica, Carmen, and the pastor's wife laid hands on them and prayed.

grants

I reflected on giants during their prayer. Were giants the threat of psychic and physical pain that had to be endured without material comforts, and without substances? Were the giants the exclusions and rejections that these converts faced outside of the ministry? The story of David and Goliath seemed apt, I thought about the barriers that these converts faced, as penniless ex-addicts in economically depressed, millennial Puerto Rico. By rhetorically placing the giants inside of each convert, and framing Pentecostal discipline as a weapon to defeat those giants, the preacher brought the locus of control back to the convert. Yet, like David, converts did not only rely on themselves, they leveraged a force stronger than their giants.

After *culto* we filed down to the courtyard where I met two women who were graduates of the program. They had their children with them; Samaria held one on her lap, a quiet, brown-skinned 14-month-old boy. We discussed new converts who came in dehydrated and confused, in alcohol withdrawal. Samaria usually brought them to a local hospital that had agreed to rehydrate them without giving them medications. I sat myself next to Samaria on a cement wall and asked why it was important for them to *romper en frio*—to go cold turkey: withdraw without medications. Samaria took a deep breath.

> I went through so much, it made me think twice about doing it again. I said, "I don't wanna feel like that again." Some people maybe like the pain, because they come again and again. [But, for me,] it strengthened my faith because every time I had pain or couldn't sleep, I got on my knees and asked God for help. I felt better. The women attending me said you're the first I seen doing it that way—on your knees.

Pain would have been viewed differently in a clinic. Control of pain is a primary benefit that biomedical clinicians offer those in withdrawal and looking for treatment. In fact, clinicians assume that fear of pain is a major reason that people used drugs. Medical schools teach the "self-medication hypothesis:" that addicted people use drugs to bear psychic or bodily pain (Khantzian 1985). Addiction pharmaceuticals are primarily valued for their relief of withdrawal symptoms, which are, in biomedical thinking, a primary barrier to abstaining from drugs.

For Samaria, however, pain had spiritual significance; in fact, it was indispensible to her overcoming addiction: it strengthened her faith.[2]

I turned to Tata and asked how she found her way to the ministry. "I used crack, on weekends. My daughter knew. She helped so I didn't have to be on the street. I worked, I had a home. My pastor sent me here."

Tata was quiet for a moment. Her eyes were moist.

> I'm fighting with myself. I want to leave, to stay, to leave. I want to stay one month, but I have to talk with my daughter first so she understands. I'm leaving here but I'm not going to go back [to using drugs]. I'm going to be good with my God. I learned a lot here. I learned things about God I didn't know.

Tears broke over Tata's lower eyelids and streamed down her face. Samaria spoke gently to her:

> God breaks you up and puts you back together again the way he wants you. It's like falling and scraping a knee. You have to clean it first, and it hurts more. It will hurt until it's healed; that's the way the Lord works.

MONASTIC SELVES

Victory Academy emulated the earliest Christians, who, according to the New Testament, gathered in simple tabernacles on the first Pentecost after Christ's crucifixion and resurrection. There they received spiritual gifts of prophecy and faith healing, and spontaneously spoke in tongues. The impetus for the Pentecostal movement at the turn of the twentieth century had been, after all, a critique of the staid rituals and material comforts of Catholic and mainline Protestant churches. The austerity and emotional charge of Pentecostal worship were meant as correctives, directly linking worshippers to the Holy Spirit, and authenticating devotion through self-imposed pain and deprivation. For the Academy's culturally Catholic Puerto Rican converts, however, these practices might have called to mind the martyrdom of saints, or the self-flagellation of some monks. The Academy's techniques of moral reform also resembled the disciplinary project of medieval Catholic monasteries. As Talal Asad put it:

> The [medieval] monastic program was conceived in terms of . . . proper ways of eating, sleeping, working, and praying or with proper moral dispositions and spiritual aptitudes [that] are aimed at developing virtues that are put "to the service of God" (Asad 1993, 63).

Bodily rituals prescribed by medieval monasteries were thought to develop moral virtues. They demanded confession of sins and rites of reconciliation (penance), including abstinence from food, sleep, baths, and social interaction, which were reinforced by a vigilant community of monks (Asad 1993).

The monks' pursuit of perfection involved re-channeling memories of prior, profane experience (e.g., desire for sex, murderous impulse) into mental states that conformed to Christian teachings (e.g., desire for unity with God, humility through penitent self-torture). Through their ascetic practice they recrafted the body, the soul, and mind. Menial labor physically inscribed a posture of humility, on the premise that "idleness is the enemy of the soul." Sanctity was achieved through proper conduct, a "practical science of good living [whose] principle is humility" (Leclercq 1300 as cited by Asad 1993). Humility was a central Christian virtue because it signaled ascetic discipline as well as obedience to God's law. Humility required self-surveillance and self-correction to re-cast one's identity and desires in relation to Christ (Asad 1993).

Asad's reading of monastic discipline was inspired by Michel Foucault's theory of biopower, in which people not only are externally controlled by institutions (religious, clinical, educational, or carceral), but also internalize institutional authority through self-monitoring, and sculpt themselves into conformity. Victory Academy employed the techniques of monasteries: the requirement for public confession (testimony) and retribution through humbling menial labor, as well as ascetic practices such as fasting, sleep deprivation, and sexual abstinence. As Foucault might have predicted, group surveillance in the ministries habituated self-surveillance, and the re-channeling of sinful impulses into Christian passions. What Foucault might not have predicted was that, through self-imposed suffering, converts at the Academy cultivated an air of consecration and nobility reminiscent of elite monks in the middle ages, achieving a symbolically reversal of their marginalization.

Reversal of power relations through self-sacrifice has been a recurring theme in the history of Christianity, however. In the medieval period, hair represented masculine strength: in war, victors shaved the heads of vanquished kings. Monks voluntarily shaved their hair into tonsures, partaking of

> an ethics of self-sacrifice—which perhaps explains what endowed them with the ability to convey authority and social power. Indeed, this was a sleight of hand that was performed routinely in Christian discourse. Just as, for medieval martyrs, voluntary submission to pain often was represented as a source of power and transcendence (Mills 2004, 122–123).

Medieval friars recruiting warriors to the monastery, for instance, argued for the superiority of heavenly knights to earthly knights, as "heavenly knights are capable of enduring much more difficult trials," including domination of one's own bodily functions through celibacy, fasting, and self-torture (Heinonen 2004, 82–83). Self-domination through monastic discipline, then, holds long-established Christian cultural currency. Contemporary street ministries hold up self-domination as a form of liberation. They attempt to use internally entrained limitations and desires to overcome externally imposed limitations and desires.

Through daily practice, converts gain knowledge of sacred rites and texts, which they then interpret for newer converts. They also learn techniques to channel spirits. Are these forms of power illusory? From one perspective, they are. Street ministries separate themselves from this world in favor of an alternate, mystical realm; they do not attempt to overthrow the secular social order to which the burdens of poverty, joblessness, and addiction's misery could conventionally be ascribed. They avoid worldly political and economic entanglements, and support their bare necessities *"por fe"* (by faith)—through donations and small-scale industry—engaging with the State only enough to maintain conditions for worship, while citing Matthew 22:21 ("Give to Caesar what belongs to Caesar, and give to God what belongs to God.").

power through
submission

From another perspective, successful converts gain spiritual abilities, and significant influence over others. Yet, if this is a form of power, it is a form that is gained through submission. Accruing spiritual abilities requires accepting discipline from the ministry's leadership. Preachers speak of the "spirit of service," an attitude that marks spiritual growth. They frame accepting ministerial authority as an exercise of personal power.

The spirit of service is the cornerstone of the leadership training that they call *discipulado* (discipleship). One year into my study of the Academy, I was invited to observe *discipulado*. *Discipulado* involved a series of evening meetings, in which twelve leaders from the ministry's homes sat on either side of a long table with Pastor Mendoza at the head in a high-backed chair. The pastor selected disciples to learn the fundamentals of leadership so that they might rise to the tasks to which they were called.

At the *discipulado* we bowed our heads while the pastor led us in prayer. We then placed our Bibles and notebooks on the table, our pens poised to copy the title of the evening's lecture: "The spirit of service is caught, not taught." The pastor directed us to Psalms 2:11 (Serve God with fear), and Hebrews 12:28 (Serve Him with loving adoration). "It is a privilege, a pleasure to work for God. For instance, if I carry your child in my arms, I'm going to get tired. But if I carry my own child . . . something gives me the strength. . . . Those who are the most servile are the leaders, they are the kings."

Here the pastor was speaking of ownership, of responsibility, of self-possession, that molds the spirit and practices of ministry leaders and others, as directed by God: an exercise of choice and power rather than subordination. His reference to having the strength to carry his own child made sense in this light. The pastor's argument was that agency and power are relational and attitudinal: obligations to others are oppressive if one does not identify with those making demands, but the same obligations are empowering if one is aligned with those to whom one is obligated. An internal adjustment of perspective can therefore transform an experience of domination and entrapment into one of voluntarism and agency.

This framing of agency has specific implications for addicted people for whom control is a central concern. Although psychiatrists define drug-dependent people as those who are out of control, their patients often describe drug use as an effort to gain control. Addicted people might describe themselves as self-medicating psychic pain (Southwick and Satel 1990, Damphousse and Kaplan 1998) or achieving fine control of their brain and body function through complicated daily drug regimens (Courtwright, Joseph, and Des Jarlais 1989). Addiction requires the mastery of a set of skills; it might involve small, everyday achievements, such as "scoring" drugs (buying them on a perilous black market), and injecting them intravenously into scarred veins. It requires competence at a way of life in which survival is difficult. Some ethnographers describe a form of pride that addicted people take in their skill in navigating their marginal status. Bourgois and Schoneberg (2009) report that African American homeless heroin injectors speak of themselves as "righteous dopefiends:" "outlaws" committed to "dying with their boots on." Decades before, Jackson (1978) found that heroin users identified themselves as "addicts" because naming their outsider status "permits them to survive" (Jackson 1978, 275).

Like narcotics addiction, evangelical Protestantism places adherents outside of the mainstream: defecting from the Catholic Church historically has been an act of political resistance in Puerto Rico and other parts of Latin America, where the Catholic church was hegemonic (Romberg 2003, Brusco 1995). Evangelists refer to themselves simply as *Cristianos* (Christians), a name they do not grant to Catholics. They contrast the Biblical authenticity of their worship with what they see as the empty ritual of Catholic services. As Director Menocal of Restoration House put it, "Christianity is not a title, you have to live it." Preachers in *culto* at Victory Academy and Restoration House often speak with disdain of *religiosos* (religious ones), the nominal Catholics that comprise most of the Puerto Rican population.

Pentecostalism requires followers to identify themselves as *Evangelios* (Evangelists) or *Cristianos* (Christians), and requires public behaviors that validate this identity. Authentic Christianity must be visible in action. Converts are taught to evangelize by setting an example through Christian acts.

In contrast, Spiritism and Santería—two other popular religious movements in Puerto Rico and throughout many parts of Latin America—have adapted to Catholic religious repression with vows of secrecy and with syncretic, Catholic iconography (Romberg 2003, González-Wippler 1996). Neither Spiritism nor Santería require public practice; their practices can be secret or ambiguous, and public identity might not be congruent with personal practice. The Catholic Church requires members to publicly identify themselves, but some question whether it holds members accountable. As converts at Victory Academy and Restoration House told me, "The Catholic church lets you do anything—smoke, drink," and absolves sins by confession. Many of them had children by multiple Catholic partners and had not thought of marriage until their conversion.

Ex-addict evangelists, for their part, are preoccupied with matching word and deed. External acts authenticate their internal transformation. Their external acts, however, are made possible by the austere community of ministries. In the ministries, work, self-sacrifice, and humility are enacted through relationships of reciprocity, recognition, and mutual responsibility. Converts described a *relational* form of personal agency; a sense of possibility awakened by contact with the Holy Spirit and sustained by solidarity with other ministry members.

AUTHENTICITY

A few months after my stay at Victory Academy, Ricardo, an Academy leader, asked me if I knew that Victory Academy was changing its name to Walk in the Light. Many things are changing, and changing for the better, he said. "We're going back to our roots, to God, nothing more. We had become too professional."

I asked what he meant.

> When someone was sick we'd take them to the doctor. We didn't pray for them. We didn't work with them in the beginning, as we should. We're going to have a big lesson for the leaders on Saturday—the pastor is going to hit them hard with that. I can't wait. Because we had been different from other programs, but now we are getting to be the same.

I asked what he meant by the program having been different. Ricardo talked about authentic evangelical practice. "We went to God for everything, prayed on everything. That's what made the program special. That's what got me. If I hadn't had (a direct experience with God) I wouldn't be here, I'd be on the streets. That was something I'll never forget."

By this time, I had come to feel that charismatic Christians in Puerto Rico were obsessed with authenticity. As if to underscore action over appearance and the spontaneity of communion with God, accessories to worship fell away. A canvas tent covered Victory Academy's chapel: it lacked walls for the ornate windows or portraits of Christ and Madonna that would have embellished a Catholic church. The Academy's pulpit was a raised plank of unfinished wood, and the podium was marked only by a microphone. This contrasted with the embroidered cloths, floral arrangements, candles, and brass-work I had seen at Catholic mass. In place of cushioned pews of the Catholic Church, the Academy's rusted folding chairs seated worshipers during *culto*, doubled as elbow rests for people in prayer, that were neatly stacked and stored away when not in use so that the bare concrete floor might be swept daily.

For Pentecostals, any place could be a chapel: a park, a living room, or an abandoned building. The church, in its members' literal Pentecostal reading of the Bible, was a community of worshipers, not a physical place. The word "church" was rarely used at the Academy; converts preferred the word "ministry," which invoked the verb to minister and its emphasis on action over the more passive, or sedentary noun church. The word ministry, as opposed to church, also distinguished them from Catholics, who were invested in elaborate church buildings at established hours for mass rather than spontaneous worship. Among Pentecostals, loud group prayer could break out without warning, in homes or on street corners, wherever two or more converts gathered. *Culto* had no printed order of service, which enhanced its ethos of spontaneity and action. Bibles were not provided at *culto*; worshipers brought their own dog-eared copies, some zipped inside of a leather cover with care, pages highlighted and notes in the margins reflecting personal study. The Bible was a tool for active personal use, not for ceremonious display as on Catholic altars.

At the Academy, authentic worship was signaled by spontaneous outbursts of emotion, such as crying or screaming with the ecstasy of contact with the Holy Spirit, by falling on the floor unconscious, "slain in the Spirit," or by speaking in tongues seemingly against one's own will. This spontaneity, however, was paradoxically achieved through habituation to a daily ritual of Bible study, prayer, and street evangelism. These rituals entrained worshippers to host visitations of the Holy Spirit. Authentic worship was thus an example of what Bradford Verter (2003) called embodied spiritual capital: a practice that appears spontaneous but is actually taught and then naturalized—rehearsed until it feels natural and is taken for granted.

The street ministries' emphasis on authenticity made sense in light of the shame that many converts had about having lied and stolen while using drugs. Their preoccupation with rejecting worldly desires could allay the doubt that others might have about their sincerity and—even more critically—the doubt they had about themselves.

Charismatic evangelists across Latin America speak of other-worldliness, of a transcendent World of the Spirit apart from the World of the Flesh that is achieved within an ascetic Christian community (Chavan de Matviuk 2002). Their rituals of purification stem from the nineteenth-century Holiness movement (Dayton 1987), and are designed to align the worshiper with the Holy Spirit and achieve harmony of belief with action. As a leader at Victory Academy put it, "Our behavior reflects God's presence."

Themes of harmony and authenticity are not unique to addiction ministries. Three other addiction treatment modalities common in the United States—biomedical programs, Twelve-Step meetings, and secular therapeutic communities—also employ a concept of an authentic self, of restoration to a balanced state. The self that is addressed in biomedical treatments is an integrated chain of biochemical reactions. Biomedical treatments, such as opiate maintenance on methadone, opiate receptor blockers including naltrexone, or the sedatives prescribed for withdrawal symptoms, attempt to restore neurotransmitters to their pre-addiction levels of activity and approximate the "natural" function in the brain: the chemically balanced self. Twelve-Step programs focus on breaking through denial—the inauthentic self—to reveal the true self: sober but chronically vulnerable to relapse. Therapeutic communities, modeled on confrontational techniques of the 1950s secular residential program, Synanon, assume that addiction is an attempt to avoid negative feelings such as fear, self-doubt, and resentment. The goal of these therapeutic groups and institutional reward system is catharsis; residents are pushed to be "honest about true feelings," to "kick out these emotions we'd been hiding and pushing down" (Casriel and Amen 1971, 123, 125) to uncover the self.

The authenticating practices of ministries are rituals of harmonization with the Holy Spirit, rather than the rituals of neurochemical balance and pharmaceutical dosage adjustment in biomedicine, the rituals of confession and redemption in Twelve-Step programs, or the rituals of confrontation and catharsis in therapeutic communities.

Although it is true, as Asad writes, that when viewed with contemporary lenses, archaic Christian "rituals of humiliation and abasement are now symptoms of patients, not the discipline of agents" (Asad 1993, 167), the self-sacrificial asceticism of street ministries bears a family resemblance to medieval Christian practices. Street ministries, however, add a contemporary discourse of authenticity to these practices. Medieval models of selfhood did not conceptualize a private identity or inner dialogue in conflict with society. That dialogical concept of self-developed during Europe's Enlightenment to account for the individual in a modern post-Reformation hubris of personal rights and responsibility for one's own destiny (Thiher 2004). Late-twentieth-century philosopher Charles Taylor (1992) argued that this separation of self from society was the basis for a modern ethos in which individuals prioritize self-realization over human relationships; for what he termed the "ethic of authenticity," which—in its most distorted form—promoted private fulfillment over collective good. In this version of modernity, no transcendent authority, especially religious authority, could mediate the values and choices that were legitimated by individual sentiment.

Pentecostalism has absorbed this construct of an authentic self while reconnecting it to the collective. I noticed this in my discomfort when evangelists refused to respect my privacy. Director Menocal of Restoration Home challenged me when I was interviewing Juan, "You still studying? Are you studying the Bible?" I avoided the pastor from Ponce who ignored my claim to be a researcher and demanded to know why I was not saved; I avoided the co-director at Victory Academy who always asked if I had chosen Christ. Throughout my field research, I held onto a separate, inner life, filled with agnostic social theory that I used to distance myself from the cultural logics of the people I observed. It was the part of me that was "real," and not strategically presented in order to build rapport with my informants. My informants saw themselves as helping me to foster my "real" self by encouraging—even pressuring—me to take steps to achieve it. For them, finding one's real self was not something achieved alone: it required a community of mutual aid among believers, which was what justified evangelism.

 I did not expect to feel ashamed, yet their constant probes made my sitting in the front row with the converted women at *culto*, and my participation in group prayer before Bible study, seem disingenuous. Each time we were asked to speak about the work of Christ in our lives I sat silent, part of me wanting to convert so that I, too, could experience the harmony of inner with outer self that was being promised. I was subject to the same technologies of desire that the ministry used on its ex-addicted recruits, by having them practice *as if* they were fully converted, until promises of harmony and authenticity led them to affectively align themselves with their practice. I began to see how personal testimony given at *culto*, at Bible study, or in street evangelism reworked the links between shame and desire, between private responses and public representation. In Carmen's words, evangelicals are not ashamed. They see the problem of shame as one of a mismatch between thought and act, between the will of mortals and the will of God. Evangelical testimony attempts to reconcile these oppositions, by making what is private public, and narrating the arc of addiction to conversion as alignment with the Holy Spirit.

When individuals perform testimony, asceticism, and worship within the collective of the ministries, they come to embody authentic, internal motivation and sentiment through externally imposed habits that are monitored and reinforced by the group. In this way, the community of converts becomes incorporated in the individual—a folding of social forces into the self, to borrow from Deleuze (1988). It is a reciprocal process; those who internalize the group's habits, motives, and emotions in turn strengthen the group itself, making it more coherent and heightening its effects on other members. This reciprocity holds for the members' relationship with Christ: collective worship and group prayer elicit sentiment that enables members to feel a personal connection to the Holy Spirit, deepening their commitment to the collective, in a version of the "collective effervescence" that nineteenth-century sociologist Emile Durkheim described as constitutive of totemic religions (Durkheim 1965). The Pentecostal self being fashioned in street ministries therefore is both intimately personal and authentic on one hand, and a collective product on the other; authenticity is based not on the expression of an individual quality that can be extracted from its environment, rather, authenticity is produced in relationship to the Holy Spirit (as apparent to practitioners), and in relationship to other converts (as apparent to observers like myself). This contrasts with the essential biochemical self of clinical medicine, a congenitally formed self that has the same fundamental deficiencies and vulnerabilities before and after treatment.

In his classic study of Pentecostal Catholic faith healers, Thomas Csordas (1994) calls attention to the self as shaped by practice, harnessing imagination, memory, language, and emotion to engage and orient itself in the world. He writes that the self is embodied and experiential, it is always "en route" and subject to hermeneutical intervention such as healing systems. A worshiper in his study who lost consciousness during services reported that, during her trance, she retraced memories of childhood abuse, adding a loving Christ to rescue and soothe her. By inserting Christ into these childhood memories, she was able to forgive her past aggressor and become more Christ-like in her own conduct.

At Victory Academy, evangelists re-worked their personal histories, inserting divine intervention to make meaning of their suffering. Carmen's Bible study narrative of her rape, its retribution, and her re-valuation as part of the body of Christ demonstrated this re-working of personal history. Converts also incorporated competing concepts of the self—such as biological views of the body—into their re-worked senses of self. Take Samaria, who told me that when the state health department came by Victory Academy and she tested positive for HIV,

> People were surprised that I took it so well. Even Mama Tita and the pastor sat me down and said "aren't you worried?" They were afraid I'd leave the ministry, that I'd go out again. But I said [that] God wouldn't have given me this if I wasn't ready for it. Maybe God is giving me this so I can help others with the disease. There were two girls here who were crying, they couldn't understand it. I said, see, that's why God didn't give it to you, because he knew you would react that way . . . the doctors, they told me I had to take medicines, [that I] had to avoid getting wet, to avoid people with colds. I took the medicine for a while but it made me feel sicker. Now it's just sitting in the office. And I feel great! My doctor says it's a miracle, she's never seen it before. They hold me up as an example for the others. I'm down to [a viral load of] 400 as of December, from 168,400 in October, without medicines. And I told [the doctor] where I live, that I care for people who come in off the street, with sores, their body broken down. I can't put a mask on, I can't wear gloves because I'd be saying I didn't want to touch them. The girls here are always getting sick but I haven't been sick.

Samaria added that she had been retested for HIV and the results were negative.

I wasn't sure which she saw as greater evidence of God's work in her life; her apparent cure without medicines, or her reaction to the news that she was infected. She had not read her infection as a curse, but took it as a sign of God's confidence in her faith. Ironically, it was a state public-health van that identified her infection, and it was her doctor who identified her remission through laboratory tests. Yet it was Victory Academy that encouraged Samaria to get tested and provided her transportation to her doctor's visits. Samaria's evangelical worldview and her biomedical events were not contradictory; rather, in Samaria's interpretation, biomedical events only helped to confirm her faith. As far as she was concerned, it was because she was close to God that she learned of her HIV infection; she then felt called to evangelize others with HIV.

As any leader at the ministries' homes will tell you, however, recognizing God's gift in an apparent curse takes more than a thought. As Tanya Luhrmann shows in her study of contemporary evangelists, they go beyond the cognitive and linguistic techniques of Bible citation and study; they use metakinetic and relational learning techniques—those that cultivate bodily and mental trance states—enabling them to feel God's presence and converse with God (Luhrmann 2012). Addiction ministries strove to invert private to public, shame to authority, and self-absorption to responsibility through affective experiences with the Holy Spirit, brought about by prayer, fasting, emotive worship. As Luhrmann observed in the United States, evangelical discourse focuses on "walking with God," a metaphor for daily bodily engagement as well as an affective sense of personal, emotional connection to the Holy Spirit.

Walking with God also meant developing spiritual eyes and ears: converts looked for mystical evidence of God's will in their everyday lives. This represented a style of seeing and living that Kathleen Stewart—an ethnographer of poor people in Appalachia who are looking for reasons to hope and for ways to survive—called "scanning for signs" (Stewart 1996).

In street ministries, externally visible bodily discipline and emotive expression cultivated internal states of heightened self-awareness and vigilance to produce an authentic self. This self was continuously in the making, the product both of the convert's willpower from the inside and of the action of the Holy Spirit from the outside. Because pain plays a productive role in this self-making, and because it is transformation through painful experience that anoints converts to become disciples and conduits of spiritual authority, the healer status of street ministers is validated by their suffering. This is not unlike the moral authority that physicians gain through self-sacrifice in clinical training (Becker et al. 1961; Merton, Reader, and Kendall 1957) or the "wounded healer" figure of narrative theorist Arthur Frank (Frank 2013) and of psychoanalyst Carl Jung, someone who is compelled to treat others in order to care for his or her own wounds, and whose "own hurt . . . gives the measure of his power to heal" (Jung 1966, 239). Pentecostal street ministers were not the first to convert pain to power, but—unlike allopathic physicians, largely drawn from the privileged classes—Pentecostal ex-addicts engage in elaborate practices of social alchemy to achieve a symbolic inversion (Alexander 1991) of domination and submission, weakness and strength, in what they would call "spiritual victory."

And it turns out that zealous enchantment and alchemic conversions of pain into power pervade the origin myths that Pentecostals on Puerto Rico and the United States mainland tell about themselves. In these stories, the Pentecostal movement itself is ignited by a direct visitation from the Holy Spirit, a visitation that backlights the bleak landscapes of rapidly industrializing, class- and race-segregated cities, opening possibilities for self-production, thriving, and unity with the rest of humanity. In interviews with street ministry founders, and in reading biographies of early Pentecostal leaders, I saw this narrative of visitation as the thread connecting nineteenth-century Millenarians with contemporary struggles against narcotraffic.

ALTERNATE ORIGINS

When I interviewed her in 2003, Judith Rossy was a wiry woman in her eighties. She wore a long-sleeved black knit dress that fell just above her ankles; her gray bun was pinned neatly on the nape of her coffee-colored neck. Sitting erect at her office desk, she gave no hint of her recent spine fracture. She told me that she accepted Christ more than six decades before, as a student in a Catholic high school near San Juan. She had always been afraid of the *evangelicos* in the Pentecostal ministries in her neighborhood, but was suffering from a grave illness that her doctors could not diagnose or treat. In the course of a few years she converted and was cured of three illnesses by faith.

She met her husband when he was an inmate and she was a volunteer in the San Juan prisons. He had gotten addicted to heroin in New York, and came back to the island where he was liberated from drugs by faith. Mrs. Rossy was employed as a secretary in the capitol building at the time and, through a friend of the governor, she got her husband released from prison. The Rossys began converting addicts, helping them enroll in classes and find work.

Drug-treatment programs were almost non-existent at the time, so Mrs. Rossy and her husband soon opened a detoxification center in San Juan. They testified in the street to their triumph over addiction, and the 4 people who first came to stay on the floor of their small house soon grew to 35. Within a month and a half, the Rossys were forced to move to a building that housed 70 people to accommodate the flow of referrals from the court, local churches, and the police. Desperate families brought their addicted members, and some made donations to the center. Otherwise, Mrs. Rossy explained, addicts often died because their parents did not know what to do.

That was 1966. The center was named *Silo Misión Cristianera*. Local churches helped to staff the growing mission with volunteers, and raised funds for the mission to move to a more spacious location. By the 1980s, *Silo* was also getting funds from the United Way, municipal and state governments, Lions Clubs, and a radio telethon. Addicts came to the ministry from as far away as New York, St. Thomas, and Guatemala. As a result, *Silo* graduates later opened addiction ministries in Chicago, Guatemala, and Venezuela, among other places. Graduates also helped to multiply addiction ministries on the island—one started the *Misión de Refugio* in Ponce. Three early graduates of *Silo* founded the Christian rehabilitation program *Corda* in Humacao. Mrs. Rossy, now a preacher in the Pentecostal Church of God, still ran *Silo*. Her office walls were lined with photos of *Silo* graduates and the ministries that they had founded with her training. Yet, I discovered that *Silo* was only one of several genealogical lines of ministries founded by ex-addicted converts on the island, lines that stemmed from an even larger African American and Latino Pentecostal revival that was born at the peak of Jim Crow segregation in the United States.

WHERE AND HOW DID PENTECOSTALISM BEGIN?

The best-known origin story of Pentecostalism is set in Topeka, Kansas, on New Year's Eve in 1900. A student in the Methodist Bible school there, Agnes Ozman,[3] felt a supernatural euphoria overtake her during group prayer, and began to speak in a foreign tongue. Witnesses later identified it as Chinese. The tongue spread to the other group members who experienced a three-day visitation of the Holy Spirit. The group— worshippers who found mainline Protestantism uninspired and institutional—wanted to return to the authentic roots of Christian faith, and had been studying the Book of Acts before the prayer session. Their discussion had centered on speaking in tongues as one of the gifts of first-century Christians who worshiped on the Pentecost before the resurrection of Jesus. When Ozman's speech became unintelligible, the group saw it as a sign that Christ's return was imminent, and that the ancient tribes of the world, once disbanded at Babel, were being reunited.

The school's white teacher, Charles F. Parnham, became the founder of the Pentecostal movement, preaching on speaking in tongues as a sign of baptism in the Spirit at revivals in the Midwest, the South, the West, and eventually the East. These revivals fostered Pentecostal organizations, independent churches, and missions, and led to a Pentecostal style of worship in some mainline Methodist, Baptist, and Catholic churches (Dayton 1987). Speaking in tongues, or "glossolalia," became emblematic of Pentecostalism's ecstatic worship style,[4] in a tradition that emphasizes that any worshipper can be baptized in the Holy Spirit and receive the gifts of speaking in tongues, faith healing, and prophecy—described in Acts 2 as occurring during the first Pentecost after the death of Christ.

Some say that it was not until 1906 that the Holy Spirit truly recreated the original Pentecost, however. It was then that William Seymour, a black minister who had listened to lectures through the window of Charles Parnham's segregated Bible college in Houston, Texas, led a revival at a store-front mission on Azusa Street in Los Angeles, California, that caught the attention of the nation. It began after ten days of fasting and prayer in the home of a nearby black couple who welcomed Seymour after he was shunned for preaching on the controversial topic of speaking in tongues. On the tenth day of their home vigil, the group received a visitation of the Spirit and began speaking in tongues. Their speaking in tongues, faith healings, and trances reached such a crescendo that white onlookers joined in, and the revival moved to an abandoned African Methodist Episcopal church building where worshippers rearranged the pews into a circle, symbolizing oneness for the interracial group. The growing congregation recognized that they were experiencing the worldwide restoration of the Pentecost that heralded the apocalyptic second coming of Christ, according to nineteenth-century Holiness movement doctrine. National newspapers covered the event (fig. 11), reporting that Seymour had prophesied the destruction of non-believers at the moment that great earthquakes hit San Francisco, California, and Los Angeles, California.

The revival continued nonstop for three years; Seymour's desegregated Apostolic Faith Mission hosted 3 services every day for more than 800 people. The preachers and council of elders leading the church were female and male, black

Los Angeles Daily Times

WEDNESDAY MORNING, APRIL 18, 1906.

WEIRD BABEL OF TONGUES.

New Sect of Fanatics Is Breaking Loose.

Wild Scene Last Night on Azusa Street.

Gurgle of Wordless Talk by a Sister.

Breathing strange utterances and mouthing a creed which it would seem no sane mortal could understand, the newest religious sect has started in in Los Angeles. Meetings are held in a tumble-down shack on Azusa street

for his church, head down, eyes absently fixed on his coming sermon. Suddenly his book went flying one way; his hat another. His two arms widely clutched the empty air. With a furious sprawl, he measured his length along the gravel walk.

From behind a neighboring hedge came very suspicious snickers. Mr. Gould brushed himself off as best he could and proceeded sorrowfully to church.

He had just started in on his "first-ly" when here came an ominous thump and a startling ker-bang on the roof; everyone in the congregation jumped with a start; then smiled and resumed attention to the sermon.

Another thump sounding like Vesuvius getting busy! One of the deacons ran outside. Snorts of laughter, but the thumping ceased.

But just as the congregation was getting rapt in attention to the sermon, there came a most dismal sound, seemingly from the regions under the earth. It was a most lonely, piercing and doleful howl

The sermon came to a dead stop. Out from under one of the pews crawled the most forlorn-looking kitten that ever existed. It was not happy and it desired the world to know of its state of mind. Scared by

AMAZING SUIT FOR DIVORCE.

Pretty White Wife Weary of Black Husband.

Friendless Girl's Story of Sorry Match.

Claims She Loved Negro When Married.

The wife: a dainty little pink-and-white Dresden china girl. The husband: a big, loudly-dressed negro.

These are the characters in an amazing divorce suit filed yesterday in the

LOS AN HO

A DISTINCT hon feet of another C.A. girl, Miss C for the past year ar educational secretar sociation. Miss Pat pointed general secr

good taste, seen before hey are fresh

t Suits

ks

FIGURE 11. Los Angeles Daily Times reports the babble of tongues on Azusa Street prior to the 1906 earthquake.

and white, and under the shadow of Jim Crow laws even white Southern pastors traveled to Los Angeles to receive blessings with "the negroes." By 1908, the mission mailed 50,000 copies of each newspaper issue and had sent missionaries to 50 countries: "not only had poor drunkards and dope addicts found salvation but learned clergy and veteran missionaries embraced the movement" (MacRobert 1988, 58). The pneumatic experience of possession by the Holy Spirit "qualified and empowered those whose hearts were converted" (MacRobert 1988, 84). Because the Spirit operated on them directly, color and education no longer signaled the abilities of converts; rather, speaking in tongues, casting out demons, and healing through the laying on of hands was evidence of their baptism in the Holy Ghost.

It was not until Seymour married Jennie Evans Moore against the wishes of the two white women who published the mission newsletter that this equalizing vision of power unraveled. Incensed, they left the congregation, took the newsletter roster with them, and the nascent Pentecostal church splintered into black (Church of God in Christ) and white (Assemblies of God and the United Pentecostal Church). The belief in a power that could bridge race, class, culture, and denomination through pneumatic experience, a power to heal the wounds of racism through charismatic healing and possession, was once again confined to black congregations where the black person "could have his humanity and dignity affirmed . . . [and] find an outlet for the self[-]expression, creativity, and diverse abilities stifled by white society" (MacRobert 1988, 94).

The legacy of Azusa Street Mission did not end in black and white, however; it also spawned Latino Pentecostalism. It was at the Azusa revival that Mexicans began to worship with black and white American Pentecostals, until a conflict between Seymour and the Mexican contingent led to splintering and the formation of the Latino Pentecostal movement. This movement can be traced to the Latin District Council of the Assemblies of God, founded in 1915, and the Oneness Apostolic Assembly of the Faith in Christ Jesus founded by Antonio Casteneda Nava and Francisco Llorente in 1916. In 1917, two former Azusa Street participants also converted Francisco Olazabal to Pentecostalism, and Olazabal was to act as a major catalyst for Latino conversion in the United States, Mexico, and Puerto Rico (Espinosa 1999).

A graduate of the Wesleyan School of Theology in San Luis Potosi, Mexico, and the Moody Bible Institute in Chicago, Illinois, Olazabal was a fully bilingual and bicultural ordained minister who started Methodist missions to Spanish speakers across California with support from white congregations. At some point, however, his wife fell ill and was cured by Pentecostals who laid on hands. Asserting that baptism in the Holy Spirit was necessary for Christian life, and that divine healing was available to all who asked in faith, Olazabal became a Pentecostal. Olazabal began preaching and performing dramatic faith healings in revivals across the nation for thousands of Mexicans and Puerto Ricans in migrant farm labor camps, factories, and inner cities. He broke with the Anglo-led—and, in his mind, patronizing—Latin District Council of the Assemblies of God, and was pursued both by the famous Four Square Gospel founder Aimee Semple McPherson and by the Anglo-American Church of God with offers for a merger. Olazabal attracted extensive crowds of migrant Puerto Ricans in New York, and the Puerto Rican paper El Mundo reported that during a 1934 tour of the Puerto Rican island he converted 20,000 people.

Although by his death in 1937, Olazabal's hopes for an interracial and interdenominational Christian movement were dashed by attacks from mainline white Protestant and Catholic churches, he had succeeded in founding the largest Latino Protestant denomination in North America, and the fourth largest Pentecostal denomination in the world. By all reports, Olazabal exuded the charisma of the Holy Spirit in his persona of "the Mighty Aztec." His appeal was enhanced by the fact that during the peak of American Jim Crow policies (and the Great Depression) "His authority was not dependent upon Anglo-American approval but allegedly came directly from God" (Espinosa 1999, 613).

Charismatic Protestant evangelism had arrived in Puerto Rico well before Olazabal's mass conversions, however. The field was tilled for evangelists in 1898, when the United States took possession of Puerto Rico from Spain in the Spanish American War and ended centuries of Catholic prohibitions of Protestant proselytizing. The following year (1899), North American Protestant leaders held an interdenominational prayer meeting in which they laid plans to evangelize then-Catholic Puerto Rico as the gateway to the rest of Latin America. Baptist, Methodist, Presbyterian, and Congregational leaders developed a comity agreement, dividing the island geographically into four sections, each denomination responsible for missionizing one section. The following year five more denominations joined the comity agreement and the island was further divided into nine missionizing territories. By 1910, the island was considered fully occupied by eleven North American Protestant missions (Moore 1969).

Yet, it was a Puerto Rican who brought Pentecostalism to the island. In 1916, Juan Lugo, a migrant who had become Pentecostal in Hawaii, was drawn back to Puerto Rico by a vision of Ponce that he received in prayer. When he reached Ponce and was joined by two fellow Puerto Rican migrants returning from Hawaii—Salamon Feliciano and his wife—the three saw twenty souls saved in the first two months of their street- and home-based preaching. Converts from the growing Ponce congregation in turn felt called to preach in other towns, more Puerto Rican Pentecostal migrants returned to the island to missionize, and by 1920 a Pentecostal conference was held in Ponce, representing 600 members and 11 congregations from across the island. The Puerto Rican Pentecostal Church of God, by then a part of the U.S.-based Assemblies of God, was incorporated in 1922, with its membership concentrated in rural areas and led largely by native Puerto Rican pastors, among them illiterate sugar cane cutters (Moore 1969).

From early on, ethnicity and identity politics strained the relationship between the native leadership of the Puerto Rican Pentecostal Church of God and its stateside counterpart, the Assemblies of God. In an incident that highlighted the political marginality of Puerto Rico, the Pentecostal Church of God leadership in Puerto Rico thought of itself not as a Latin American mission, but as a U.S. district body, and was surprised when its petition for recognition as a state district was denied by the U.S. Assemblies of God. As a result, in 1947 the Puerto Rican leadership declared itself independent of the Assemblies of God and formed its own missions to Latin America, and to the United States, including New York City. This newly independent Pentecostal Church of God expanded rapidly in the Puerto Rican industrial-economic boom of the 1950s and '60s. Observers pointed out that Pentecostal pastors were of the same educational background and salary level as the people they evangelized, and that their prophetic evangelism appealed to disinherited workers; Pentecostalism grew most quickly among low-income Puerto Ricans. The mountainous Puerto Rican terrain, lack of transportation, and the tendency of Puerto Ricans toward *caudillismo* (following a strong leader) all contributed to rapid splintering of congregations. By 1966, the membership of the Pentecostal Church of God had long surpassed that of other Protestant denominations at 19,000—nearly twice that of the Baptists and more than twice that of the other Protestant groups it rivaled, including Methodists, Disciples of Christ, and Adventists (Moore 1969, 5, 13). Thirty years later, by the 1990s, Pentecostals comprised almost 30% of the island's population (Cleary and Stewart-Gambino 1997).[5]

As ministries multiplied on the island, new forms of ministry developed among mainland Puerto Ricans. In his autobiography (adapted in the 1970 film *The Cross and the Switchblade*), David Wilkerson describes himself as a young white Pentecostal pastor in rural Pennsylvania who, in 1958, received a vision calling him to minister to teenaged Puerto Rican gang members on trial for murder in New York City. A white man of slight build from the countryside, upon his arrival to Brooklyn, Wilkerson got the leaders of two of New York's largest black and Latino gangs to kneel and pray in front of a housing project. The same year, Wilkerson and a Spanish-speaking Assemblies of God congregation put on an outdoor rally for gangs from all New York boroughs. It ended with the mass conversion of gang leaders who had been at war with the police; after the rally, they turned in their weapons to the police station, Bibles in hand.

Wilkerson left his parish in Pennsylvania to work with the gangs in New York full time. Increasingly aware of the economic and social conditions that fostered gangs, he denounced the racial segregation which trapped black and Latino families in overpriced, rundown tenements, as well as the urban-renewal policies that concentrated the poor families in marginal neighborhoods (Wilkerson, Sherrill, and Sherrill 1963). Yet, Wilkerson stated that his mission was not worldly politics; it was to bring the Holy Spirit to the neediest youth in the City so that the Spirit could work miracles on them directly. He called on worldly men of wealth and influence—eventually the presidents of Bonwit Teller and of Tiffany's served on the board of Wilkerson's organization—but their role was to raise money for the ministry so that the Holy Spirit could work through it. Wilkerson educated business and religious leaders not about social policy, but about the gifts of Pentecost that were available to all classes, ethnicities, and races. He felt that rebirth in the Holy Spirit in itself solved the social-economic problems of the converts, who through church contacts found jobs, stabilized their families, and furthered their educations, often by enrolling in Bible colleges.

In time, Wilkerson focused on "the one depravity that surpasses them all: dope addiction" (Wilkerson, Sherrill, and Sherrill 1963, 50). Addiction, he argued, was the cause of the high rates of robbery, murder, and abandonment in the ghettoes; craving for drugs drove people to a level of desperation beyond that of their intense poverty. Yet, there was only one crowded hospital in all of New York's boroughs where an addict could get help, and almost all people treated there relapsed upon discharge. Wilkerson worked with addiction on the principle that "The heart of Christ's message is extremely simple: an encounter with God—a real one—means change" (Wilkerson, Sherrill, and Sherrill 1963, 44). He saw this transformation as the key to curing addiction. Addicts are lonely, he wrote, their families have deserted them, they are hungry for a sense of significance in their lives. Wilkerson argued that when they are born again in Christ, they start their lives again, they are cleaned of their violent and shameful pasts, and they have a second infancy surrounded by love (Wilkerson, Sherrill, and Sherrill 1963).

One of Wilkerson's successes was the conversion of Nicky Cruz, the Puerto Rican leader of the most feared gang in Brooklyn. In Cruz's own autobiography, he relates his encounter with Wilkerson at a time that Cruz feared for his future and felt isolated, despite his control of more than 300 gang members. Cruz had little education, spoke broken English, had severed his ties to his family, his best friend had been murdered by a rival gang, and Cruz had a long record of arrests by policemen full of contempt for "Spics" like him. He was "baptized with love" during Wilkerson's sermon on inter-ethnic understanding and emotional freedom (Cruz and Buckingham 1968, 128).

Sponsored by Wilkerson, Cruz graduated from Bible School, became a Pentecostal preacher of international renown, and founded a Christian residential center for addicts. He recruited ex-addicts to testify in the streets about the God of love rather than judgment, and combined this message of love with strict discipline in a detoxification and rehabilitation center where there was "no medicine but Jesus" (Cruz and Buckingham 1968, 219). Cruz collaborated with Wilkerson to found Teen Challenge, a street evangelist movement first directed to youth gang members that soon expanded to serve adult narcotics users. The ties that Cruz and other Wilkerson followers had to Puerto Rico helped Teen Challenge get a foothold on the island; Teen Challenge opened its second residential addiction ministry in Puerto Rico in 1967, a year after _Silo_ opened.

This unique brand of street evangelism inspired a second generation of converts who started sister ministries. Sonny Arguinzoni, a Puerto Rican-Italian teenager on heroin, converted when he met Nicky Cruz in New York in 1962. Cruz helped Arguinzoni attend Latin American Bible College in California. There Arguinzoni married a fellow student from East Los Angeles whose converted ex-addict brother had evangelized her. The couple founded Victory Outreach Ministries, a ministry dedicated to addicts, in 1967. Arguinzoni's biography states, "It wasn't enough to unburden himself. Where others wanted to put away the criminals in the inner city, Sonny wanted to set them free" (Victory Outreach Ministries 2003). In 1984, Arguinzoni opened Victory Outreach School of Ministry to provide ex-addicted converts with pastoral training. Graduates opened new ministries and rehabilitation homes not only in U.S. cities but also overseas. Starting with Mexico and going as far as Manila and the Netherlands, by 2001 Victory Outreach Ministries had founded 500 ministry sites in 18 countries (Victory Outreach Ministries 2003).

Victory Outreach Ministries reached Puerto Rico rather late: in 1996 it opened its doors in Bayamón. The first directors of rehabilitation for the Puerto Rican mission, Yvette and David Quintero, were Mexican Americans who had journeyed from California. During my interview with them in 1999, they explained that the ministry was internationally known for its work on addiction; 90% of its pastors were ex-addicts. The Quinteros had arrived in Puerto Rico without any local contacts, but because of Victory Outreach's reputation among Pentecostals they received referrals and assistance almost immediately: within days they had twenty people asking to join the ministry. Three years later they had a storefront center just outside of San Juan that served 120 members. Ministry recruits themselves supported the center with their earnings by doing local paint jobs, distributing promotional fliers, and selling newspapers. Some recruits found themselves called to missionary service, others attended the Victory Outreach Urban Training Center in Bridgeport, Connecticut, for leadership and job training. Two women who needed to avoid old triggers for drug use transferred from the island to Victory Outreach in New York.

Before Sonny Arguinzoni founded Victory Outreach ministries, when he was fresh out of Bible school and running a Teen Challenge center in Los Angeles, he oversaw the conversion of Freddie García. García was a Mexican American ex-heroin addict from San Antonio whose family sent him to California in a desperate attempt to find him a cure. As García writes on the jacket of his autobiography, he was the product of racially segregated Texas in the 1960s who "sought his identity in angry rebellion . . . and supported his heroin habit with crime" (García and García 1988). Not until García heard words of love and forgiveness in Teen Challenge's makeshift chapel did he let go: "Suddenly, it hit me—*I hugged a White guy!* The hostility and hatred I had toward the Anglo was gone!" (García and García 1988, 60).

As García describes it, he was instantaneously liberated from his self-destructive urges, and found himself in the Latin American Bible Institute in La Puente, California, only months later, giving sermons in which he was "not speaking on my own authority but on the authority given me by God" (García and García 1988, 77). The next few years found him back in San Antonio, Texas, presenting himself as a preacher to his incredulous father, converting his mother, opening a home for ex-addicts, starting a bilingual, bicultural ministry for Mexican Americans, and gradually building a fellowship of disciples that by 1987 were pastoring forty churches, some as far as Mexico and Peru.

As García allowed the Spirit to lead him to the streets of San Antonio, he writes, he was an instant celebrity because "San Antonio has never seen such a thing as a 'cured' drug addict" (García and García 1988, 124), much less the choir of ex-addicts that he and his wife Ninfa directed on a tour of local churches. His disciples quickly ascended the ranks to pastor, and Garcia assured those who doubted their promise for Bible school that "any man who is able to steal over two hundred dollars a day to support his heroin habit—without getting caught—has to have a brain" (García and García 1988, 135). García's crusade blended pride in ethnic heritage with the sense that street smarts was convertible to a pastor's wisdom, a blend that led to yet another international network of street ministries called *Clamor en el Barrio* (Outcry in the Neighborhood).

Clamor en el Barrio reached Puerto Rico in the mid-1990s through a mission headed by a Puerto Rican. The Puerto Rican pastor, trained in García's fast-growth method of discipleship, opened four homes for ex-addicts across in the island in five years. His Puerto Rican recruits accompanied him once a year to Texas for spiritual reinforcement, preparing themselves to bring *Clamor en el Barrio* missions to Costa Rica and Peru.

In the Pentecostal origin myth, a polyvocal outburst of multiple languages heralds political unity. This has particular meaning on an island whose exclusion from federal elections has been justified on the basis of its dominant Spanish language and cultural divergence from the United States. Pentecostalism promises a spiritual order that supersedes the worldly order, and offers evangelical employment to people who have been excluded from the post-industrial economy. It offers citizenship to those excluded from neocolonial America on the grounds of language, miscegenous race, or syncretic cultural practice. It offers a new spiritual family to people whose families are splintered by narco-violence. Finally, what the autobiographies of the Pentecostal street ministers reveal is an imagined community of ex-addicts who, through discipline and earnestness, become authentic members and even leaders of a global Christian movement that unites converts across differences in nationality, language, race, ethnicity, class, and drug-use history.

3

Visitations and Gifts

I first visited Puerto Rico in 1997, the same year that the Center for Addiction Studies at the Caribbean University in Bayamón conducted a survey of addiction treatment programs across the island. It found that three-fourths of addiction programs licensed by the state were evangelical (Centro de Estudios en Adicción 1997). This despite the fact that the U.S. federal government had devoted significant funding to building a biomedical system of addiction treatment in Puerto Rico—significant, at least, compared to the funding available in neighboring Caribbean islands. This also despite the fact that Puerto Rico's second-term governor, Pedro Roselló, was a physician who had declared modernizing the island's healthcare infrastructure to be a top priority. How, then, did this formerly Catholic island, with U.S. funding to biomedicalize its treatment system, become an epicenter for Protestant addiction evangelism?

I began to make sense of this puzzle when I juxtaposed the stories that Pentecostal Street ministers tell about their own origins with the histories that Puerto Ricans and their observers tell of the Island's economy. There were, of course, pragmatic reasons why the Puerto Rican state embraced street ministries in the midst of a crisis of narcotraffic: street ministries did not require the monetary investments that biomedical clinics required, and were politically attractive at a time when the popular media called for moral uplift (rather than medical care) as an antidote to drug use. There were, however, more subtle ways that the cadences and grammar of Pentecostalism on one hand, and of Puerto Rico's "industrialization" as a territory of the United States on the other, complemented each other— through motifs of liberty and dependency, of unrestrained growth and implosive debt, of marginality and divine selection. Together they present mirror images of

73

Puerto Rico on the world stage alternately as "spiritual Wall Street" on one hand, and as the backwater of racialized post-industrial fallout on the other.

The evangelical ethos of unrestrained expansion through mass conversions—a form of redemptive spiritual bounty—has a corollary in mainstream free-market discourses of growth of capital and market expansion; a form of redemptive material bounty. This is not accidental. The Puerto Rican state is constrained by its subordination to the United States, and its residents look for ways to transcend the state and the economy, including the "spiritual Wall Street" described by Victory Academy's disciples.

Together, the mirror images of Puerto Rico's economic constriction and of Pentecostal growth paint a picture of people attempting to overcome systemic limitations. Like biomedical clinics, street ministries draw on the rhetoric of addiction as a character flaw, and of individual reform as its solution. In the ministries, however, the process of reform is relational. Conversion puts an individual into a relationship with the spirit world and with communities of other converts. These communities of converts are imagined as transnational and trans-racial; in ministry discourse, mass conversion is what promises to redefine the relationship of Puerto Ricans with Anglo-Americans, and to eliminate the exclusions and hierarchies of racial and national orders. Street ministries strive for a looping effect (see, e.g., Hacking 1995): Through a realignment of their perception with an alternate spiritual reality, each convert helps to create a milieu in which new relationships are cultivated, and the milieu in turn encourages more conversions, ultimately changing the social order and the material reality. Converts thus see spiritual practice as a political act which can level hierarchies of color, language, and geography.

To flesh out the connections between the moral economy of street ministries and the political economy of post-industrial Puerto Rico, I reconstruct two parallel histories: one is a brief economic history of Puerto Rico's evolution from a Spanish colony to its current status as a "territory" of the United States, with partial eligibility for U.S. federal entitlements while serving initially as a labor pool and later as a tax shelter for U.S. industry. Another is the story of more-recent debates surrounding the island's drug policy and addiction treatment under health reform, given that health reform has been a key element of the island's efforts to elevate its status in relation to the United States. These two stories of economic "development" and of addiction treatment illustrate how political and clinical motifs of dependency are entangled on an island dominated by narcotraffic in the face of corporate disinvestment.

These two histories take on yet another valence when read alongside the history of Pentecostalism, told from the point of view of street ministers (provided above). Through the Pentecostal movement, ex-addicted people learn to see themselves as gifted; as among a select few who are chosen to foment a spiritual revolution, and to experience spiritual growth, spiritual wealth, and power. Their Pentecostal narrative of humble beginnings, democratically distributed spiritual gifts, and exponential returns on the prudent use of those gifts, echoes the capitalist American trope of limitless growth through hard work and investment; a form of spiritual bootstrapping. At the same time, however, Pentecostalism works against the racialized exclusion of former addicts from capitalist accumulation by affirming their membership and deservedness. As shown by the recent history of addiction treatment in Puerto Rico, the spiritual-social technologies of street ministries therefore could revalue addicted, non-white people in ways that the "biotechnological embrace" (Delvecchio Good 2001) of clinical medicine does not.

ISLAND OF POVERTY?

The unification narrative of Puerto Rican street ministries dovetails a colonial history of disinvestment and subordinate political status of the island relative to the United States. Economists' histories of Puerto Rico, for instance, are consistent on one theme: the indeterminacy of Puerto Rican material life. Located in a liminal zone between North and South America, Weisskoff describes it well: "Is Puerto Rico poor or wealthy?" he asks.

> If Puerto Rico is within the United States, it therefore should be compared to states like Mississippi or Louisiana, or regions like Appalachia or the Ozarks. However, if Puerto Rico is outside the United States, it should be treated like other small developing nations. This is precisely the historical dilemma of Puerto Rico: it is internal and external to the United States at the same time" (Weisskoff 1985, 2).

Geographically, politically, culturally, and economically located between North America and Latin America, Puerto Ricans have a double consciousness (*see, e.g.,* Du Bois 1969). Thanks to foreign capital seeking U.S. tax shelter on the island, and to U.S. federal transfers for benefits such as welfare and food stamps, Puerto Ricans have a higher per capita income and more even distribution of wealth than their Latin American neighbors. Yet, the territory's industry and capital are controlled by North Americans, and Puerto Ricans have less income and more local inequality than North Americans.

In an attempt to maintain a North American standard of living, Puerto Rican consumption expenditures have risen more rapidly than incomes in the later part of the twentieth century, with debt financing 60 cents of every dollar spent on imported goods (Dietz 1986, 271). With little local agriculture or manufacture for local markets, Puerto Ricans have become completely dependent on imported goods bought with federal funds and heavy state and individual level borrowing.

> An air of false prosperity pervades Puerto Rico.... The availability of [federally backed] loans gives the impression of confidence and a flashy superstructure within which private borrowing is also carried out on levels far in excess of the real producing power of the economy (Weisskoff 1985, 71).

Constructed image

Many working class and middle-class Puerto Ricans that I met thought that the island were well off. A psychologist from Ponce who had also worked in Massachusetts told me that there was more child abuse among Puerto Ricans on the mainland United States than on the island, because Puerto Rico had exported its poorest and most problematic residents to the United States. Doña Antonia, my hairdresser, felt that the image that North Americans have of Puerto Ricans has been marred by the poorer, less-educated people who left the island for the mainland, "The island has more professionals. It's easy to get an education because of scholarships from the U.S. They graduated 1,500 engineers from (the University of Puerto Rico) Mayagüez last year."

Not all the graduates found employment, however. Doña Antonia's own daughter, a chemical engineer, was considering a move to the mainland given the uncertain future of the pharmaceutical firm that employed her in Puerto Rico.

Despite its established albeit insecure middle class, urban poverty is deeply entrenched in Puerto Rico. By the 1980s economic historian Weisskoff pointed to mass unemployment (67% of Puerto Rican adults at the time were unable to find work or were out of the labor force), and a Puerto Rican "two-fold strategy: one, encouraging mass emigration . . . and two, for those who remain at home, providing a life dependent on federal subsidies" (Weisskoff 1985, 72). A formerly rural society of sugar cane harvest had been transformed into a chain of post-industrial cities at breakneck speed.

When I arrived in Puerto Rico for the first time, taxis advertising Wendy's hamburgers and Hertz car rentals greeted me at baggage claim. Panhandlers approaching me in the shadows of San Juan's high-rises looked like those I had left behind in Manhattan, but they were dressed in flip-flop sandals and tank tops instead of tattered boots and blankets to guard against the brisk New York winds. Tourist shops in Old San Juan featured palm-leaf ceramics made in China, their banjo-playing tree frogs alluded to an agrarian past of which no trace was to be found in the asphalt and steel of Puerto Rican convenience stores.[1] In low-income neighborhoods, shantytowns had been replaced by U.S. Housing and Urban Development–financed projects that looked like East Harlem tenements near the center of San Juan, and then more like the stucco, single-story government housing of East Los Angeles on the city's outskirts. That year, official unemployment hovered at 14%, adult labor force participation rates were 45%, and in Washington the Drug Enforcement Administration testified to Congress that "cocaine and heroin traffickers from Colombia have transformed Puerto Rico into the largest staging area in the Caribbean for smuggling Colombian cocaine and heroin into the U.S."[2] (U.S. DEA 1997).

By 2000, when I moved to Ponce to start research, the southwest cities of Ponce and Mayagüez formed the second largest epicenter of narcotics consumption on the island after San Juan (Colón, Canino and Robles 1998). San Juan, in the north-east, was a sprawling metropolitan area of one million people, and lovingly nick-named the sixth borough of New York City, not only because so many residents cycled to and from New York, but also because its size, crowded conditions, and pace of life approached those of New York. By comparison, Ponce, the second larg-est city in Puerto Rico, was a sleepy town of 180,000 people where feral horses roamed the abandoned lots bordering K-Mart and Taco Bell.

Ponce's historians attribute the city's founding—in 1692—to Juan Ponce de Leon's great-grandson, Loiza de Leon; its Spanish colonial history is tangible in its elaborate central plaza, replete with an ornate cathedral, fountains, and colonial mansions. Ponce has long been a cosmopolitan center attractive to European and Caribbean immigrants, a major seaport conveniently located near southern sugar cane fields and attracting trade in contraband (Edmondson 1994). At the time of U.S. occupation in 1898, Ponce was Puerto Rico's largest city. It was, and remains today, Puerto Rico's principal shipping port on the Caribbean Sea.

In the industrial transformation of the mid-twentieth century, Ponce also became known for cement production. Ponce Cement Inc., originally part of an experiment in state-owned industrial plants and which was sold to the multimil-lionaire Ferré family, still dominates the town. Evidence of its activity can be seen in the razed hillsides surrounding Ponce, thoroughly mined for their chalky soil, and can be seen in the thick layer of dust on the windows of any house near the cement factory. A large Roche pharmaceuticals plant also dominates the view of Ponce from its southern highway, another remainder of the once industrial land-scape of the town. Ponce still produces significant exports; rum, cement, and canned tuna are its major products, and as recently as the 1980s canneries in Ponce and Mayagüez supplied 40% of the U.S. tuna market (Dietz 1986, 255). These days, however, the canneries have been razed and the center of gravity has migrated to the Plaza del Caribe, the second largest indoor mall in Puerto Rico. On any given day, from its 10 a.m. opening to 9 p.m. closing, the mall's parking lot is filled with freshly washed cars. The mall's fast food restaurants, J. C. Penny, Sears, and other North American chain stores are jammed with shoppers who long ago abandoned the local merchants of the once elegant Spanish colonial downtown plaza, leaving empty buildings and active drug trade in the town center.

Given the strategic location of its ports, Ponce has been a trading post for contra-band goods since Spanish colonization (Edmondson 1994). By the 1990s, Puerto Rico's status as a U.S. territory, and the lower level of scrutiny given to goods entering the U.S. mainland from Puerto Rico than from other Latin American regions, helped Ponce to become the center of Caribbean-U.S. mainland narcotics smuggling opera-tions as well (U.S. DEA 1997; Booth and Drummond 1996; Johnson 2004). During my field research, I lived in a city that subsisted on labor in the global narcotics trade, U.S. federal transfer payments, and consumption of imported consumer goods.

culture of poverty theory

To understand how Puerto Rico achieved this state of affairs, requires examining the island's social and economic transformations over the last century, as shaped by its colonial relationship with the United States. To understand the differences between how Puerto Rican islanders see their own economic position and how U.S. mainland whites imagine the economic position of Puerto Ricans, one must acknowledge the unique role that Puerto Rico has played in anthropological understandings of marginality. I took up my study of street ministries in the aftermath of anthropologist Oscar Lewis' culture of poverty theory, the theory that poverty in industrial society is reproduced intergenerationally by cultural traits (such as poor parenting, impulsivity, inability to defer gratification or plan for the future, insecure gender identity) that are both cause and consequence of frustrated social mobility.[3] With the publication of Lewis' nationally best-selling book, *La Vida: a Puerto Rican Family in the Culture of Poverty* (1966), Puerto Rico served as a conduit for culture of poverty to be applied to U.S. welfare policies, where it surfaced in Assistant Secretary of Labor Daniel Patrick Moynihan's report on "The Negro Family," and in President Lyndon Johnson's War on Poverty. Lewis' description of a family in the San Juan slums shocked middle-class readers in the United States: hard-edged mothers who prostituted and turned away their grandchildren; men who drank away their women's income at the local bar; young children who cursed at adults.[4] With these images, Lewis invented the version of the urban poor that contemporary policy makers now take for granted: a geographically and culturally isolated population of very low-income blacks and Latinos that constitute the analytic social science category of the "underclass" (Briggs 2002).[5]

The urban slums depicted in *La Vida* reflected that by the 1950s the island sat in the eye of an industrial storm. Operation Bootstrap, the rapid modernization scheme of the first native Puerto Rican governor of the island, Luis Muñoz Marín, began in 1947 with a program of "industrialization by invitation." In the wake of the depression and a wartime economic crisis in which the agricultural workers were dislocated, the Puerto Rican government recruited U.S. capital. It took advantage of the exemption that corporations earning income in Puerto Rico had from U.S. federal taxes, and also exempted corporations from paying taxes to Puerto Rico. The financial press in the United States immediately billed Puerto Rico a "bounty for industry" and "a taxpayer's paradise" (Dietz 1986, 211). The effects of Operation Bootstrap were dramatic. Between 1948 and 1965, 1,027 new manufacturing plants opened in Puerto Rico. In 1940, 67% of Puerto Rican islanders were rural, by 1960, 77% were urban. The per capita income of Puerto Ricans rose from $121 per year in 1940 to $900 per year in 1965 (Knight 1990).

This economic transformation was accompanied by social change as well, including a "revolution of rising expectations." The 1950s and '60s were characterized by economic and geographic mobility, with people moving in droves from countryside to towns, and from towns to the U.S. mainland in search of work.

Migration to the U.S. mainland rose from 1,000 per year in the 1930s to 40,000 per year in the 1950s (Knight 1990, 271), reflecting on one hand that unemployment on the island remained high despite rapid growth in income, and on the other hand that in 1950 the average hourly wage in the Puerto Rican island's manufacturing sector was less than one-third that of manufacturing on the U.S. mainland. Dietz (1986) points out that low wages accounted for an even greater share of the profits made by U.S. firms in Puerto Rico during Operation Bootstrap than did tax exemptions, and that this "sweatshop" phase of development lasted many decades. By 1979, manufacturing jobs in Puerto Rico still paid only 54% that of manufacturing jobs in the United States.

The distinctive form that industrialization took in Puerto Rico emerged from its history of Spanish colonization prior to 1898, followed by U.S. colonization after the Spanish-American War. From the sixteenth to the nineteenth centuries, Puerto Rico was a tangential Spanish colony, relegated to the status of military outpost and trade station after its minimal gold reserves were exhausted. Initially Native Americans, and later enslaved and free Africans, worked alongside European peasants and mixed free laborers (*pardos*) on sugar plantations on the coast, coffee plantations in the mountainous interior, and on subsistence food plots (Steward et al. 1956). Spain controlled Puerto Rico's modest agricultural economy through a white creole elite, despite slave revolts in the 1840s, when the percentage of slaves in the population reached a high of 15%, and despite periodic uprisings against Spain, such as the *Grito de Lares* of 1868 (Knight 1990).

After 1898 however, U.S. occupation of Puerto Rico during the Spanish-American War, and its transfer from Spain as a U.S. possession, led to infusions of capital from the United States for export crop production. This fueled intensive commercial agriculture focused on sugar and tobacco, and a cash economy. The value of Puerto Rican agricultural exports grew from less than $25 million in 1900 to $360 million in 1950. New divisions of labor in crop production and the increased flow of manufactured products to the island generated occupational groups such as processors, transportation workers, wholesalers, and local merchants leading to urban growth, a service sector, a new middle class, and a burgeoning group of landless laborers. Fertile coastlands were in the hands of American corporations. The low wages and poor working conditions that accompanied this channeling of wealth to landowners on the U.S. mainland were only counteracted, in some measure, by labor unions that in 1949 included half the island's labor force (Steward et al. 1956).

Puerto Rico also underwent political change after U.S. occupation. Puerto Rican governors were appointed by the U.S. president and were always North American. In 1917, the U.S. government passed the Jones Act which established a locally elected Puerto Rican House of Representatives and made Puerto Ricans citizens of the United States, but without the granting the right to vote in U.S. elections. The U.S. citizenship of Puerto Ricans laid the ground for mass migration between the island and Northeast mainland in times of economic hardship, yet Puerto Rico's continued subordination to mainland policies and lack of voting rights fostered anti-U.S. sentiment and Puerto Rican independence movements. The depression of the 1930s was a turning point in island politics. The majority of the population lived in serious poverty, and independence activist Luis Muñoz Marín formed the *Acción Social Independentista* (later the Popular Democratic Party, PDP), which lobbied Washington for Puerto Rico's inclusion in New Deal programs. By 1948, Luis Muñoz Marin became Puerto Rico's first elected governor; he had avoided turning Puerto Rican independence into an election issue and instead made economic development his mandate (Steward et al. 1956).

The ambiguous political status of Puerto Rico was codified into law by the 1952 plebiscite in which Puerto Rican voters accepted Muñoz Marín's proposal for commonwealth status for Puerto Rico. The proposal formalized politically what was already the dominant relation with the United States: a semblance of cultural autonomy and a set of Puerto Rican–elected representatives belying the financial and political influence of the United States. It is revealing that the constitution of the new Puerto Rican commonwealth had to be approved by the U.S. congress, and that it passed in congress with one section of the Bill of Rights eliminated—that guaranteeing rights to a free education, a job, and an adequate standard of living for all islanders (Dietz 1986, 237). With the commonwealth plebiscite, Muñoz Marín established an attitude of compromise that has continued in island politics until today. Puerto Rican voters—many of whom are pro-independence in sentiment but afraid of the economic impact that withdrawal of U.S. federal subsidies, American capital, and trade agreements would have on the local economy—have repeatedly affirmed Puerto Rican commonwealth status over either independence or U.S. statehood. Commonwealth status affords Puerto Rico a degree of local autonomy (e.g., to retain Spanish as the official language), and entitles the island to export tariff exemptions and to federal subsidies given to states, but it gives islanders no influence on mainland U.S. elections.

Although the standard of living in Puerto Rico rose significantly in the quarter century after Muñoz Marín's Popular Democratic party (PDP) came to power, it was a one-time gain resulting from the wholesale industrialization of the island by U.S. capital and from new government subsidies of housing, public health, and education. By the post-industrial period starting in the 1970s, the standard of living stagnated. Industrial jobs generally pay more than do agricultural labor jobs, the industrial transformation of mid-century Puerto Rico led to a one-time jump in average income. All of the manufacturing expertise, however, remained in the hands of U.S. firms,[6] and little Puerto Rican economic leadership developed in those years. As a result of the lack of local control of industry and of the tax incentives that the state of Puerto Rico offered to U.S. firms to encourage their investments, the vast wealth generated by Puerto Rican manufacturing did not stay on the island and instead flowed back to investors in the United States. By the 1970s—when East Asian countries offered even more advantageous tax exemptions and cheap labor to U.S. firms, manufacturers left Puerto Rico—and left Puerto Ricans without the expertise or capital to generate alternative industries. In 1980, the per capita income in Puerto Rico was less than one-half that of the poorest state in the United States (Mississippi); in 2000 this ratio remained the same (Dietz 2003).

Twentieth-century Puerto Rico has long had a transnational economy, serving as a link in an international chain of U.S.-based firms and their international subsidiaries that have deposited earnings in Puerto Rican banks and kept manufacturing bases in Puerto Rico to take advantage of tax shelters and to avoid paying trade tariffs. These U.S. firms siphoned-off profits and used Puerto Rico merely as a production point—one that did not create local multiplier effects or proportional gains in local incomes. As a result, the Puerto Rican government has had to borrow extensively to make up for taxes lost on exempt profits. This arrangement unraveled in the 1970s when the United States experienced a financial and oil crisis. United States manufacturing firms based in Puerto Rico slowed down, and because U.S. economic conditions were poor, unemployed mainland Puerto Ricans returned to the island at greater rates than emigrants left. The resulting sharp increase in unemployment and underemployment in Puerto Rico led to rapid growth in the informal economy, from street vending to drug traffic. It also led to a 1,974% increase in federal transfer payments to Puerto Rico between 1960 and 1976, most of them for food stamps, rent subsidies, welfare, and government jobs (Pantojas-Garcia 1990, 123). In 1980, 70% to 80% of the population was eligible to receive food stamps by virtue of low income, and it is only because of such transfer payments that disposable personal income grew (Dietz 1986).

The economic crisis of the 1970s affected not only working-class people but also local Puerto Rican capitalists and political elites, motivating them to rethink their industrialization strategy. By the mid-1970s Puerto Rico had lost many of the advantages it had as a manufacturing base for U.S. firms. The minimum wage was greater than that of wages in East Asia and Latin America, shipping costs had increased, and energy costs were higher than in the United States. To stave off these threats, Puerto Rican economic and political elites developed an economic restructuring scheme designed to transform Puerto Rico into the high-finance capital of the Caribbean and the business service gateway to Latin America for U.S. firms. This strategy has been called "peripheral post-industrialization"; other, countries such as Hong Kong, Ireland, and Singapore also have pursued it by specializing in transnational services for high-tech and knowledge-intensive industries. These countries market themselves to transnational firms by pointing out that—relative to richer countries—they provide inexpensive skilled labor and few industrial regulations, but relative to poorer countries their infrastructure is developed and they are politically stable. By 1986, the Puerto Rican tax codes, combined with President Reagan's Caribbean Basin Initiative, made the Caribbean "a huge tax- and duty-free export-processing zone and financial center, allowing the legal tax-free repatriation of profits to the United States" (Pantojas-Garcia 1990, 157). In fact, in 1986 Puerto Rico became the top single source of income for U.S. capital, reflecting that it was "one of the largest tax havens in the world" (Pantojas-Garcia 1990, 166). *how ppl were affected*

As the Puerto Rican economy shifted toward service employment, wages for most workers fell, unemployment and welfare dependence remained high, and the informal economy—especially drug trade—grew. As a result, although Puerto Rican executives and professionals enjoyed the benefits of international high finance, wage earners and the unemployed were further marginalized from the legal economy (Pantojas-Garcia 1990). By the late 1970s, unemployment in Puerto Rico reached levels seen in the United States only during the Great Depression.

Unemployment was particularly acute among male workers. The Puerto Rican unemployment rate has been greater for men than women since the 1960s, and the labor-force participation rate has been decreasing for men and increasing for women, as women compensate for missing men's economic contribution to their households (Dietz 1986), and U.S.-based firms specifically recruit lower-wage female workers in the Caribbean (Safa 1995b, Freeman 2000).

Peripheral post-industrialization has replicated the influx and outflow of North American capital that raises hopes of local wealth but ultimately flies above the reach of island natives. A frustrated aspiration permeates Puerto Rico, one in which the high technology and status of North American consumer culture trickles through one's fingers the harder one grasps it. Ironically, by the end of the twentieth century, the Puerto Rican state attempted to solve its dilemma of political-economic liminality by privatizing its health care system and shedding its image of dependence on federal aid, embracing U.S. mainland trends in a bid for full statehood. This strategy went hand in hand with legally redefining addiction as a spiritual and social problem rather than a medical problem.

ADDICTION: A "SPIRITUAL-SOCIAL" PROBLEM

It was September 2000—an election year. The month was dominated by a hotly debated contest between supporters of U.S. statehood for Puerto Rico (New Progressive Party, PNP) and supporters of the status quo, commonwealth status, for Puerto Rico (Popular Democratic Party, PDP). Campaign vans with loudspeakers circled the neighborhoods of my sleepy corner of Ponce, spilling over with rally supporters dressed either in blue (for PNP) or bright red (for PDP). The headlines in the Puerto Rican papers, which two years before had read "Mental Health Privatized"; "Deficient Attention to Mental Health"; and "Toward Comparable Coverage for Physical and Mental Illness;" now read "Away from Defining the Addict as Ill;"

"(Reverend) Raschke Holds Up Mental Health Law for Second Time"; and "Legislators Accused of Succumbing to Religious Groups" (Valdivia 1999, Blasor 1998,
Valdivia 2000d, Ramírez Alers 2000a, Rodríguez 2000, Valdivia 2000c). Addiction
and evangelism obsessed Puerto Rican legislators. In the end, the governor—a physician whose major campaign promise was to make modern biomedicine accessible
to all Puerto Ricans—achieved passage of a law which defined addiction not as a
treatable mental disorder, but as a spiritual and social problem. *debater*

The Puerto Rican Mental Health Law of 2000 was a bill of rights for mental
health patients. By leaving addiction off of the list of mental health disorders for
which a minimum standard of psychiatric care was required, the law facilitated
public funding for evangelical ministries as licensed rehabilitation centers and
reduced funding for biomedical addiction clinics. Debate over the law was fueled
by disparate framings of addiction—as a sign of organic disease or as a sign of
moral depravity. Suddenly, the seemingly obscure Pentecostal ministries in which
I was deep in research had been thrust into the Puerto Rican and U.S. national
limelight. What would the other-worldly Pentecostals do with the political opening that the Puerto Rican Mental Health Law, on the heels of the U.S. President
Bush's Faith-Based Initiatives, seemed to provide?

The debate about the law opened a window on the political economy of addiction treatment in Puerto Rico. For their part, however, street ministries were
remarkably indifferent to the Mental Health Law and to government support for
their work. The robust growth of street ministries on the island over the preceding
decades had little to do with the Puerto Rican governor's politically expedient
embrace of faith-based programs. Rather, street ministries multiplied because they
addressed a deeper historical dilemma of Puerto Rico as a post-colonial (and some
argue currently colonial) state starved for capital, with aspirations for political
autonomy and for U.S. standards of living long frustrated by its marginal position
in between North and Latin America. The ministries combined a "victory" discourse with a discourse of care for the wounded and vulnerable, particularly dis-
possessed men, for whom the ministry positioned itself as a surrogate family, or
even a substitute for a state that had abandoned the common welfare.

THE PUERTO RICAN MENTAL HEALTH LAW

In the throes of the Mental Health Law debate, evangelical and biomedical practitioners claimed to use mutually exclusive approaches to well-being. Yet, over the
three decades prior, addiction ministries had coexisted peacefully with public mental health programs in Puerto Rico. In that era, the bulk of U.S. federal funds for
drug abuse went to the Puerto Rican Mental Health and Anti-Addiction Services
Administration (ASSMCA, formerly DESCA), a state agency which ran inpatient
and outpatient addiction treatment clinics. The ASSMCA licensed evangelical

rehabilitation programs that got referrals from the court system and from health clinics in the same way as biomedical mental health centers. Starting in 1998, however, the question of who was a legitimate addiction treatment provider and whether the State should fund or regulate all providers became politically charged. The story, as I reconstructed it from the Puerto Rican newspapers and from interviews with key players in the debate, is as follows.

In 1998, Puerto Rican governor and physician Pedro Rosselló gathered a group of psychiatrists, psychologists, social workers, counselors, and hospital administrators to solicit advice on how to proceed with his last campaign promise, a new Mental Health Law guaranteeing minimum standards of care for mental health patients. It was prompted by his controversial health-reform program, which privatized the health-care system, putting care for the poor in the hands of managed-care companies. Health reform closed public mental health centers, and managed-care contracts made little provision for psychiatric patients, prompting public outcry against the State's neglect of mental health (Blasor 1998). In his response, the governor included addiction as a mental health problem, perhaps because drug abuse and crime were ranked among the top-two problems most disturbing to voters in opinion polls for the third year in a row.[7]

In 1999, with election year looming, the Mental Health Law became a hot political issue. Psychiatrists and hospital administrators pressed for a psychiatrist-led treatment team as the minimum standard of care, including addiction treatment. They also pressed for universal adoption of the American Psychiatric Association's DSM-IV manual criteria for diagnosis, and a Patient Bill of Rights abolishing limits on coverage for psychiatric care. Managed-care companies warned that requiring unlimited mental health coverage would bankrupt them. Meanwhile, evangelical and community-based groups called on the governor to recognize them as legitimate providers of drug abuse treatment, pointing out that they ran the majority of the rehabilitation programs on the island.

By the election of 2000, the governor and Puerto Rican legislators drafted a Mental Health Law that required psychiatrists to lead treatment teams. It also abolished limits on mental health coverage that distinguished it from physical health coverage in an effort to elevate mental illness to the same status as physical illness. The president of Hogar Crea, a network of peer-driven therapeutic communities,[8] protested the law's requirement that psychiatrists treat addiction, pointing out that addiction is a spiritual and social problem, that ex-addicted people and community-based organizations provide the most accessible and motivational rehabilitation services (Garcia Rios 2000). The outspoken evangelist Jorge Raschke threatened to mobilize Christian voters against politicians who supported the law, causing the Puerto Rican legislature to delay consideration of the law and to consult with evangelical leaders about revisions (Ramírez Alers 2000a). In response to this pressure, Governor Rosselló declared that addicted people would not be defined as mentally ill, thereby securing the place of religious and community groups in their treatment (Rodriguez 2000).

The Puerto Rican psychiatric society swiftly accused legislators of succumbing to religious groups, opening the door to the possibility that anyone without training could practice medicine (Valdivia 2000c). The administrator of the state mental health department declared that addiction should be defined as a mental health problem because "We are not a third world country of ignoramuses who are going to use criteria that are not established in the scientific literature" (Valdivia 2000a). Psychiatrists referred to extensive scientific literature cataloging drug abuse and dependence as a mental health diagnosis, asserting that drug addiction "has a neurobiological basis" (Valdivia 2000b). They demanded a moratorium on voting on the Mental Health Law, saying that impending Puerto Rican elections prevented an objective evaluation of the law's contents. Not heeding this demand, legislators negotiated the contents of the law until midnight on the day of voting. They made last-minute changes to forty-one lines of the law, adding a statement that addiction is not a mental illness, defining a new class of treatment professionals called "specialists in community treatment," and exempting from State regulation all community-based organizations that use spiritual-pastoral counseling to treat addiction (Ramírez Alers 2000b).

A week later—and one month before election day—Governor Rosselló triumphantly signed this Mental Health Law, which he said treated mental health on par with physical health problems (Estrada Resto 2000). While Reverend Raschke proclaimed Puerto Rico a model for U.S. President Bush's Faith-Based Initiatives, psychiatrists accused the legislature of compromising patient care in an effort to limit biomedical treatment in favor of lower-cost, non-credentialed peer or pastoral counseling. Public drug-treatment programs continued to close and addicted people were referred either to outpatient for-profit clinics for a limited course of pharmaceuticals, or to evangelical programs, many of which received government grants for their services while their protocols and staff credentials remained unregulated.

Thus, the principle of separation of church and state that first opened the Catholic stronghold of Puerto Rico to Protestant evangelism upon U.S. possession in 1898 was challenged a century later, in 1998, by a law that formalized state support for evangelism.

How do we explain these events? Why did legislators solve the problem of treatment standards for addiction by declaring that addiction is not a mental illness? What were the models of addiction employed by the actors in this conflict, and what motivated the actors who promoted each model?

Let us first examine the behavior of the legislators. Within the bureaucratic logic of the Puerto Rican State, declaring that addiction was not a mental illness but rather a social or spiritual problem allowed the governor to declare both that his administration was providing uniform, modern biomedical treatment for mental health problems, at the same time that it helped him to cut mental-health expenditures. It also enabled him to please an evangelical constituency and demonstrate his support for nongovernmental solutions for social problems, an approach very much in line with political currents toward privatization and decentralization in the United States, as exemplified by the Faith Based Initiatives of President Bush.

In 1994, when Governor Rosselló launched his health-reform plan, he saw as symbolically important the creation of a managed care system in Puerto Rico patterned on the privatized U.S. system, in the hope of controlling costs and rationalizing allocation of services. This focus on health reform might have reflected that Dr. Rosselló was a surgeon before entering politics, but it also reflected the political weight of the managed-care movement among potential statehood supporters in the U.S. Congress. A policy consultant to the Puerto Rican state told me that Rosselló was committed to accomplishing one of the fastest and most complete transitions to managed care in the Americas[9] to show U.S. politicians that Puerto Rico was in sync with the rest of the United States politically, economically, and technologically. This made sense in light of the fact that Rosselló and his party sought to make Puerto Rico the fifty-first state in the Union.

As a commonwealth of the United States, Puerto Rico is politically and culturally marginal to the United States, and Puerto Ricans struggle against images of their backwardness in the eyes of North Americans. These images were evident in the U.S. media in 1998 when Congress considered the option of offering Puerto Rico to become the fifty-first state in the Union. Conservative U.S. commentators who objected to Puerto Rican statehood emphasized that Puerto Ricans spoke Spanish, not English, and were not interested in assimilating to North American culture as evidenced by the fact the Puerto Rican migrants to the U.S. mainland are the least educated and poorest "Hispanic" ethnic group in the country. They pointed out that Puerto Ricans have a 20% unemployment rate, are more dependent on welfare than mainland Americans, and that their average income is one half that of the average income in the poorest U.S. state (Chavez 1998, Buckley 1998). Therefore, the type and quality of health services offered in Puerto Rico had special symbolism for Puerto Rican politicians, and served to index the modernization and professionalism of contemporary Puerto Rican society.

ADDICTION: A SPIRITUAL, BIOLOGICAL, OR POLITICAL DISORDER?

In Puerto Rico, North American–style biomedicine is well-funded relative to other Caribbean and Latin American countries, and is delivered through institutions that are roughly comparable to U.S.-based public-health institutions. As a territory of the United States, Puerto Rico has access to U.S. federal funding for public health services and infrastructure. This makes provision of state-supported drug-abuse services a potentially lucrative enterprise.

As part of Puerto Rico's Health Reform of 1994–2000, biomedical treatment for addiction was taken out of the hands of the public health system, privatized, and subcontracted by managed-care companies to behavioral health care organizations (Alegría et al. 2000/2001). Such organizations employ teams of licensed counselors and nurses, directed by a psychiatrist, to provide outpatient medication management and brief individual or group therapy, which are cheaper than in-patient rehabilitation.

When I visited a clinic run by a behavioral health care organization for publicly insured patients, the psychiatrist directing the clinic explained that he was the only psychiatrist available to see the more than 500 patients scheduled for treatment every Friday, "addiction day." Patients were told during the first of their brief weekly sessions "You are going to be an addict all your life," that they would always be predisposed to abuse drugs. The psychiatrist prescribed pharmaceuticals that mimicked the effects of the drugs used by the patients, gradually reducing the dosage to achieve abstinence while buffering severe withdrawal symptoms. Clients also were assigned to group therapy sessions with a licensed addiction counselor. Counselors charged families with monitoring the patient's progress; as the manager of the clinic noted in conversation with me about patients who lie about relapse, "If they are here voluntarily [without legal pressure], we punish them. We take them off of their medicines and cancel their psychiatry appointment for the week. They may lie because of their family, spouse, or work. It is rare that they really come voluntarily. We tell the family everything—they are our conspirators."[10]

The psychiatrist's philosophy that "once an addict always an addict" contrasted with street ministries' concept of Christian rebirth. The clinic director's commentary about the family's involvement in monitoring patients suggested that the patients' families were unproblematic structures of support. Because clinic patients lived at home and came to the clinic only once a week for services, they did not move out of their homes to establish a more autonomous identity as they did in residential evangelical programs. Additionally, the clinic's policy on relapse showed how biomedical addiction treatment could be punitive.

Yet advocates for biomedical addiction programs pointed out that their problems stemmed from inadequate investment in their services. Subcontracts between large health maintenance organizations and for-profit behavioral health companies limited the number of visits per patient, and budgeted for only a minimal number of credentialed staff to treat large patient loads. Furthermore, as of 2000, only a handful of Puerto Rican physicians and health counselors were certified to treat drug abuse.[11] To compound matters, the idea that largely self-supporting, non-professional self-help groups such as Christian ministries would respond to the demand for addiction treatment also reduced the political pressure to invest in public biomedical treatment. Further privatization of the community clinic network on the island after 2000 through health reform and managed care contracts has further reduced the accessibility of behavioral healthcare (Mulligan 2014).

SOCIAL REMEDIES

A small group of Puerto Rican health activists are promoting a third alternative in addiction treatment, a combination of harm-reduction programs such as needle exchange for injection drug users at risk for HIV, with political reform efforts to decriminalize drug use and empower the urban poor. An outspoken leader in this effort, Dr. Victor Vargas—a family physician and former nondenominational pastor—offered me his own critique of both the biomedical and evangelical approaches to addiction. He argued that Christian programs put so much pressure on their clients to convert that they end up lying about their belief, making clients feel guilty and powerless, ultimately reducing their chances for recovery. He also pointed out that the puritanical doctrine of Christian rehabilitation programs is a barrier to recovery, because Christian programs only see abstinence as success: "They don't see reduction [in drug use] as something positive . . . [and they] don't allow for relapse. Relapse is to go to the Devil, to lose your faith."

In the best-case scenario, Dr. Vargas argued, the "Christian centers exchange dependence on drugs for dependence on the centers." As a former pastor of a nondenominal church, Dr. Vargas offered a theological critique of their puritanical approach. "Perfection excludes compassion. It has nothing to do with humanity."

Dr. Vargas also had a critique of a biomedical approaches to addiction, which he saw as apolitical, saying that medical "professionals and the government require that you see [addiction] only as an illness. For me, it is also a social problem. You can't just give medication . . . [psychiatrists] see it as a source of income in the health care system . . . addiction is related to inequality.

Dr. Vargas construed addiction not as a discrete illness or individual moral failing, but as the result of the result of broader political-economic trends. He cited unemployment after the withdrawal of U.S.-based manufacturing firms, and the criminalization of drug abuse which served to imprison a surging population of men who were excluded from the formal economy. Dr. Vargas and his collaborators lobbied for the decriminalization of drugs and drug-use paraphernalia, and his nonprofit organization opened needle-exchange sites across the island with public health grants, as well as drug-treatment program for women based on peer support with the goal of regaining control of one's life rather than complete abstinence from drugs.

When I visited Dr. Vargas' needle exchange site in Ponce, it proved to be an active center of social exchange as well. Heroin and crack cocaine users chatted with the exchange staff at their booth in front of an abandoned building-turned-shooting-gallery. A small group of women drug users gathered in a park building nearby to go over condom techniques with a health educator from the project. I had two memorable conversations that day: when I asked the women in the condom workshop what their experiences had been with evangelical treatment programs, they expressed positive feelings. The women said that compared to the staff at other programs, evangelists were kind, provided for necessities such as clothing and food, and were less punitive. Their complaint was that the evangelical programs did not provide medication for withdrawal symptoms, which forced them to drop out.

My second memorable conversation was with a man in his thirties who came to the exchange site for needles, but was introduced to me by the staff as an evangelist. He talked extensively with me about his conversion; how he went cold turkey in his apartment, then found a local Pentecostal church where he accepted Christ and began to study the Bible. Christ helped him stay off drugs, he said, and sometimes he used a little bit, but never like he did before. Even when he came to buy drugs at the shooting gallery, he brought the Word of Christ to other addicted people. These conversations revealed to me how people with drug problems do not necessarily see their treatment options in distinct categories. A man can identify himself as evangelist even as he frequents a needle-exchange site. Sex workers might find evangelical treatment programs nonjudgmental and nurturing, even if they do not convert. Addicted people combine elements of addiction programs as necessary, such as symptom relief from medical detox programs; with needles and condoms from public health activists; with food, clothing, and a sense of meaning and belonging from Christian ministries.

The pragmatic approach that sex workers, syringe exchangers, and street ministers took to addiction treatment included working against the state's primary response to narcotics: the Caribbean drug war. Street ministries had more in common with social activists like Dr. Vargas than he or they acknowledged. Although addiction ministries accepted referrals from drug courts, serving a "rehabilitative" function for inmates that made law enforcement against narcotraffic more palatable to Puerto Ricans, street ministers nonetheless were critical of the punitive state. They held the drug war at an uneasy distance and sought to distinguish their motives and logic from that of state control. In some cases, the ministries even adopted a language of social welfare and the responsibility of the state to assist a disenfranchised generation of young Puerto Ricans.

SOFT HEARTS AGAINST HARD HANDS

In 1993 Governor Rosselló launched *Mano Dura* (Strong Hand) as part of the U.S.-sponsored War on Drugs (Poitevin 2000). He had the National Guard round-up and search public housing project residents, and staged mass arrests with ample news coverage. Since 1990, Puerto Rico had been a major port for Colombian cocaine to enter the United States, and Puerto Rican murder and drug-related crime rates had surpassed that of any state on the mainland (Booth and Drummond 1996, Abel 1998). Rosselló showed zero tolerance to drug lords and street-level users alike, flooding the media with images of handcuffed addicts being loaded into police vans.

These images played into and fostered public anger toward drug dealers and users as the cause of the island's social and political instability, and street ministries saw themselves as offering an alternative to *Mano Dura*. Although they employed individualist rhetoric of addiction, they also opened spaces of social analysis which reflected their social position as working-class Puerto Rican men.

At Restoration House, Brother Menocal explained that addicted men come to the House injured, having been abused as children: in his words, they have a heart of stone which has to be turned into a heart of flesh (*corazon de carne*). This required a gentle approach, a form of corrective emotional experience in the hands of ministry leaders who were mediums for restorative powers.

At Victory Academy, Pastor Mendoza lectured program leaders on the modern mindset of disposability; disposability of food, of products, and of people. He told them that a life of service to others was the antidote to this mindset.

The Mendozas saw themselves as offering an alternative to the incarceration of jobless Puerto Rican men. Brother Menocal saw the vulnerability of young, addicted men. But both the Mendozas and Brother Menocal had a complicated, dual relationship with the military State. Both ministries functioned as an arm of the prison system, as they accepted referrals from the court systems and filed reports with parole officers. Given the Puerto Rican legislature's move to privatize addiction services, Puerto Rico increasingly relied on street ministries to provide surveillance of convicts, as well as detoxification and rehabilitation.

Brother Menocal worried that privatization would reduce public funding for his professional counselors. He started to refuse clients sent by the courts, saying that those most suitable for Christ-therapy were those who sought it voluntarily. The Mendozas also restricted their court referrals, preferring to recruit volunteers directly from the streets. They had never accepted government funds, saying that they were called to live *por fe* (on faith alone) and that they did not want the government to influence their work.

As the director of an evangelical program sixty miles north of Brother Menocal's said, "The government is not interested in addicts. The plan is *Mano Dura*—closing doors. With a drug record, you can't work or study—the only alternative is to sell drugs ... [the system] marks them, locks them up for a short time, and cycles them through. It's recycling."

Brother Menocal described the consequences of *Mano Dura* on his clientele, "[We're at] capacity: 60 clients. We are full a lot—in [this town] there is a lot of demand. Rosselló with his *Mano Dura* did not support rehabilitation. It's not a good approach for addicts. They're very wounded, they have lots of problems."

Neither the Mendozas nor Brother Menocal accepted the criminalization of drug users. They framed addicts as casualties of a corrupt society, rather than the cause of corruption. They also used criteria for moral judgment that, unlike those of mainstream Puerto Rican society, did not privilege material success. Surviving *por fe* (by faith alone), refusing to accept government subsidy, and embracing an ascetic life, ministries did not see poverty as a sign of moral weakness but rather as a source of moral authority.

Ultimately, street evangelists saw themselves as revolutionaries, creating a world-wide community of peace and equality one convert at a time. As the speaker on a Puerto Rican Christian radio show commented, "Christians are good for society. You know you can leave your child with a Christian neighbor and they will be safe."[12]

This imagery of a worldwide Christian family created through mass conversion, in which children are nurtured and neighborhoods are safe, was a recurrent theme in street ministries. The reimagined kinship in these post-conversion families is what made possible new relations of inclusion and care, intended to reverse the displacement and exclusion of the political order. The Christian families to which ministries aspired was formed through gender-specific strategies, however; strategies that opened new paths to domesticity and moral authority for men, and foreclosing options for domestic contributions and authority of women.

male dominance ——>

4

The New Masculinity

The New Masculinity: No vulgarity, no discourteousness, a man who is a model for children, who gives kisses and affection, who cries when sad, is a hard worker, and never loses sight of his principles.

FROM A POSTER HUNG ON THE DOOR OF A PENTECOSTAL
STREET MINISTRY FOR MEN IN MAYAGÜEZ.

In trying to explain the mass conversion of Latin Americans to evangelical Protestantism, social theorists first proposed that the cause was (North) Americanization—the encroachment of capitalism necessitating a more individualist cultural practice than that of Catholicism—and also was a reaction to political instability and the need for emotionally expressive rituals to balm the wounds of war (Stoll 1990, Lalive d'Epinay 1969, Martin 1990). Elizabeth Brusco, in *The Reformation of Machismo* (1995), proposed an intriguing third alternative: Protestantism as gender strategy. Based on fieldwork in Colombia, Brusco argued that the Protestant church is a female-dominated institution and that women convert their male partners to domesticate them.[1] Enforcing the clean-living program of evangelists, Colombian women brought men into the domestic sphere as heads of household, and forced men to give up the male subcultural pursuits of alcohol, adultery, and domestic violence. Here, I use Brusco's argument as a point of departure. I saw conversion among addicted men in Puerto Rico as a male-driven—rather than female-driven—gender strategy that changed the relationship male converts had to their families and their work.

When I started fieldwork in Puerto Rico, I suspected that recovery from addiction would involve overcoming the stigma of addiction. What I did not anticipate, but which surfaced again and again in my interviews, was how central redefined gender roles and negotiation of one's position within one's family were to ex-addicts' newfound identities as Christians. This resonated with the findings of Brusco, which identified the effort to change male behavior (such as drinking) as a key motive for conversion. Rather than seeing street ministries as female dominated, as Brusco did, however, I found them to be male institutions. Rather than hearing stories of wives and partners who pressured men to convert, I heard stories of men who, through conversion, met their need for an alternative route to respect as men. <u>Conversion involved a renegotiation of the status of converts in two domains;</u> in the way converts identified themselves as men and performed masculinity, as well as in the way converts related to members of their families and performed their roles as sons, brothers, spouses, and fathers. The ministries provided arenas in which men could rehearse and perform these roles, ranging from a newly masculinized domestic sphere as spiritual head of home, to an austere, monastic sphere of honor through sacrifice and denial of bodily needs. At times, these two poles—masculine domesticity and insular monastic restraint—conflict with each other, highlighting a tension between individualist and relational elements of spiritual power.

DOMESTIC BLISS

Wilson and I pulled up to the middle school parking lot in twilight. It was August, just after a tropical downpour. Mosquitoes circled at the car door, waiting to land on my bare arms. I drew a deep breath of cool air from the air conditioner, and braced myself for the humidity that would pour in once I opened the door. Wilson was unaffected. His floral-print shirt stayed pressed and buttoned as he motioned me toward the fluorescent lighting of the gym windows. He moved his six-foot tall, three-hundred-pound frame briskly to the door, not wanting to miss his nephew's solo.

Inside, mothers and small children pushed metal folding chairs toward a makeshift arena marked by a rectangle of tape on the floor. Four pre-teen girls in matching pink sweatshirts and one thin boy in a white T-shirt and spiked leather wrist cuffs moved into formation as the volume was adjusted on a beat box. Wilson motioned to the boy in the T-shirt: "That's him—we got here in time!" His nephew's sun-streaked hair brushed his shoulders, he danced in formation with the girls until it was time for his solo. Pop-locking his arms and sliding backwards in a moon walk, the audience gasped when he made a full flip and ended in the splits. Amid a standing ovation, Wilson beamed. "I *told* you. That's how he got three trophies last year!"

It was the first dance tournament of the year. Wilson had no doubt that his nephew would win it—and many more—on his way to the island-wide finals. Wilson's aging Jeep was broken down that night, but he planned to repair it and drive his nephew's team to tournaments across the island. Wilson's sister Jessica had been coaching his ten-year-old nephew and four girls from their housing project daily through the summer. Jessica had danced herself when she was young, but for years she lost that side of her life to an abusive, heroin using husband who ultimately left her with two toddlers. Jessica was arrested in the desperate years after he left. Not able to clothe her children, she shoplifted. Wilson blamed himself. "I was in the penitentiary. I was not there."

Wilson told me that the Holy Spirit had intervened to give Jessica probation and to make her the coach of the dance troupe: "She was called to work with the children ... she doesn't know it was Jesus because she's not Christian." In turn, Wilson felt called to support her. When he was not in *culto*, Bible study, or working his father's hotdog stand, Wilson chaperoned Jessica, his nephew, and his niece. He also accompanied his mother—who was weakened by a heart condition—on trips to the grocery store and to the doctor.

I joined Wilson and his mother on the day that a popular Latin American soap opera, *Betty La Fea* (*Ugly Betty*), was scheduled for live taping inside the city's shopping mall. The crowd was too thick to glimpse the actors, so Wilson, his mother and I headed to a five-and-dime store. Wilson searched for toothpaste, and his mother greeted a friend, a woman with thick makeup who looked to be in her sixties.

Her friend described her own son's struggle to overcome drugs; her son embraced the church at first but then lost interest and stopped going. She congratulated Wilson's mother on Wilson's regular church attendance. Overhearing the conversation, Wilson called out: "Amen! Glory to God!" But as we left, the smile on Wilson's mother's face faded. I sensed she was wondering how long Wilson's churchgoing would last; she had shared such doubts with me before.

Despite his mother's doubts, Wilson wove himself into her domestic space. In the drug world he had survived by using violence, but home life provided a different point of re-entry. In his mind, a churchgoing man was a family man, and he performed both roles with gusto. Although marginally employed, he had become a provider for his family, lending moral and practical support to his ill mother and his abandoned sister. He was also physically transformed. As we thumbed through an aged family photo album, he said "See, I used to be so skinny. Now I have meat on my bones," pointing to a shadowy Polaroid shot from the 1980s and then to his round belly. Wilson felt he had achieved substance, both bodily and spiritually, by following God's plan and caring for his home.

Months before, I'd spoken to Wilson on Father's Day, wishing him a good day and asking about his children. He told me "They made me cards—I'm going to pick them up right now." He explained that his children, ages 9 and 12, were in the custody of his ex-wife's mother, and that he worried that their stepfather might be abusing them. "When I get my certificate of good conduct, I'm going to get custody of them." Later that day, I spoke to Wilson's mother on the telephone. "Are you going to see your grandchildren, Wilson's children, today?" I asked innocently. Wilson's mother was confused: "Wilson's children—what children? Wilson doesn't have any children!"

At first, I was taken aback. Was Wilson lying to me? Was his mother in the dark? But soon I saw that Wilson coveted the role of father and protector to the point of claiming the children of an ex-girlfriend as his own. And I saw how Pentecostal testimony worked as much on the speaker as the listener to rewrite not only pasts but also futures. Through testimony, Wilson had convinced himself of his paternity. It held the key to his own rebirth into the home.

The family home was one of the few places where ex-addicted (and ex-convicted) men might carve-out a space for themselves. For Wilson and many other converts, their newfound domesticity opened traditionally feminine routes to respectability through the moral authority that comes from suffering and sacrifice in the service of others, and from recasting oneself as an interdependent subject.

In Wilson's case, it also provided a way around violent male codes of domination and retribution. Wilson told me that he had made hits for a drug cartel and had served six years in prison for murder. But he did not want to dwell on the details from that time in his life.

I asked Wilson how he met Jesus.

> I went to prison; I had been in the street. I said, I don't want to be in the streets. I opened my heart to God. In prison there is a Christian community. . . . Every day they held *cultos* for Jesus. There were lots of problems in my life. I owed money. People wanted to kill me. A brother in the church presented God's plan to me. I opened my heart. I had been using drugs in jail. I went cold turkey with Jesus in the jail: I didn't feel any symptoms. I felt like I feel today: happy.

When time came for Wilson's release, Wilson was considered a Christian leader in his ward of the prison. He chose to go straight to Restoration House rather than go home on parole. By the fourth day at Restoration House, Wilson gave his testimony at a revival held in front of a shooting gallery. He had been in treatment programs before and had been on methadone but, as Wilson put it, conversion changed his life. In the past he had gone right back to drugs, but this time, he said, "Jesus took the desire out of my heart."

Conversion also helped Wilson with dilemmas posed by the tradition of vengeance in street culture.

> There was a guy at *Hogar Restauración*. [Before I converted] I had shot him 21 times, he couldn't walk because of it. [Since then] he also became Christian. We talked; I said I'm sorry—the Devil had me. When a person goes to Jesus He takes out his old heart and puts in a new heart. I couldn't live with [this guy] in prison because he accused me—he had [hired] security. When I saw him [in prison] I didn't have Jesus in my heart. I would say "I'm here because of you, I'll kill you!" But at *Hogar Restauración* I said, "Forgive me." He said, "No, forgive me, because I was looking for you to kill you, too." Jesus took a killer and gave him a new heart. . . . Jeremiah says that Jesus takes out the heart of stone and puts in a heart of flesh.

Although Wilson described himself as a killer before his conversion—a "hitman," in fact—I sensed that he had had little autonomy in his use of violence; that he instead had been a cog in the narcotraffic machine, a desperate mercenary at the whim of his heroin supplier. Conversion and his family's reliance on him empowered him more than his gun had. And the evangelical discourse of forgiveness enabled him to speak to his former adversaries in the grammar of testimony. By attributing the power to Jesus to replace hardened hearts, Wilson was able to symbolically disarm his adversary through the intervention of a (divine) third party, an intervention that reset the terms of their feud as a matter of faulty hearts; as a deficit of—rather than an affront to—their manhood.

Wilson left Restoration House a few months before graduating, because the director accused him of unauthorized leave while at a doctor's appointment. The director later apologized and asked Wilson to come back, but by that time Wilson was humiliated. Rather than graduate from the program, Wilson chose to live with his parents, helping his father to sell hotdogs at a concession stand outside of a high school, and attending a local Pentecostal church every evening. Wilson stood tall outside the church, dressed in buttoned floral-print shirts and pressed slacks. Resting his hands on the belly overhanging his belt, he bellowed "*¡En Victoria!*" (In Victory!) at church brothers across the road.

A year later, he married a woman who he had known in the streets. A former sex worker, she struggled to stay off of crack. Her looks captivated Wilson, "She's like a model!" He bought her a small house in a heavily drug-trafficked neighborhood near the beach and supported them from the concession stand.

Wilson was determined to remain faithful to her through her bouts with crack; he called programs across the island and found her treatment—not a small feat given the island's lack of drug-treatment programs for women. He enrolled her in a residential program located two hours north of their home. There he visited her on Sundays, which was family visitation day, whenever his Jeep was running.

AWAKENING THE SENSES

Juan, who at Restoration House had taught me about spiritual eyes and ears, had his own strategies for managing his masculinity at home and work, strategies that had not changed much with conversion. This dawned on me one night when I invited Juan out to dinner at a restaurant in Ponce. I asked Juan to pick the restaurant, and he chose a neighborhood standby, a place that had stayed in business for forty years by selling home-style *criollo* (Puerto Rican, or creole) meals. Juan settled into a familiar seat and went over the menu with gusto, deciding on a steak. He reminisced about life before conversion, "There was this one guy who always ordered this dish. We came here all the time and he always ordered this one and loved it. He got shot in his sleep by a man he'd been with all day, who he'd shared drugs with and eaten with."

Intrigued by Juan's flat delivery of the story, I asked why his killer did it. Juan answered that it was for money and for drugs. Wouldn't it have been easier just to rob someone than kill him, I asked? Juan explained that his friend was *agriado* (cranky). The man who killed him would have been in danger because his friend would have hunted him down.

> Street people will do anything. I know God had plans for me because there were so many times I was on the street and I came close to dying, but God saved me. [Fifteen years ago] I sold drugs. I was only twenty-one, I did it for fun. I was in the house of the *dueños* [drug dealers], and they asked me to pick up food [from a restaurant]. When I came back I was at the front door, and four men with masks came up and put a gun to my head. They told me "Knock!" and I hesitated. They said "Knock or we'll kill you!" and I hesitated again, but then I knocked. The people inside opened the door because they were expecting me, and the men with masks ran in the house looking for the money and the drugs. They threatened the people in the house to get the location of the drugs, but the people didn't know. Finally, they searched and found the drugs under the refrigerator. They had me on the ground with a gun in my mouth. I knew I was gonna die, I saw my life run backwards to the time I was in my mother's womb. Finally, one of the people in the house said "Let him go—he doesn't know anything. We just sent him for food." And they did. But the men with masks had gotten all of the drugs and money, thousands of dollars, in just five minutes.
>
> Later, the owner of the drugs called me. He wanted to kill me for letting in the robbers. I said okay, but it was the people in the house who were not guarding the drugs well. I just did what they told me and went out for food. The owner knew this was true and he let me go.

Juan was not a violent person. I asked how he survived in the streets all that time. He answered that he was always friends with the guy in charge. Not the people working for him, he said. With *him*. Juan had used his interpersonal skills to navigate the treacherous hierarchies of male dominance in the violent drug trade. His talk of aligning with people in power reminded me of his effort to win favor with powerful spirits, and ultimately the Holy Spirit, by developing his spiritual eyes and ears, and passing spiritual tests in his daily life. It was a game of alignment with power, and Juan was able to transfer a feel for the game[2] from his prior life to his new life in the ministry.

Juan was so engrossed in his memories he almost forgot to pray before putting the first slice of steak into his mouth.

> I used to come here all the time when I washed cars for the doctors at [the hospital]. I was earning so much money then. That was a bad time in my life, I prefer not to think about that . . . because I was spending it all on drugs. The dealers used to bring me their cars. They loved the way I did it. I would wash everything, the tires, the vents, using Q-tips. I would even put the car on that thing they use to lift cars for oil changes, and clean the bottom. That impressed them because no one ever looks down there. I would tell them, look, you can only see it from a distance. Then I'd [hoist the car up] and show them. They used to just hand me the bills and I didn't even count them. I looked at them later and saw that they gave me $100. . . . The

doctors, I used to drive their cars. People used to ask what kind of work you do? One day I'm driving Mercedes, one day BMW. I used to put on a white coat and stethoscope and pretend I was a doctor [laughing].

Juan's mixed images of professional achievement—sidewalk entrepreneurism through car washing, donning a doctor's coat in luxury cars—revealed one way that he had pursued male honor before conversion. Another way involved mutual aid to other drug users.

One day I was in a *shooting* ["shooting gallery;" a drug injection spot[3]]. I used to go and pay the owner to have a private room; I wanted to be by myself. I was in my room smoking crack and I heard someone say "Help me! Help me! I'm gonna die!" I ran out and saw a man with a needle in his arm, falling over.

"Did you call an ambulance?" I asked.

Juan laughed: "No, how I'm gonna call an ambulance? I splashed water on his face and walked him around."

"Was he overdosed?" I asked.

Juan was more solemn.

Yes. He would have died if I had not done that. Later I saw him at *Hogar Restauración*. He didn't recognize me. I said, "Don't you know me? I'm the one that helped you that time in the *shooting*." He said, "Oh, that was you? Thank you!"

I thought to myself that Juan worked by the same ideology of patronage when he was using drugs as he did now. Juan often spoke of looking exclusively to God for authorization and protection. He had considerable social skills and worked by meeting other people's needs; as a drug dealer and user, the reciprocity he generated must have helped him in the violent world he described. Juan was not a forceful man; his shoulders and stomach were as round and unassuming as his low, soothing voice. He was not physically imposing but was adept at reading unspoken thoughts.

Juan used these skills in his evangelism. After our dinner conversation, Juan looked at my babysitter, Mariana, a migrant from Colombia who I invited out with us because she had no family in Puerto Rico. Mariana had been silent throughout our dinner. Juan turned to me: "She's missing her family. Is it okay if I talk to her?"

He spent twenty minutes talking with Mariana about putting her questions to God, and waiting for His answers. He told her that God would reply if she listened. "I know what is on people's minds because God tells me," he said.

Juan talked with Mariana for a few minutes outside, out of earshot, before driving home. After Juan left I noticed tears in Mariana's eyes. Juan had guessed the question looming over her head: Would she return to Colombia to her family, but also to a jobless economy and give up her hard-earned U.S. visa? Mariana did not convert to Protestantism that night, but she said Juan had made her understand for the first time why so many of her friends in Colombia had done so. He had seen her pain. And he showed again how, in the Pentecostal logic of strength through suffering, pain brings recognition to immiserated people who would otherwise be ignored or rejected. At the same time, Juan's ability to recognize pain served as a gift that enables him to motivate and lead potential converts, rather than it being a sign of his subordination.

At other times, I heard Juan engage converts in talk about spiritual strong men that was reminiscent of male locker-room tales of athletic achievement. He told bystanders at Restoration House,

> When you are with God, you get powers. You know Randy Island? From the Dominican Republic? He is a man of God. He goes to a mountain to pray for a month, and when he comes down he sends his spirit from one kilometer away. He tells you what is on your mind, what you [will be] doing tomorrow.

Juan was thirty-six that year, and re-enrolling as an undergraduate at the Inter-American University. He had voluntarily admitted himself to Restoration House, therefore he had the right to leave at will, and one night he did. The residents of Restoration House were in shock; Juan had been counselor and spiritual medium for many of the young men there. The director had even pulled me aside and asked if I thought Juan could be convinced to come back: "The guys here, they're just crazy for Juan!"

Weeks before, Juan had warned me of his departure.

> Sometimes it gets to be too much. Too heavy. I ask God, what you want me to do? You want me to help the poor people of Africa? God, I just wanna serve you. But my mother says she needs me. God, I will leave it all behind for you. My family, everything.

Juan lost his own father at 12 years old, and did not have biological children, but had been fostering the younger men of the ministry. They came to him for help reading the motives of the people in their lives, and for divination. He had a reputation for being in-tune with God's thoughts—he told others of the troubles they carried before they said a word, he knew the names of people he had never met, and he saw angels visit him in prayer. His tattered sweatshirts and frequent fasts demonstrated his asceticism, and his sensitivity to the thoughts and moods of others instilled trust. Juan fit the image of Christ so often painted by preachers in *culto*: humble, eager to serve, omniscient.

Yet, for all the trust he inspired in his young devotees at the addiction ministry, Juan admitted that the trust of his mother and eight sisters was hard to regain: "Trust is the hardest thing to get back once you have lost it. Once you have lied to them they can never believe that you were out late because you were at church."

And for all of his asceticism and impartiality, Juan yearned for a partner. He told me "I'm lonely, I wish I had someone to share my life. But she has to be at a high spiritual level."

Intimacy with his mother and his sister, and finding a life partner was hard for Juan. Selfless acts toward strangers had always come easily to him: Years before conversion, to shield a teenager from acquiring a criminal record, in court Juan took the blame for stealing a car that he did not steal. Yet, he fantasized about leaving his mother and sisters behind to go and bring God to the poor people in Africa. "When you have God, He is all you need. He is your family, and then you love everybody the same."

Juan discovered in the image of Christ a model for his own manhood. As an evangelist, Juan was no longer a mark, but rather was someone who gave selflessly. He was not a romantic failure but rather an ascetic. He did not abandon his mother and sisters but rather followed God's call to love everyone equally. Juan identified directly with Christ, adopting the mysticism and asceticism that he imagined Christ himself exuded. Material markers of male success, like the BMWs and Mercedes Juan drove years before when he cleaned cars for drug dealers and doctors, were inapplicable to him as a Christian. Juan defined success as spiritual maturity: his capacity to serve others, to forgive.

Forgiveness was a recurring topic of sermons and Bible study at both Restoration House and Victory Academy. Preachers advised converts to ask those who had injured them for forgiveness, especially parents who had been rejecting or abusive toward them when they were children. They pointed out that all men are sinners by nature, and that to resent sinful acts in another person is hypocrisy (Matthew 7:1 "Do not judge or you too will be judged," John 8:7 "If any of you is without sin, let him be the first to throw a stone"). This resonated with the Biblical directive to, in Carmen's words at Victory Academy, "meet bad with good," setting a Christian example of nonviolence (Proverbs 15:1 "A gentle answer turns away wrath"; Luke 6:29 "If someone strikes you on one cheek, turn him the other"). But a second, parallel logic was that by asking the perpetrator or abuser for forgiveness, the victim reframed the relationship as one in which he had choice and power. Asking for forgiveness became a demonstration of strength.

This concept of forgiveness was related to the idea of Christian love as a weapon. One afternoon at Restoration House, Juan gave me a report on the *culto* of the night before.

> The closer you are to God, the more Satan's messengers alert him. He sends soldiers, captains. . . . Last night a man [in the ministry] had a demon in him. A few clients tried to take it out. They can't—only Jesus can. God used me to do it—Jesus uses love. You know what I asked Jesus? Put love in my heart.

Wilson and Juan demonstrated how evangelists use the doctrine of proper male behavior modeled on Christ to invert the meaning of humility, domesticity, and emotional sensitivity. In the underground culture of illicit drug trade, these qualities in a man could be seen as signs of weakness (Bourgois 1998a and 1998b). In the ministries they are markers of spiritual strength that legitimated male authority. This inversion enabled Juan and Wilson to escape rigid codes of male behavior in the drug economy. Juan empowered himself by healing others. Wilson achieved mutual respect for a murderous enemy. The "new masculinity" to which they subscribed thus helped them to bypass ideals of male dominance, control, and achievement that positioned them as failures and targets for aggression.

THE LAST WILL BE FIRST

Evangelical doctrine also could invert the meaning of suffering for men. Octavio, who had taught me about occult forces during his round-the-clock prayer at Restoration House, told me that his humble origins were the source of his connection with God. He had left school after repeating the eleventh grade three times, going on to develop crack addiction as well as being infected with hepatitis and AIDS.

> God takes us addicts. He doesn't like those who think they know a lot. The Bible says intelligence comes from God. No matter how much education you have, if you don't have the Holy Spirit you can't understand. . . . I could be a millionaire, but still missing something. Like a machine assembled but missing one piece without God.

After our interview, Octavio walked me to my car from the chapel and said, "I suffered a lot, I lost a lot. But it doesn't matter how much if I can help another. [Lowering his voice] Can I ask you something I haven't asked anyone, except maybe my wife?"

Unsure of where he was going with the question, I mustered, "Yes!" in my most convincing voice.

"Do you think I could write a book about how God has changed me?"

I said, "You're filling my notebook!"

Octavio continued: "Good. Because I'd like to help others who suffer. Not for my own benefit. I'm not an educated man—God gives me knowledge."

Octavio related how his painful life and humble status took on a sacred character upon conversion. Marginally literate, he felt called to write an autobiography; one that would inspire other men. In my conversations with him, however, Octavio gave few details about his own life. He deferred to biblical citation, or began speaking with God, asking God the questions I posed him, and relaying parables and citations that he received in response. Octavio was, in a sense, too humble to tell his own story. He gave himself over as a conduit for the voice of God. That is what elevated him as a Christian, it was why other converts said his name with great respect.

Padín, a serious, dark-skinned man who had been a prison guard when he started using heroin, would select an appropriate Biblical verse to open each of our interviews, and asked God for wisdom to share with me. When he liked an observation he had made, he consulted his Bible for a parable or verse that corresponded to it. He felt the more humble and obedient his attitude, the more authority was given him by God.

At Victory Academy's Bible study, a ministry leader explained how humility related to Christian authority.

> Ecclesiastes 9:3: [W]hen God wants to give you responsibility, if you don't take it, you are ungrateful. When I preach I put myself behind the pulpit so no one sees my knees shaking. . . . The Bible says, our thoughts are not our thoughts, our path is not our path.

Padín described accepting responsibility, and therefore the authority, as a pious act. His responsibility was tempered by his references to the ultimate authority of God.

Historically, monks in medieval Europe also constructed an alternative masculinity that inverted cultural logics of gender and submission. Craun (2004) describes ascetic monks in Christian late antiquity as feminized; submitting completely to God's will, describing their desire for Christ using sexual imagery of union with the Beloved, to the point, at times, of referring to themselves as "Brides of Christ." The proof of their masculinity, he argues, was that monks chose to submit their will to Christ; they were not forcibly dominated.

Other historians of medieval masculinities expand on the theme of the will, arguing that allegories of martyr-kings of that era blended with images of Christian holy warriors whose "masculine-holiness [was] premised on the mastery of the self" (Christie 2004, 155). This heroic image then applied not only to Christian kings and crusaders but also to solitary ascetics, for whom complete mastery of the body, especially its sexual urges, became an unearthly feat. Celibate monks could have been seen as effeminate, in an historical era in which "the intrinsic connection between manliness, sex and procreation" was taken for granted, but a monk instead presented himself as a knight of God, with sexual drives who was nonetheless "so masculine that he does not give into these" (Heinonen 2004, 82). Biographers of monks detailed the extreme measures they took to conquer their carnal passions (bathing in icy rivers, binding limbs and genitals with spiked leather thongs during sleep), asserting that " 'it is not their nature that afforded them victory . . . for that is mortal and full of innumerable passions,' rather, it is 'their resolve, attracting divine grace' " (Craun 2004, 47).

In medieval Europe, then, monks secured respect in their broader society by converting suffering into a source of power; overcoming bodily desires was the heroic feat that founded that power. Monks appropriated military language, as a monk "donned armor against the flesh, soldiered against himself, and himself overcame himself, both conqueror and conquered in one and the same conflict" (Murray 2004, 30). This technology of desire attracted new recruits to the ranks,

many of them from nobility. The connection between individual chastity and public power was not unique to monks; as medieval historian C. Leyser points out,

> [A]scetic writers were making an appeal to received ethical wisdom. Every ancient
> man—not just a few philosophers—would have understood the consummate need
> for those who claimed power to demonstrate their physical self-control . . . it was in
> the broadcasting of his "private" virtue of temperance (sophrosune) that a public
> man might hope to substantiate his claims to the allegiance of his hearers. . . . In a
> symbolic code that sounds alarmingly familiar, discussion of a man's sex life stands
> in for analysis of his financial and political probity" (Leyser 1999, 111).

More recent Christian history shows a parallel discourse of nineteenth-century
evangelical temperance and masculinity movements that foregrounded conquer-
ing temptation (alcohol and extramarital sex) as a way to build spiritual strength
(Baxter 2011, Berkley Fletcher 2007). Twentieth-century Puerto Rican addiction
ministries present the self as conquerable terrain, and add an element of venture
capitalism: "winning (other men) for Christ." Recruitment into the ministry could
be seen as a pyramid scheme, with each person who succeeded in building a base
of converts being heir to the expanding number of converts brought in by those
below.

An addicted man's liabilities in the secular world became assets in the inverted
corporatism of evangelists; his time in the street became his credential for recruiting in the street, and his testimony regarding his past wrongs became not a source
of stigma making him unemployable, but rather a sign that he was called to do
God's work.

Victory Academy leaders and their assistants wore polo shirts inscribed with
the Academy logo and drove vans with the ministry's logo painted on the sides.
Among Puerto Rican working-class people, uniforms generally signaled employment. The ministry uniforms—collared, buttoned, and pressed—give leaders an
air of professional expertise. Leaders also had managerial and clerical duties such
as filing reports on clients to the State probation office, ordering supplies, and
keeping financial records. They started small businesses that generated income for
the ministry and gave residents the opportunity to learn marketable skills. Yeyo,
the co-director, had been an auto mechanic before joining the ministry; he opened
a repair shop that generated ministry income from local clients and provided ministry recruits with an apprenticeship. The Academy's discipleship prepared the
most successful graduates as pastors to open ministries in new territories. *Discípu-
los* (disciples) had to prepare sermons and preach in *culto*, teach Bible-study
classes, and train new recruits in evangelist technique. The ministry's designation
as an academy indicated vocational training for an evangelist career.

At the same time, ministry leaders spoke to converts as if they were enlisted
in military service. Images of spiritual warfare were ubiquitous at the Academy,

starting with the stages that initiates pass through to become leaders, named for various official ranks of combat: *Reclutas* (Recruits), *Soldados* (Soldiers / Warriors), *Vencendores* (Victors), and *Conquistadores* (Conquerors). In sermons and Bible study, preachers invoked *La Guerra* (the War), *El Ejercito de Dios* (God's Army), *La Lucha* (the Struggle), *La Victoria* (the Victory), and *El Enemigo* (the Enemy), in reference to the spiritual battle with Satan for which converts were preparing themselves. This war imagery lent a military cast to the hierarchy at the Academy, justified its rigid chain of command, and heightened the emotional tenor of conscription. Although the titles of each rank (except pastor) were applied to women as well as men, the martial idiom referenced a traditionally masculine career. The personal discipline demonstrated by punctuality and precision in dress and speech, the physical and mental stamina as entrained by hours of cleaning duty and Bible Study, as well as assuming a kneeling prayer position four to five times for half an hour each day reflected the Academy's military notion of training. In fact, many in the Academy's leadership—including the head pastor and two program directors—had careers in the U.S. military before becoming saved and dedicating their lives to the ministry. The professionalization that the Academy offered was based on a masculine model of self-development through rigorous basic training.

In contrast to Victory Academy, the ambiance at Restoration House, with its mango and banana groves, barbershop, frame-making, and print shop, was a sanctuary from a hostile world. As the director explained it, the men had been emotionally injured in childhood, and the House was to nurse them back to spiritual health. Despite this language of healing, however, leaders at the House also spoke of battle preparedness. Daily worship and Bible study prepared converts for exorcisms performed by late-night prayer chains. Spiritual practice helped converts to resist temptation when they returned to the war in their neighborhoods and homes.

MEN CLAIMING THEIR PLACE

Scholars of gender roles in Latin America on one hand, and of drug trade in North American cities on the other, invoke what I call the "Theory of the Displaced Male." The theory is salient in Puerto Rico, where, since 1950, unemployment has been greater for men than for women (Safa 1995a, Safa 1995b). Classical theorists of *machismo* point out that it is often lower-class men who demonstrate the most extreme enactment of *machista* behavior, including physical aggression, excessive alcohol and drug use, and multiple sexual unions (Stycos 1965).[4] They argue that these men attempt to compensate for their lack of material power by displaying their symbolic masculine power with violence, substance use, and sex (Rainwater 1964).[5] Although contemporary critiques of the concept of machismo have demonstrated that the practices of Latin American men are far less unidimensional

(Gutmann 1996, Ramirez 1999), male aggression and substance use are recurring themes in studies of Latin American urban poverty.[6]

Similarly, studies of Latino North American drug users portray them as reacting to their exclusion from white middle-class status by creating an oppositional drug culture. Their violent subculture is filled with dramas of tenuous friendships and betrayal, ritual abuse and hyper-masculine displays that paradoxically reject middle class American norms of behavior while employing the logic of American capitalism and individualism (Bourgois 2002 and 1995, Williams 1989).

Others have argued that Latin Americans, including Puerto Ricans, emphasize kinship as a source of identity and obligation as compared with white North Americans. One formulation of this concept has been termed "familism," which "places the family ahead of individual interests and development" (Ingoldsby 1991, 57). Familism refers to the responsibilities that extended families and godparents place on individuals, leading Latin Americans to live in close proximity to extended families and lend each other material and social support.[7] As Ingoldsby (1991) points out, the concepts of familism and machismo appear to be contradictory. He concludes that "while familism may be the cultural ideal, there are many forces which push Latin Americans toward machismo behaviors instead" (Ingoldsby 1991, 57). For Ingoldsby, symbolic masculinity and family obligations are opposing cultural forces.

Ministries diffused the tension between the masculinity of the drug involved, indifferent male and that of the responsible family man through a life-cycle view of male development: Men passed through stages of acting out male aggression and accepting male responsibilities. Such models of adult development can be found in other parts of Latin America. Matthew Gutmann (1996) observed that men in Mexico City contrasted youthful binge drinking with the sober domesticity of middle age. In Puerto Rico, converts were not only reborn; they also matured into spiritual patriarchs. Ministry leaders spoke about this spiritual maturation using analogies from child development. As Juan told me, when he explained Biblical concepts to new converts, he built them up gradually, "First I give them milk, then milk and rice, then rice and beans, then meat." Padín paraphrased a Biblical verse, saying "When I was a child, I did the things of a child. Now I'm a man, doing the things of man." As Pastor Marrero explained in a lecture on discipleship, the role of ministry leaders was to "support [new recruits] in a process of growth," guiding them through the steps to spiritual development that eventually would make them collaborators.

Converts could escape the permanent male adolescence imposed by the unemployment of the local economy,[8] framing conversion as a rite of passage in which rebellious youth learn from their errors and replace adolescent willfulness with wisdom. According to preachers at *culto*, mentoring by Christian leaders enabled men to truly become men, qualifying them for legitimate unions through Christian marriage and then for fatherhood, preparing them to guide their children toward Christ. In fact, the director of Restoration House and the pastor at Victory Academy themselves determined when converts would wed their long-term domestic partners in church ceremonies.

Rapid industrialization in Puerto Rico, leading to disproportionately male unemployment due to the targeted recruitment of women into low-wage industrial labor, and later due to disinvestment of manufacturing from the island, has drawn social researchers to examine the ways in which labor patterns influence gender roles, as well as the ways in which men and women have resisted such influences. Safa (1995a) concludes that, in Puerto Rico, the image of the male breadwinner persists to the point that chronically unemployed men are considered household heads, and their employed female partners are considered supplemental breadwinners.[9] Safa and others, such as historian Martinez-Fernandez (2000), argue that major institutions such as private industry, the Protestant church, and the Puerto Rican State historically have promoted ideologies of patriarchy within heterosexual marriage even when economic forces have created female-headed and female-supported households.[10] Although historians challenge the notion that the patriarchal ideal ever was enacted among working-class Latin American families, pointing out that many poor Latin Americans customarily have lived in female-headed households,[11] the complex reality of Puerto Rican families does not diminish the power of the patriarchal ideal as an ideal, as a cultural frame of reference. It even could be argued that the elusive nature of patriarchy strengthens its aspirational value, and raises the stakes for men who repeatedly fail until they "come to Jesus."

Evangelist men who had disqualified themselves from being the head of household during their addiction, used spiritual practice to restructure a less problematic social identity for themselves—which proved a useful tool to the extent that addiction was seen in moral terms rather than in biomedical or social terms. Identities were articulated primarily in terms of kinship, both fictive and biological, through men's roles in their families, and a primary audience for their gender performance was their families. Adopting the "new masculinity" of addiction ministries, then, might be seen as a strategy for ex-addicts—considered social failures by the mainstream—to put themselves on a track to middle-class respectability by pursuing a spiritually-based, rather than economically-based patriarchy.

SPIRITUAL FAMILIES AND WORLDLY FAMILIES

Sunday *culto* at Victory Academy was for family visitation and was well attended by the mothers, fathers, domestic partners, children, brothers, and sisters of program residents. Extra rows of folding chairs were assembled at the back of the chapel, and a makeshift canopy was constructed to provide shade for those who could not fit inside the chapel. The group assembled promptly, thanks to a ministry rule that families who did not arrive before the beginning of *culto* did not get visitation privileges.

One Sunday the preacher advised recruits that the only way to soften their hearts, hardened by past abuses toward and from their families, was to ask their families for forgiveness. The preacher turned to the parents of the recruits and asked them to search themselves for the will to forgive. Then he had program residents to stand, find their parents, and ask them for forgiveness.

Within minutes the most of the recruits clung to their middle-aged and elderly mothers and fathers. Men whose parents in were not at *culto* embraced the preacher or program leaders, who served as surrogate parents. A broad-shouldered man in his thirties clutched the program director at the podium, his body shook violently with rhythmic, inaudible sobs. The chapel was silent, except for the dampened sniffles, for at least five minutes.

Images of family reconciliation were powerfully resonant for converts. They often struggled with rejection by their families or having failed their families. Men who are estranged from their families are displaced in the Puerto Rican social landscape.[12] Sermons at *culto* in both Victory Academy and *Hogar Restauración* often alluded to the Biblical parable of the prodigal son (Lucas 15:11–32). After citing the parable in a Wednesday evening *culto*, a guest preacher from a Methodist Church described the disappointment and pain that he caused his father, a prison guard, when his father learned that he was an addict. "He saw [me] at a drug spot. He invented a case to put me in prison and then locked himself up in his office and cried. He prayed: 'God has to change my son's life.' How many of our fathers have cried?"

At another culto in the same chapel, a guest preacher from a Pentecostal Church in Guayama talked about how he now felt in relation to his family, after converting and leaving drugs, "I walk with my head high because I am a new man. I have repented the person that didn't respect my mother. I'm not ashamed of being *evangelico*, of being in the presence of God."

Yet, family members were not always quick to accept that evangelists were new men. For example, Nilde, the wife of Tito, a new but enthusiastic convert at Restoration House, talked about her fears that Tito was easily influenced both by drugs and the Church.

> He is a weak person—he convinces himself of things easily . . . he wants to sanctify himself too much . . . but he is weak, weak, weak. This is how I know. He was with . . . an *espiritista* (spiritualist). This man was smoking a cigar. Tito never smoked cigars but there he was with a cigar. I said, "Tito—you smoke cigars?" [He said] "Yeah—it's good!"

Tito's wife leveled a significant critique of Tito's masculine self-image, implying that he converted because he was impressionable. She challenged the potential *machista* connotations of drug use by calling it a sign of weakness, and challenged evangelical constructs of strength through individual choice by attributing conversion to group pressure.

Addiction ministries themselves could be seen as a shelter from the "real" world of responsibilities and choices, a crutch for those unwilling to face the consequences of their pasts. As Juan's sister said, when I called her to locate Juan after he left Restoration House, "Juan left because he needs to face the world. He needs to stop running away from his problems."

Regardless, joining the ministry offered a place to rehearse family reconciliation, and the experience of acceptance and competence in their roles within the ministry. In cases where men could not reconcile with their families, the ministry served as alternate family.

Program pastors and leaders talked about the ministry and a broader fellowship of born-again Christians as their *familia espiritual* (spiritual family) in contrast with the *familia del mundo* or *familia carnal* (worldly family or family of the flesh). For instance, when Yeyo's young assistant in the ministry's automechanics shop told me that he did not have any family on the south side of the island, Yeyo turned to him in mock disgust, saying, "You have family *here*, don't you? Who am *I*?"

The very terms used to address colleagues and superiors in the ministry, such as *hermano* and *hermana* (brother and sister) to indicate a fellow evangelical Christian, or *Mama* in the case of the wife of the head pastor of Victory Academy, reflected the pervasiveness of kinship imagery in the ministries. Converts did not use the word *Padre* (Father) in reference to authority figures in the church, probably because of its association with Catholic clergy. Instead *Padre* was used in reference to God as the nurturing, forgiving paternal figure that recruits often felt their families lacked. The ministry, acting as surrogate spiritual family, served as an alternative source of affiliation for converts from problematic worldly families. Yet, in the process it created its own set of demands upon members, which could conflict with their obligations to worldly families.

GOD BEFORE FAMILY OR FAMILY THROUGH GOD?

As ministry staff told me many times, "it is rare that anyone comes truly voluntarily." They meant that even among those who were not forced into treatment by the legal system—those who were called *voluntarios* (voluntary clients)—ultimatums from relatives and partners were strong incentives to get treatment.

 Learning how to be a good father, husband or partner, and son was a recurring theme. Many equated successful treatment with success in family reconciliation. Jorge, a gentle, soft-spoken man who oversaw the wood-crafts workshop in Restoration House, described an agreement that he had with his twelve-year-old daughter: She would get good grades in school if he stayed off drugs Jorge said, "This semester, she has straight A's!"

Ministry leaders portrayed the converted man as gentle and not too proud to help women with domestic chores, and as someone who, while providing leadership and material support for the home, always acknowledged that God was the true leader and provider for the family. As a guest preacher at Victory Academy put it, "Serving God has a price, but serving God also brings compensation. [You might say] I have school, work, a family to care for . . . but look to the Provider [God] first."

At a conference on domestic violence at Victory Academy led by an evangelist couple who ran a Christian shelter for battered women, the husband explained that at the shelter,

> My wife is the boss, I'm the worker [laughing]. We have to share our work. When I come home from work, do I kick one shoe here and one shoe there, sit back and ask for a soda? No! They teach us that the man is the *macho*. Before, I thought that way, but the Lord [said] [shaking his head and clicking his tongue] you're mistaken!

what is it?

His wife then explained that it is not only beatings that count as domestic violence. "If a man says to his mother, '[C]ook this! Iron that!' this is also a form of violence." Demands for domestic servitude and restrictions on a woman's liberty were "infractions against Christianity. You have to examine yourself." She explained that mistreatment "is based on *machista* ideas, for example, the idea that the Bible says that the wife is a slave." Conversely, she placed the burden on women—if their abusive partner could not be rehabilitated through Christ, then "find a partner who also accepts Christ." She drew a parallel between drug addiction and women who return to abusive men, saying that returning to abusers "is also like an illness. It is also a vice, it is obsessive." The portrait of the evangelical family painted by this couple was one in which by practicing Christianity correctly, both the man and the woman are responsible for sharing domestic chores and cultivating relations of respect, relations which are free of violence and conflict because they are mutual and equitable.

On the surface this appeared to contradict the patriarchal model of masculinity promoted in the ministries but, in practice, evangelical rhetoric spoke the languages of both patriarchy and egalitarianism: A Christian man both protected the family as its head, and respected his wife. The addiction-treatment programs taught men that they were accountable for providing for their families spiritually and materially, but also for minimizing conflict by sharing domestic labor and allowing their wives autonomy.

Just living at the addiction treatment programs could create conflicts for men who were trying to be accountable to their families, however. A week after our first interview, Octavio struggled with whether to go home to his family or stay at the ministry. He had only spent four months at *Hogar Restauración*, and the full course was 12 months, but his wife was having a difficult time supporting and raising their children alone.

> I have a wife and two sons. They need a head of the house. God put me here but it isn't healthy [to leave my family]. Yes, sometimes God takes us out to reestablish us. But . . . when God comes to man *for real* there is a transformation. God asks one thing: tell others what he's done. . . . There are situations that mark being human, that change your life. For example, [someone] has an accident, recuperates, but it changes their way of being. God prepares everything ahead of time. I've made the decision to put myself in the hands of God.

Octavio justified leaving the program by talking about his transformation as permanent. He identified giving his testimony as his primary responsibility as a Christian, which he could do outside of the program. But he was obviously torn, and while he claimed that he had put himself in God's hands, Juan disagreed, saying that if he was truly following God's will he would finish his treatment at Restoration House.

> Octavio is a man of God, he knows the Bible very well. But you have to have a balance. If we have a marriage, the Devil has a way of ruining it. . . . In your house, God comes first, then the home. People without food—God comes with food. God is never late. Octavio uses the Bible, but if he really did, he'd be here. If you're in the hands of God, God has to give you food, money, anything you need.

Octavio's dilemma revealed a tension between the family values rhetoric of the ministries and the way that evangelism is practiced. Octavio's transformation into an evangelist promised to save his marriage, but also required that he temporarily abandon his family responsibilities. As a leader in the ministry, he focused on fathering his spiritual children, rather than raising his biological children. Leadership in the ministry promised him something akin to a mainstream social identity, yet it required him to give up conventional family life.

The individualism of Protestant evangelical doctrine was visible in this tension of the Puerto Rican family's determination of identity, the individual nature of evangelical salvation, and the demands of ministries. The ministries urged recruits to "die to self" as the first phase of being reborn into a new family in Christ. Family members who had not accepted Christ were left behind in the carnal world. Conversion itself was an intensely intimate, and thus individual, encounter with the Holy Spirit. In this sense, a convert's existence was radically separate from that of his unconverted family. It put him in a privileged relationship with God, potentially inverting family hierarchies.

The majority of the men and women who sought treatment at Victory Academy and Restoration House had lived with domestic partners of the opposite sex who they referred to as *mi esposo/esposa* (my spouse) but to whom they are not mar-

marriage → both Converts

ried. In this way they mirrored the majority of working and lower-class men and women in Puerto Rico. Ministries encouraged all converts to marry their domestic partners in the church, but required partners to convert. The effort to convince partners to convert could go on indefinitely. In difficult cases, pastors sometimes advised converts to divorce and to live unpartnered or find a new spouse who was ready for a "marriage blessed by God." This highlighted the extent to which the evangelists placed evangelism before family unity.

Protestant narratives of adult rebirth, self-elected baptism, and salvation reflect a more individualist approach to status attainment than that of the historically family-based, collectivist ethos of Puerto Rican Catholicism. It mirrors North American tropes of honor through self-reliance and individual achievement regardless of origin. Historically, nineteenth-century North American fundamentalists who were the precursors to modern evangelists rejected the Victorian idealization of the family and domestic sphere, which they felt absolved the mother and children of original sin. These early fundamentalists encouraged strict upbringing of children that avoided emotional indulgence, as well as an individualism which adopted "Christ's lonely example as a model of holiness," and rejected "the conflation of godliness with the middle-class family" (Lamberts Bendroth 1999). The family values rhetoric of late-twentieth century U.S. evangelists is thus a reversal of earlier fundamentalist doctrine and is internally debated among evangelists themselves[13]: some argue that family values rhetoric is a superficial and politically motivated gloss to evangelical individualism.[14]

Ministry leaders used the doctrine of Christian servitude to promote both a relational concept of self, and a hypermasculine image of self-reliance. On one hand, the pastor at Victory Academy glorified and feminized Christian servitude: "Christ died to be a servant, that was his highest calling . . . God is not looking for a girlfriend, He is looking for a wife." On the other, he spoke of Christian perfection through service in a way that discouraged reliance on others—self-sacrifice as independence; a Christian as "here to serve," not to ask others to meet his needs.

Protestant individualism is tempered by the image of the ministry as surrogate family. A convert does not abandon his family, rather he adopts an alternative family in the ministry. This is one way that Puerto Rican addiction ministries adapt North American evangelism to their time- and place-specific needs; that of escaping the paradox of the dysfunctional Latin American extended family as the source of both shame and sustenance. Positioning of men in a field of power outside of their families of origin is critical to the spiritual capital building that allows subjugated men to reinvent themselves as successful. I was to find, however, that this inversion of the violent victimhood of addiction into masculine victory came with uncertainties and costs, to women in the ministries, to families of origin, and, at times, to converted men themselves.

Spiritual Mothers

Mornings at Victory Academy were pleasant. Samaria greeted me and handed me a broom, a saucepan, or a desk chair for Bible study, depending on my time of arrival. In kitchen conversations, the ministry's women advised me on my sleepless one year old and tutored me in the art making *sofrito*, the sauce base for Puerto Rican beans. The women's home took up the first floor of the three-story former motel. A female zone, it was a relief from the gendered vigilance that leader exercised over my interviews in all-male street ministries. And it was the only Pentecostal home for women on the Island.

A year later Samaria was gone and the women's home was closed. Mama Tita, the pastor's wife, said something that I had heard at other Christian homes: Women addicts are more difficult to treat than men; they had a lot of emotional needs, and the ministry did not have the resources to work with them at the time. Mama Tita assured me that the ministry would reach out to women again in the future. At the moment, Jessica was the only female convert they had. She ran Sunday school for the children of male recruits whose families attended *culto*.

In my three years of field work in Puerto Rico, I saw Victory Academy double the number of its men's homes from two to four, while the number of its women's homes dropped from two to zero. With time, and despite the prominent discourse of "women's greater needs" as the reason for failed sites, I came to see that this had less to do with women's faith or emotional needs than with their inability to gain authority in the ministry. In its bid to cultivate the respectability and upward mobility of its recruits, the Academy had adopted a middle-class, patriarchal model of family relations and proper womanhood. This often stood in marked contrast to the realities of working-class, woman-centered extended families from which most of its membership had come.

My observation that women were in some ways shut out of addiction ministries flew in the face of research on gender in the Pentecostal movements that flourished in the Caribbean, Latin America, and Sub-Saharan Africa from the 1980s on. Field researchers had counterintuitive findings: The same conservative ministries that advocated the separation of men from women in public space and for men to assume the role of spiritual heads of home were, in practice, dominated by women who benefitted when converted men gave up substance use, gambling, and adultery to focus their resources on their nuclear families, and by women who found support and shelter from violence in gender-segregated ministries. A number of reports highlighted the ways that Pentecostal women used the discourse of equal access to spiritual gifts to empower themselves and to legitimate the leadership of female preachers and missionaries (Lawless 1991; Rabelo, Ribiero, and Almeida 2009). Scholars referred to this phenomenon as the "Pentecostal gender paradox" (Martin 2001), by which they meant that, "Pentecostalism appeals to women while at the same time reproducing gendered hierarchies. The argument is that Pentecostalism offers women certain kinds of empowerment, but unlike Western middle-class feminism it does so in ways that are relatively unthreatening to men" (Lindhardt 2015, 257).

This theme of women's paradoxical empowerment under Pentecostalism has been so pervasive over the past two decades that current scholarship on Pentecostals in the Global South is now challenged to explain the empowerment of men and cultivation of masculinities within a movement that is numerically dominated by women, one that encourages affective vulnerability and interdependence. The Pentecostal men's strategies described range from creating a "softened" patriarchy focused on domestic life (Reihling 2015, Chitando 2013, Thornton 2013) to Pentecostal "technologies of gender" involving deliverance from what was believed to be demonic possession that causes adultery and homosexuality (Rey 2013), to the enactment of spiritual power through repackaging of conversion as "victory" and an expression of agency (Maskens 2015, Lindhardt 2015).

The transformation that Victory Academy promised addicted men—from marginality to moral authority and a sense of domestic place—translated poorly for ex-addicted women. Ex-addicted women often are trying to shed abusive men and histories of sex work, but women's authority at the Academy hinged on their attachment to a man of status in the ministry. At the same time, the spiritual power of converted men derived from their image as providers of guidance and protection, which in turn depended on the victim status of women. Samaria, a women's home leader who taught me about the contradictions of being a female ex-addicted Pentecostal, did not fit the mold of victim, nor was she attached to a man in the ministry. The ministries' reliance on the victimhood of women as a key resource in the reformation of masculinity narrowed women's routes to spiritual power and capital.

equity → programme?

The ministries' rhetoric of women's victimhood coexisted with one of gender equality in moral standards: The insistence that both men and women demonstrate monastic discipline and dedication to the ministry over their families of origin. This apparent equity in expectation ignored the differential family responsibilities and relational histories of women. Building spiritual capital upon ascetic self-discipline required systematic misrecognition of socially structured, gendered circumstances—such as the ability to leave children in other people's care and go missionize, or to serve as an unmarried ministry leader—as a matter of individual resolve. More fundamentally, the fate of Victory Academy's women reminded me that addiction treatment is profoundly gendered, because addiction is profoundly gendered. Although male rejection of alcohol and drugs figures neatly into the Pentecostal narrative of reformed *machismo*, there is no clear corresponding narrative of women's reformation. Samaria showed me how costly this could be.

. . .

On a misty February morning, I awoke to the calls of tree frogs on the lawn, and noticed I had voicemail. It turned out to be two messages from Samaria: "Helena, I'm in Sabana Grande. I need a ride. Could you call me back?" The number she left was muddled. The second message was clearer: "Helena, it's really urgent. Can you call me in Sabana Grande?"

I was happy that Samaria had finally taken me up on my offer of rides. Samaria was stubborn and had once walked five miles in the rain to see an HIV specialist rather than accept a ride in the ministry van. But I was also confused. Why was she in Sabana Grande? Did she have another doctor's appointment?

The number she left did not go through, so I called the Academy to make sure that she had gotten a ride. Leader Pedro answered. "I don't know how to tell you this but Samaria left. She left Tuesday. She made a mistake and didn't want to take responsibility for it." He did not give me details but told me "There is one thing you can do. Pray."

Two hours later I arrived in Sabana Grande, through a maze of dirt roads, using the sparse directions that Samaria had given me over the static of a payphone. There were no sign posts for the street names she gave me, but an elderly man flashed recognition when I asked for Samaria; he turned out to be her half-brother. He chased off two small dogs with a stick so that I could climb the stairs to his door. Samaria sat silently in the dark of his living room, a backpack and overnight bag at her feet.

In the car, Samaria and I talked about Eli. Eli was, at eighteen, the youngest of the women at the Academy, and she could always be found at Samaria's side. Samaria, thirty years Eli's senior, was the only one that seemed to get through to Eli. Eli did not speak to me at first; Samaria explained that it would take a while for her to open up, given how much she'd been through: at age six to losing her mother cancer, at age nine being raped by her foster father, and then being admitted to the psychiatric ward after her suicide attempt.

> When Eli first came to the Academy, she was very rebellious. She would yell at me and tell me she hated me. I didn't fight back. I just told her God loved her. I tried to be patient. That's what works: don't fight her. She would have nightmares, couldn't sleep at night. I had to get in bed with her so she could sleep. She would scream in her sleep and move as if she was fighting someone off.

Samaria had swatted Eli's bottom once, when Eli was making trouble, telling her: "That's what you need, a good spanking!" Conversely, Samaria often told Eli, "I won't let nobody here hurt you." It seemed to work, because as Samaria pointed out to me, "Eli's very affectionate now."

Driving from her half-brother's residence, Samaria turned in her passenger seat to face me saying, "I'm gonna tell you what happened now, why I left the Academy." I told Samaria that she didn't have to, she didn't owe me an explanation.

"I know. I want to." Samaria said. "It would be good for me. I haven't told nobody. . . . [W]e go through things that seem hard at the time, we don't know why they're happening, but in the end I always learn something from it."

Samaria told me that weeks before, a rumor began circulating at the Academy. A male recruit had gotten a letter from an admirer that they thought was a woman at the home. Gabriel had asked Samaria to tell him who it was on several occasions.

> Gabriel called me in the office, asked me if I knew anything. I said no. He told me not to cover up for the girls. I said, please Lord, hold my tongue, don't let me say anything. But he kept going and going. So finally I said, "[L]ook Gabrielito, before I came here I did all kinds of things, but I did them all out in the open. I didn't care what people said. All my life I been like that. You think I'm gonna change now?"

After a while Samaria realized that Gabriel was accusing Eli. "I asked Eli please tell me if you know anything and she said, 'No, no.' I didn't want them messing with her because she could leave over this, they could hurt her. She's not as spiritually strong as I am, she could go back to using drugs."

In the end, Gabriel contacted the pastor's wife, Mama Tita, who was at an evangelist conference in the United States. Mama Tita called back for Samaria and told her that Samaria had completed her nine months at the program and was free to leave.

Samaria was hurt at the unceremonious ending to her work at Victory Academy, but told herself "[T]his isn't the end of me. The Academy is just a step in the path for me, I can do other things." She was more worried about the impact of her leaving on Eli, who needed her protection. She suspected that Gabriel's next move would be to kick Eli out of the ministry.

I don't care what you do to me, but you're not gonna hurt Eli. She's staying. When I left Eli was crying, hugging me. I said, "Eli, I'm going but you're gonna stay. I don't care what happens, you're staying. You belong here. You stay and do the work you're meant to do."

I had a hard time believing that Gabriel—the self-effacing, grandfatherly man I knew—could orchestrate such warfare. But Samaria told me there was a lot about him I did not see.

One time I went in the office to get some keys and Gabriel was there, he grabbed my hands and tried to kiss me. I was carrying a metal bucket, you know, that kind you use for paint. I said, Gabriel, if you don't let go of me I'm gonna hit you with this bucket. He didn't think I'd say anything, but I did. I told Jorge, Yeyo, everybody. He said, "What you do that for?" I said, "Don't do something and expect me not to tell. I'm like that, I say what I'm doing. I don't hide things like you." He never liked me after that.

We pulled into Rincón and I offered Samaria something to eat at the bakery. She ordered a doughnut and juice, I ordered a sandwich and asked her if she knew what she was going to do now. She mentioned knowing doctors and lawyers who would write her a letter of reference for a job. For the time being, Samaria had no specific plans to find a new ministry. She planned to stay with her friend Ana and attend church with her. We stopped on a dead-end street and Samaria gathered her bags. She wanted to go to *culto* at the Academy so we agreed to meet on the same street that Sunday so that I could give her a ride.

The next day I drove through sheets of rain to the Academy. Along the way I stopped to buy meat patties for Eli and the other women at the Academy, only to find that I'd locked my keys in my car. An ominous sign, I thought. An old man with a machete pried my door open, and I thought, maybe I'm meant to go to the Academy after all.

The Academy looked deserted. It stopped raining and I saw a man meditating behind the chapel. I entered the office where Gabriel shook my hand, kissed my cheek, and pointed me toward the women's quarters. I gave Eli the message from Samaria that she was fine, and she was planning to come to *culto* on Sunday, that she was thinking a lot about Eli, and that she loved Eli a lot. Eli looked confused. No one understood why Samaria left, she said. Samaria was fine at the Academy. Eli asked if I knew why Samaria left. I told her that I couldn't say, but that I imagined Samaria would give her an explanation in person on Sunday. Eli asked if I saw the friend she was staying with in Rincón. I said no. Eli looked worried. "Are you worried?" I asked. "Yes," said Eli, "because Samaria doesn't know anyone good in Rincón."

On Sunday I arrived at the designated site with my infant daughter to pick up Samaria. Fifteen minutes passed, then twenty-five, so I dialed the number that Samaria had given me for Ana. It turned out to be a church. The man who answered didn't know Samaria but knew Ana. Finally, Samaria appeared in a crisp white shirt and floral wrap-skirt, smelling of perfume, her face carefully made up. Her fingers were moving more than usual and her voice shook. She told me that nothing had changed in Rincón except that the addicts were younger. One girl who was standing on the corner told Samaria that she wasn't up to anything, but when she took off her jacket, Samaria said, "Oh my God. There were track marks everywhere. . . . She had a baby, a one-year-old boy. She was only seventeen."

I missed the turnoff for the Academy. Samaria and I laughed at how distracted I was. I told her: "Samaria, I give you a lot of credit. You are brave to go back to the Academy right now and face Gabriel."

When we got to the Academy a young man at the gate told Samaria that Gabriel wanted her to come to the office. I struggled to keep my smile looking natural, and said, "I guess they're expecting you." The young man motioned us into a parking spot, and I told Samaria, "I bet you he feels bad about all this. Maybe he's going to apologize to you. I hope that's what it is." She looked away, and walked to the Academy office as I herded my daughter toward Wanda and three toddlers in the children's room. Carmen did not look me in the eye but talked with my daughter, who hid behind my skirts. Within a few minutes Samaria emerged from the office with Gabriel, looking serious. Gabriel motioned me over and told me that Samaria had to go, by direct order of Mama Tita, the pastor's wife. He told me: "We have rules here. This one comes from Mama Tita, so there's nothing I can do. I tried to call you before but I could not get through."

Samaria asked Gabriel for water and he sent a young man to get two glasses for us. Samaria drank quickly and walked toward the car, her back straight, a stiff smile on her face. We drove out in silence. Samaria was still smiling. As we got on the highway I touched her hand. "Samaria, please forgive me if my passing by the home last week and telling them you planned to come to *culto* had anything to do with this." Samaria told me that it was okay. I lowered my voice, "I can only imagine how bad that felt. I know I felt bad." Tears welled in her eyes.

Once we got to Rincón I invited Samaria to eat at a bakery again. She lifted my daughter from the car and carried her inside. My daughter was unusually calm, resting one hand on Samaria's chest and another on her shoulder. I cautioned that my daughter was heavy for a one year old. Samaria shrugged.

My second son was only three pounds at birth, but at six months he was forty-five pounds. I gave him three meals a day, plus milk before bed. I gave him *biandas*, rice mixed with milk. He was walking by seven months. The doctor put him on a diet, he was too fat. He was so cute, he had lots of rolls. The diet didn't work, he kept gaining weight. He's still a big guy, five-eleven and two hundred-something pounds.

She looked at my daughter. "Kids are great. My father used to say, children fill up the house. It's not a home without the children. And he was right."

We finished eating our sandwiches and walked back to the car. We drove to Ana's street and I told Samaria that she'd helped a lot of people. Samaria said plaintively: "I got a lot from my family. I try to share with other people what I got." I asked her how I could keep in touch with her. She gave me her half-brother's address in Sabana Grande. Out of the car, she lifted her skirt and set foot on the overgrown palm tree-lined path to Ana's house. Her pressed white shirt disappeared into the shadows, and I shivered, feeling that it would be my last sight of her.

One month later I sought out Mama Tita, the pastor's wife, at her home and detox center in the mountains. Converts at the Academy called Tita their spiritual mother. A poised Mexican American woman who converted after her Puerto Rican husband was saved from alcoholism, she wore the embroidered skirts of indigenous Mexicans to *culto*. The bright folds of her skirt looked large enough to shelter many children, spiritual and otherwise.

Ordinarily reserved, Tita seemed even more formal than usual. She pulled a chair out for me from under a red tablecloth lined with white doilies. Wanda, with whom I'd scrubbed toilets the day before, emerged from the kitchen to offer me a glass of water on white napkins, symmetrically arranged on a tray.

Without prompting Tita began telling me her story. It was a *testimonio*. She met her husband in the army, he spent their money on alcohol, she thought that the only way out was divorce, "like anyone without the Lord in the center." Then her mother called about a new church with a Puerto Rican pastor who she thought her husband could relate to. "We went to that church for a movie . . . we got saved that night."

Mama Tita saw the women who came to her as broken, because their families were broken, something that biomedical addiction clinics missed.

> Take someone with heroin problems. [If] they go to a psychiatrist they just give medicines, just give one drug for another. Even with medicine they still use [drugs]. [At the ministry] we get involved with them. We live here. We are the father and mother they didn't have. Their parents are divorced, the mother doesn't know where the father is. We live in community with them, we are role models for the family they don't have. . . . We try to take a woman who was destroyed, beat up in the street, prostituting. If the desire is in their hearts they're going to change. You have something to work with. When you drop a vase that was precious, you're gonna try to restore it because it was precious, you value it. That's the same way God is with us. He values us because of the price he paid for us. He puts women in our hands all broken up. What are you gonna do, put them in the trash?

Tita's theory was that they needed to experience unity in a spiritual family to heal the fractures from their worldly family.

> A lot of addicts come from broken homes, that's why they're on the streets. [They're surprised] when they see a good family talk to each other without arguing, fighting.

A lot of them reject your affection, they don't know how to take it. They can't stand it when you say I love you. . . . God inspired us to have Sunday services for families. At first we had services for the guys only but we saw there wasn't love in the families. Sundays we have a rule, they can visit family but the family has to come to services.

Tita saw the women as condemning themselves, struggling with feeling "down and dirty," unable to accept that they'd been "cleaned by God," meaning that God had forgiven them. Her role was to help them to embody responsible Christian womanhood, teaching them classes in table manners; how to walk, talk, and dress; and how to care for children. Many of the women had not seen their children while in the throes of addiction; they told Tita, "Grandma took care of my kids, I don't know how to be a mother." Tita also taught bookkeeping to this group of women—who had on average a sixth-grade education, and some of whom even could not tell time. "Before the army I went to bookkeeping college. It helped me a lot. A lot of people are not so fortunate."

Walking me to the door, Tita showed me a book about Christian womanhood that she often assigned to women converts for book reports. Its cover featured the portrait of an English Victorian woman, strolling the boardwalk in a high-necked dress and white gloves, holding a parasol. Tita sighed and said that there were times when women did not make it, when she had put people in charge who were not ready, and that put other people in danger. I took my cue. "I meant to ask you about that. For instance, Samaria." Tita looked pensive. "She did know a lot. But she didn't want to accept discipline for her mistakes . . . I guess she wasn't ready . . . the problem was, she was after a man in the program." Although I never got definitive confirmation of either Samaria's side of the story or Gabriel's, it was clear that the gendered authority structure of the ministry had landed in favor of Gabriel.

On the surface, Pentecostals offer a more egalitarian vision of gender and authority than does the Catholic Puerto Rican mainstream. As Mama Tita asserted, the Academy teaches that "It's not a different path spiritually. . . . Women have the same teachings as men." In contrast with the gendered iconography of the Catholic Church, Pentecostal sermons and Bible lessons speak of Christian principles in gender-neutral terms. Historically, Pentecostal doctrine was that all individuals had direct access to divine knowledge, without needing to go through (male) priests such as in the Catholic Church. Victory Academy does not ordain women, but some Pentecostal ministries do, and several prominent early twentieth-century Pentecostal evangelists were women, among them Aimee Semple McPherson, founder of the Foursquare Gospel Church in Los Angeles, California, who in her time was more popular than Billy Sunday.[1] Scholars of gender in evangelical churches have described the ways that women subvert masculine texts and pulpits to their own ends, by using the Spirit's predilection for His "weaker vessels" as a rationale for women's anointment and sainthood, by showcasing women's oratory in tandem with male preachers, and by staffing ministry offices that exert administrative control (Goldsmith 1989/90, Lawless 2003).

In Latin America, Protestants contend with a deeply rooted Catholic image of womanhood: The Virgin Mary. It is hard to overstate the pervasiveness of references to Mary in the daily lives of Puerto Ricans; one of the most common expressions people use when disappointed or frightened is "¡Aay—Virgen!" The virgin mother of God, she is worshiped and solicited with almost as much fervor as Jesus himself. Pentecostals identify this worship as idolatry and thus as blasphemous. They campaign to eradicate the images of Mary and the religious festivals in her honor that are so ubiquitous in Latin America. Gabriel, for example, struggled to convince his aging mother to discard her collection of figurines and paintings of Mary to complete her conversion to Protestantism. In my time at Victory Academy, I heard Mother's Day sermons cite exemplary women in the Bible but make no reference to Mary, while nearby Catholic churches held Mother's Day mass in honor of Mary. Victory Academy segregated Bible study groups by gender, but told both men and women to emulate Jesus in their conduct, and provided identical curricula for men's and women's groups. Both women and men could become *Soldados* (Soldiers), *Guerreros* (Warriors), and *Vencedores* (Victors) for Christ. On the surface, spiritual power appeared less determined by gender in these ministries than in Catholic churches.

Nonetheless, preachers at *culto* in both Victory Academy and Restoration House referred to biblical passages such as Ephesians 5:22, "Wives, submit yourselves unto your own husbands, as unto the Lord." For instance, in his autobiography, the founder of the street ministry Outcry in the Barrio quoted his wife as saying that according to the Bible, the husband is the head of the wife, even as Christ is the head of the church, [Ephesians 5:23] while asking his forgiveness for having taken charge when she should have waited for his decision (García and García 1988).

On one hand, street ministries challenged double standards of monogamy and childrearing by requiring men to become attentive fathers and faithful husbands. On the other, however, as Eber (1995) found in her study of problem drinking among Mayans in Mexico, Protestant movements that promote male domesticity can paradoxically shrink the already circumscribed foundation of women's power—control of the home and of family life—as men become closely involved in family affairs as symbolic heads of household. And as Sally Engle Merry (2001) discovered in her study of Pentecostal interventions for domestic violence in Hawaii, even in homes deemed dangerous to women, the ministry encouraged a woman "to have a meek and quiet spirit and not to provoke her husband, using the Biblical adage that a gentle answer turns away wrath" (Engle Merry 2001, 66), based on a reading of the Bible as requiring wives' submission to their husbands and on the understanding that "divorce is violence against God" (Engle Merry

ultimately

2001, 65). Thus, in some cases, the Pentecostal doctrine of male domesticity actually can lead to more complete and violently enforced male domination.[2 3]

In contrast to the Mary of Immaculate Conception, the authority conferred by motherhood at Victory Academy was contingent on relations to men in a nuclear family unit. Samaria did not fit the mold: she joined the Academy just after leaving her husband of two decades, and she was an independent thinker. She was no victim, and she did not use the language of suffering to describe her pre-conversion life. Although some came to the ministry in search of a surrogate family, the support Samaria had gotten from her family was her source of confidence. She talked in romantic terms about her own mother, "She brought us kids everywhere. . . . She told people, if my kids don't fit, I don't fit. It was amazing how she always made time for us. If I called her she'd drop what she was doing and come to the phone."

Samaria also posed a sexual threat to men in the ministry, including Gabriel. The pastor and his wife were vigilant of sexual dynamics that could distract the ministry leadership. For instance, they'd prevented the director of their men's home from opening a church for the surrounding community because he was not married. They told him he needed a wife to counsel women members, and to check his own temptations.

Samaria found these gender divisions tedious. Before she left the ministry, she told me that the pastor had disciplined Yeyo because he let me interview him in a private room.

> It's your problem if your mind is in the gutter. . . . Here in Puerto Rico, with the older people, a married woman doesn't even talk with any man who is not her husband. If her husband is with her, he does the talking and the men act as if she wasn't even there. I don't go for that. I've always talked with whoever I wanted and never had a problem. When I was growing up, my mother always talked to other men and people would say to my father, "Aren't you jealous?" He said "No, I trust her."

Samaria believed in her abilities, and resisted Christian narratives of women's weakness before God.

After Samaria left Victory Academy, I saw Eli, Wanda, and Alexis every week, at Bible study and on kitchen duty. I was afraid to bring up the topic of Samaria, and despite their knowing looks, they did not mention her name either. Ears were everywhere at the Academy.

Months later, Eli and Wanda were still at the Academy, but all of us had lost touch with Alexis. Alexis finished nine months of residency at the Academy and had begun working as a leader but faced difficult choices: leave the Academy to raise her three young children, or advance in the Academy while leaving her children in the care of her neighbor. According to Mama Tita, the Department of Families and Children would not allow women to live at Victory Academy with their children, because mothers seeking custody of their children were required to provide a "real home."

When Alexis told me her history, I was struck by how her children's needs, the needs of her partners, and her calling in the ministry worked against each other.

> They caught me robbing. I tested positive for heroin and crack. They told me they knew a place I could go instead of jail. I didn't want to come, but I wanted to keep my babies. I was very rebellious when I came. [I told] Samaria and Jessica I didn't want to do anything. But when you clean your body, you start to clear your mind, you start to think about things you didn't before: your family, who you robbed.

Alexis' husband followed her to the Academy but left after a few weeks. Alexis told him "You can leave but I'm going to stay. I'm tired of my old life." But she was not ready to let go of her children.

> There was a time I had problems caring for my kids. It hurts me [to think about] but in the Bible it says care for children. On my [weekend] pass [to leave the Academy] the first time I cried, I said "[L]ook what's happened!" I noticed that I had problems. But it was not like before—this time I was confronting them.

Her husband got in touch with her again, he was in prison and had tested positive for HIV. Alexis got tested, and when she came up negative, told herself "God had other plans for me and strengthened me." Her mother got sick also: "God gave me more tests, and more tests." Eventually her mother recovered. "I've had terrible experiences and I've seen how God heals me."

Alexis had not smoked or used drugs until she met her husband, when she was twenty-six. She married him after leaving her first husband—an alcoholic that Alexis barely knew when she was forced to move in with him at age twenty because her parents discovered she had spent the night with him and consequently refused to allow her to return home.

When her second husband offered her drugs, she was afraid he would leave her if she did not try them. She soon found herself buying heroin and crack cocaine for both of them with earnings from her part-time job, something she could not sustain.

> I started to rob people. I wasn't in the house, I came home late. Imagine supporting a habit, a family, and then robbing. They caught me, and I detoxed on medication but it didn't work; I had two habits [heroin and cocaine]. I ended up in jail for eight days, I got clean. But I went back to drugs when I left and my problems came back. I didn't care that I had appointments, that I had a family. I was thirty years old, I'd had a habit for four years and every year was worse.
>
> Sometimes I left [my kids] by themselves because I had to cure myself[4] while they were sleeping. Sometimes I was sick in bed, and I didn't get up, I didn't take them to school. My mamma, she was afraid [for me], but I was rebellious, I didn't want to ask for help, or to lose the kids.

Alexis knew that if she went into addiction treatment she would have to leave her children behind. "I'd never been separated from them. Your kids share in the bad and the good. It's an excuse for not getting help."

A woman who had been her neighbor was now caring for her two small daughters while she as at the Academy, and her eleven-year-old son, the product of her first marriage, was with her mother. He had her worried.

> He's had problems in school, he's rebellious. First his father left him. I was both his mother and father. Then [I left], then my mother got sick and couldn't take care of him. I have to work with him emotionally. I have to give him a lot of attention. Then I want to study computers. . . . I would like to help the women here, to tell them about my experiences. But I need to take care of my kids.

No one knew what became of Alexis after her graduation from the ministry. She left among tears, hugs, and promises to work out a plan with Mama Tita to serve in the ministry as much as her children would allow.

Weeks later I called Alexis at the number she gave: it was disconnected. The women in the home took it as ominous. They thought that if she and her children were doing well she would have wanted them to know. I wondered if Samaria's leaving the week of Alexis' graduation had anything to do with Alexis' disappearance, but I was never able to confirm that.

Alexis had looked to the ministry for a surrogate family when her own parents and husbands had failed her. In Alexis' language, God—and by extension the ministry—took the place that should have been held by each of her husbands, as head of home: "I've seen that if you're faithful to God, He provides."

The ministry provided her support and meaningful work. Yet the ministry fell short on a crucial point: it could not help her to raise her small children. Had Alexis been married to a ministry leader, she would have been able to raise her children at the Academy. But as a single mother, she could not devote herself to the ministry and meet her children's needs at the same time.

Without skipping a beat, Carmen and Jessica took over leadership of the women's home. Carmen, who always had been high strung, kicked into even higher gear. On kitchen duty I often found Carmen's bony frame in tattered work clothes, her hair pulled back tightly in a bun, her elbows cutting into the air as she scrubbed grease from the stove and blood stains from the meat freezer. Outside of Bible study, Carmen never sat still long enough to be interviewed. But she did share with me that she was excited about something. She and her fiancé, with whom she had three sons and four grandchildren, were getting married in the church. He had completed nine months in the ministry and was starting discipleship, she had already been discipled for a year. They had ambitions: they were in line for a ministry mission to Costa Rica.

Carmen's wedding took place at Sunday *culto*. The chapel was filled with recruits, graduates, and the bride and groom's children and grandchildren. The

FIGURE 12. Carmen's wedding. Photo by Helena Hansen.

altar was unadorned, and *culto* started with a sermon. At the end of the sermon, Jose, the pastor's younger son, played the wedding march on his keyboard and a procession of suited men walked the aisle with Carmen's fiancé, followed by Carmen in a long white gown, a veil over her face, and Pastor Mendoza holding her arm (fig. 12). Carmen and her fiancé kneeled expectantly at the altar.

A week later, Carmen showed us snapshots of their honeymoon. She and her husband had spent three days at a beach house in Cabo Rojo. "It's great, it's like it was when we first met," she giggled; we circled to admire the pair lounging on the golden sand. She was glad that most well-wishers had heeded her request for cash. After all, she pointed out, they'd be going overseas soon and would not know what to do with gifts.

A year later Carmen and her husband had indeed left the ministry. But they were not in Costa Rica; rather, they were at their old haunt, Vega Baja, Puerto Rico. Gabriel intimated that Carmen and her husband had left the ministry because in the end, the pastor and Mama Tita did not choose them for the mission. "They thought they were going to Costa Rica, and when they didn't get what they wanted, the true Carmen came out. She began to want things her way, she wasn't humble. God knew they weren't ready. He's preparing [another couple]."

Carmen and her husband eventually went back to live with her husband's mother. According to Gabriel, they went back to heroin, and Carmen supported them both with sex work, as she had for many years.

Carmen had hit a gendered ceiling in the ministry. Her fiancé-cum-husband converted a year after she did, and his progress as a disciple was slower than hers. The pastor considered her husband the spiritual head of family, and judged him not ready to head the Costa Rican mission. When Carmen found out that her husband did not have the status to head the mission, she asked to be considered on her own merits.

The women recruits and I felt Carmen's departure acutely. Christian marriage was a rare achievement in the ministry. Arriving at that point required consistent personal discipline, keeping commitments, and the judgment of the pastor that the candidates could set an example of Christian matrimony. For male ministry graduates, chapel ceremonies wedding them to their long-time domestic partners and to the mothers of their children established their new lives as Christians. But few women recruits in the ministry managed to marry, and even fewer married the fathers of their children.

A number of studies have found that treatment is more damaging to women's domestic relationships than to those of men. Women are more likely to lose their partners during treatment, in part because they are more likely than men to have partners who used drugs and are forced to leave their partners to stop using drugs. Drug use among women also implies promiscuity and prostitution in ways that it does not for men, which can become self-fulfilling prophecy because women have fewer ways to access and pay for drugs than men do (Tuchman 2010; Inciardi, Lockwood, and Pottieger 1993). The stigma is hard to shed. As the director of a men's home north of Mayagüez who had tried and failed to start a women's home put it, "When [women] pass old [sex work] clients in the street, they feel dirty. The process is much slower. You have to cure the emotional process [so that they] can confront themselves, and say 'I am important—*adelante* [on with it]!' "

Carmen's departure left only one female ministry leader, Jessica, who stayed on at the ministry to become Mama Tita's right-hand woman. Jessica's freckled nose and the way her ponytail swung in rhythm made it difficult to picture her using heroin. According to Jessica, she had been a counselor and youth leader long before she used heroin, "My family was stable: we moved only one time . . . my neighbors were like friends, like my brothers and sisters. I changed schools in sixth grade but I did well, I helped my teachers and I was popular. I knew everyone. They used to say I was 'like white rice.' "

Living at home in the security of a traditional family, Jessica held a series of teaching jobs after getting a bachelor's degree in primary education at the University of Puerto Rico, but because of a shortage of teaching positions she was unemployed for a while in 1999. In the same year her family life was disrupted.

When I was twenty-two my father left the house. He had problems with alcohol, and he left. It was very traumatic for me. When you have your father your whole life you count on him, you don't understand when he leaves without saying anything, without telling you where he is. My mother was very affected by it, very alone and she needed me. She didn't have relationships. [But] I wanted my life.

In her loneliness, Jessica partnered with an unlikely mate; her student in a reform school for troubled youth.

He was in prison and wrote me saying he'd look for me when he got out. He was from the streets, he knew the *puntos de drogas*, the substances. When something is off limits people want to try it. I was curious. He said it was okay, but he didn't want me to do it. He asked me to pick up his heroin and I said okay, but you have to share it with me. He was a "casual" user. It was my first experience. It wasn't like [I did] marijuana, pills, then other things. I went for the worst first. Boom! I was working, I got $1,000 a month, I went nine months without paying my bills.

By January I was anxious if I didn't have it. By May I was using every day, I was using intravenously in only five months. I lost weight, I was irresponsible. I lived for *el vicio* [the vice]. I left in the morning looking, and again at 12 at night. By June I was unemployed. Everything I had saved was gone. [My boyfriend's] father had a store that sold beer and cigarettes. He robbed his father's cash register. He took liters of rum and whiskey and sold it in the streets.

In a story with an all-too-familiar plot, Jessica's relationship with her boyfriend melded with her relationship with drugs: she followed him to drug-dealing spots, then to jail, and then squatted an abandoned building with him that they quickly turned into a shooting gallery. Jessica's first attempts at rehabilitation were foiled by her boyfriend, with whom she turned her prescriptions for withdrawal symptoms into a source of income for heroin.

I was very skinny, down to 110 pounds from 200. I had tracks on my arms. My mother looked for a place for us both because I didn't want to go [into treatment] without him, or him without me. The government health plan referred us to a psychiatrist. We went to an outpatient program. We had to use medicines in the house to cut down our drug use. [The psychiatrist] said take this much Xanax on this day, this much the next day and so on until you're not using any. But we were using eight bags [of heroin] a day. With such a strong vice what you do without supervision is to mix heroin with the medication. Also you sell the medicines. It was a business.

In desperation Jessica turned to a church that gave her a space independent of her boyfriend. She ended up living at the pastor's house and caring for his children, so the church served as a bridge from a life dominated by her boyfriend to a life dominated by service to the church. Jessica's pastor referred her to Victory Academy, where she was given responsibilities that signaled that she had God's favor.

By August I was practically in charge of the girls, and I had finished my [rehabilita-
tion] time. The pastor and his wife went to Florida for one month, for their oldest son's
wedding. They gave me the choice, to be in charge of the girls, or to be responsible for
the ministry's money. They saw I was capable, and that I always wanted to help. God
rewarded me—they say Mama Tita never puts women in charge of the money.

Jessica identified her submission to God and to the pastor as the paradoxical
source of her newfound spiritual authority.

If you're obedient, then no matter what, God rewards you. That's why I stayed. I want
to fulfill my promise to God . . . in [the Academy] they had a beautiful ceremony:
they gave me the staff of authority, because of my work with children and because
Christ also died for the children. Out of twenty-five women in the ministry I was the
only woman with a staff.

Jessica received another sign of favor in the ministry: the attentions of the pastor's
son, Samuel. Seven years her junior, Samuel had lived at the ministry all of his life,
and was looking for someone completely dedicated to the ministry. They got per-
mission from the pastor and the congregation for approval to go out together.
Jessica's mother could not be more pleased: Jessica was about to shed her ex-
addicted identity for a union that placed her in the ministry's central leadership.

Before this turn of events, Jessica had described feeling out of place because she
was not a wife or mother. Without one of these roles, she found herself at a loss
even in everyday conversation with other women. Yet, conversion and ministry
leadership helped her achieve a reversal with her own mother: Jessica's mother
converted from Catholicism soon after Jessica joined the Academy; as Jessica's
mother said: "I came to be Christian because of Jessica."

Jessica and Samuel married a year later. When Samuel was named the new
director of Victory Academy of Southern Puerto Rico, Jessica became den mother
for the men living there. She was the only woman of the women's home leaders
who successfully established her authority in the ministry, and that was through
her association with a prominent man, the pastor's son. Building up to that, Jessica
achieved the status of surrogate mother in the metaphorical family of the ministry,
caring for her first pastor's children, leading Sunday school at Victory Academy for
the visiting children of ex-addicted converts, and balancing her maternal roles
with the role of obedient wife and daughter through deference to Samuel, as well
as to her in-laws, Pastor Mendoza and Mama Tita.

The metaphor of motherhood as vehicle for women's authority in Latin America is long established.[5] As Christensen observed, "No holiday except Christmas
exceeds Mother's Day in its frenzy of gift giving and honoring of the female role in
Puerto Rico . . . the mother-child relationship in Puerto Rico at times borders on
hysteria, and mothers often seem to encourage a dependent relationship with the
children" (Christensen 1979, 58).

motherhood → authority

Puerto Rican feminist writers have argued that the ideal woman in the Puerto Rican mainstream has been the *mujer sacrificada*, the mother who gives up her own ambitions, her own pleasure, and consumption for the good of her children and family. Ideally, she even puts her children ahead of her husband, whom she infantilizes. This is a socially enforced dynamic: as one eighteen-year-old man at *Hogar Restauración* told me, "A woman ought to be a mother first and a *mujer* [wife or woman] second." Such a woman exercises power over men through her sons' and husband's dependency on her in all areas of domestic management.

Ironically, the feminization of the Puerto Rican workforce accompanying mid-twentieth-century industrialization (Acosta-Belén 1986) presented women with a dilemma as many became the breadwinners for their families through the garment industry and service work. Although some women pioneers in the Puerto Rican labor movement rejected images of feminine passivity in favor of political activism (Rivera 1986), many women workers preserved mainstream dichotomies of male and female, of public and domestic spheres by defining themselves primarily as mothers and wives, and by describing their income as supplemental (Safa 1986).

In their struggle to maintain a drug supply while they raise children, addicted Puerto Rican women have conflicts with the cultural ideal of motherhood. As in other parts of Latin America, women who either use drugs, sell sex, or both, are widely portrayed as over-consuming, pleasure seeking, and sexually unrestrained, the opposite of a *mujer sacrificada* and thus not qualified to be good mothers or good women in the cultural dichotomies of Madonna and whore (Castaneda et al. 1996) and *mujer de la casa* versus *mujer de la calle* (woman of the house versus woman of the streets) (Acosta-Belén 1986). Despite societal labeling of them as "bad mothers," addicted Puerto Rican women make heroic efforts to keep custody of their children, they report that that their children motivate them to seek treatment, and they see the quality of their mothering as a marker of treatment success (Hardesty and Black 1999).

On a practical note, Taylor (1993) analogized the reports of women drug users in Glasgow to mainstream discourses of conflict between career and family; like a licit profession, habitual drug use required women to maintain social networks, to acquire specific skills, and to keep a regular schedule (e.g., of raising funds and locating dealers), which competed with the demands of childrearing. Like many women in licit professions, Taylor's informants were initially attracted to drug-using circles by the possibility of gaining social status, skills, and increased earnings (as dealers); they later found themselves struggling to balance the demands of drug use with their need for childcare. As Taylor points out, drug use for women did not necessarily reflect loss of self-control or passivity with drug-using men; drugs provided many women with a goal-directed, meaningful lifestyle that had to be restructured into drug-free social networks and activities if they were to stop using.

Rosenbaum's (1981) path-breaking study of women on heroin in the urban United States reported that, like men, "most women see the shift to legal work as crucial to restructuring their lives and identities as non-junkies" (Rosenbaum 1981, 84). Unlike men, however, they "subscribed to the notion that motherhood . . . is the core of their own femininity" (Rosenbaum 1981, 100). The low-income black and Latino women in Rosenbaum's study described motherhood as one of the only viable roles for them, one they found they could not take for granted as the Department of Children and Families threatened to remove their children from their custody. Although a minority of these women successfully balanced their drug-using lifestyle with parenting, others found themselves torn between the two occupations; that of drug user and that of mother. Echoing mainstream societal judgment, one woman drug user told Rosenbaum, "I know that you cannot be addicted and be a good mother [at the same time]" (Rosenbaum 1981, 101).

Ironically it was Jessica—a former heroin user without children—who was able to tap and rework Puerto Rican metaphors of motherhood to exercise institutional power in the ministry. She adopted members of the ministry as fictive kin, and moved from the role of dutiful daughter to that of wife and mother through marriage within the ministry.

Of the all women in Pentecostal homes that I was able to interview, she was the one who was able to make good on the possibilities of ministries as places where "ideal husbands can be found and complicated relations with kin can be erased . . . [where] gaining access to the power of the Holy Spirit helps [women] to conquer new modes of being and doing with regard to sexuality, marriage, marital relations, kinship and love" (Van de Kamp 2011, 223). And the reconfiguration of familial metaphors parallels what others have described with regard to Puerto Rico's long list of prominent female politicians. Puerto Rico had a woman run its capital for more than twenty years, the mayor of San Juan, Felisa Rincón de Guatier; and Puerto Rico has seen many female state assembly members and female congressional representatives. A woman and mother, Sila Maria Calderón, was elected governor of Puerto Rico in 2001. Acosta-Belén (1986) argues that politically powerful Puerto Rican women extend their maternal image into that of *supermadre* (supermother), with the role of nurturing the people of Puerto Rico in the areas of education, health, and welfare. Similarly, Lavrin (1987) noted that historically Latin American women have resorted to "mother imagery or maternal metaphors to validate their political activities and goals" (Lavrin 1987, 119). In this scheme, women are able to exercise power in public space to the extent that they frame their authority in terms of their roles as mothers.

As Jessica showed me, legitimate womanhood in the ministry depended on a delicate balance of maternal discernment, self-sacrifice, vulnerability, and obedience. Authoritative women in the ministry, such as Mama Tita, had built a reputation for wisdom and service to others, but still deferred to their husbands as the ultimate agents of God's will. As Samaria and Alexis showed me, however, for women Pentecostal conversion did not necessarily lead to stable relationships and gender roles in the church. In fact, as Van de Kamp (2011) points out, the mobility that conversion offers Pentecostal women brings with it a disruptive ethos, which can increase tensions in households and with partners—and, as in the case of Victory Academy, can increase tensions within the ministry.

Among biomedical addiction-treatment providers, it is a truism that women do poorly as compared to men; that they leave treatment earlier, and relapse more quickly after leaving treatment. The treatment outcomes of women also depend more on the drug-using status of their romantic partner than do those of men (Tuten and Jones 2003), and on whether they have dependent children (Copeland and Hall 1992). The past two decades of addiction treatment research on gender has pointed to the need for specialized services for women which support them as mothers, and which acknowledge histories of trauma or abuse (Grella and Joshi 1999; Ashley, Marsden, and Brady 2003; Covington et al. 2011; Marsh, D'Aunno, and Smith 2000; Paone et al. 1992. Gender-sensitive critiques of established substance abuse treatment approaches such as Twelve-Step programs, and of therapeutic communities that employ public humiliation "interventions," have also pointed out that their power dynamics might be poorly suited to women. For example, Twelve-Step programs that initiate participants by requiring them to admit their powerlessness, based on the assumption that denial is the primary barrier to treatment, as it might have been for the affluent white men that founded the Twelve-Step movement (Bill W., a businessman, and Dr. Bob, a physician), might not be well-suited for women whose principal need is empowerment (Saulnier 1996). As the writers of a handbook for women's addiction treatment put it, "Confrontation . . . was designed to break through [a] false, grandiose self of men. Addicted women, however, generally have a diminished sense of self" (Covington 2002, 4) having experienced abuse and disempowerment. Instead, they require "strengths-based" approaches that "help the client to see the strengths and skills she already has" (Covington 2002, 11) and, I would add, the social strategies that have helped her survive, such as extended families and networks of support.

When Victory Academy closed its home for women, women looking for spiritually based treatment were often directed to Precious Gift. Precious Gift was a residence in the northern mountains that started in the early 1990s as a small program for HIV-positive women, by a female pastor from a Protestant denomination that was committed to social action. Staffed entirely by women—some of whom were program graduates—the program developed a reputation for effective work in rehabilitating women drug users. The founder soon collaborated with the Puerto Rican health department, using funds designated for HIV services to open a larger residence for women.

By the time I visited Precious Gift, it offered family housing and was adjoined by a daycare center. The program director lobbied to be designated the legal guardian of any children that had been removed from their mother's care so that women with children—including those who had lost custody to the child welfare department—would be able to live under supervision with their children while completing the program's curriculum. Some of the children attending Precious Gift's daycare already had been orphaned by mothers with AIDS, but stayed on as foster children of the staff. The program director herself adopted an HIV-positive six-year-old whose mother had died in her care. Because Precious Gift started as a residence for women with HIV, it employed an AIDS specialist, an internist, and a pediatrician, in addition to a health educator, a service coordinator, a female pastor, and a public relations manager.

The director, a petite woman with short hair and wire-frame glasses, stood squarely in a polo shirt monogrammed with Precious Gift's logo. As she explained it, Precious Gift was committed equally to the spiritual, emotional, and physical well-being of its residents. This meant that although they tried to cultivate personal discipline and self-dominion, they did not believe in denigration or punitive measures as treatment for addiction. Instead, they focused on family reunification and establishing women in socially supportive environments, with stable housing, after graduation. Yet, she did not let women continue what she saw as irresponsible behavior.

> Many of the women here say "I'm a victim—that gives me license to do whatever." The whole family gets caught up in their bad habits and their bad attitude. I don't permit that. I take the evangelical attitude that I love you but you have to change. You have to take responsibility for your actions; your past is not an excuse.

The issue in their previous lives as drug users and sex workers, said the director, had been a malformation of their character that let them lower themselves to undignified positions. They simply couldn't confront their realities, especially the demands of family life. In turn, Precious Gift's staff and peer educators focused on helping women to re-integrate their families. On Saturdays was an open house for family visitation, and during the week the staff arranged for mothers to visit their children in the community foster care. According to the director, succeeding in this work required crossing traditional boundaries between personal and professional roles. "We look for families until we find them. We help [residents to] sanitize their relationships, to clear up their legal issues. We give them gifts to bring [to their relatives], we provide rides and favors for family members, we fix up their houses."

Keeping with Precious Gift's non-punitive approach to addiction treatment, she saw relapse as part of the process, "Relapsers can come back as often as they need

previous gift [handwritten annotation]

to. Those who don't finish the [one-year] curriculum often relapse and return. We don't punish them."

Many of Precious Gift's graduates stayed on as employees, and those who did not got pastoral services in their communities. The latest project at Precious Gift was to open a minimally supervised housing facility for program graduates, given that "most of the women at Precious Gift do not want to leave; they don't feel secure. Their families are drug using, and they live in a drug using area."

Precious Gift presented itself as consistent with the social and health-service delivery model most familiar to government administrators, employing credentialed professionals and establishing formal agreements with the child welfare department, while bringing evangelical entrepreneurship to its community-based approach that was missing from state-run treatment programs.

If Precious Gift did not threaten the paternalism of the state, neither did it directly threaten male evangelist leaders with claims to spiritual authority. Precious Gift was a women's mission, founded and run not by a former addict but by a highly educated female pastor who felt called to work with the poor. The mission employed ex-addicts, but if men's discipleship at Victory Academy drew on military metaphors, Precious Gift was closer to a hospice or almshouse for the poor. Precious Gift started by catering to terminally ill women with AIDS; its ethos continued to be one of care and acceptance of human limitations. It drew on a gendered trope of victimhood[6] even as it challenged a victim mentality by disciplining clients into "taking responsibility."

Precious Gift also differed from the Academy in its use of family metaphors. If Victory Academy, in its pursuit of a middle-class version of respectability, attempted to model and mold recruits into something resembling a nuclear, patriarchal family, the model for Precious Gift was an extended family. Despite Precious Gift's director's assertion that it honored marriage and family as directed by the Bible, in practice it drew on an extended family arrangement far more prevalent and established in Puerto Rico. As historian Eileen Findlay argues, from the turn of the century, Puerto Rican elites had tried to impose a nuclear, patriarchal, "white" middle-class model of family structure on working-class women in their campaigns for moral reform, and extended families—headed by women in serially monogamous consensual unions—persisted as the predominant form among the working class (Findlay 1999). Women at Precious Gift developed support systems that included their own consanguineal relatives and the staff at Precious Gift, but not always the fathers of their children. The family housing offered at Precious Gift was for mothers and their children; no men lived on the premises. What Precious Gift did, in practical terms, was to enhance the viability of women's networks of (often fictive) kin, making them less dependent on men as providers or fathers of their children. Where Victory Academy framed God as the patriarchal provider, and male converts as patriarchs in their homes, Precious Gift gave women the tools to be independent of men. And to the extent that Precious Gift dispersed government resources to their clients through grants from the state, the state itself entered this network of support.[7]

Precious Gift enhanced a strategy that resource poor women in many parts of the Americas have historically used to survive where reliance on a male breadwinner has not been an option (Stack 1974) and where women have resisted patriarchy (Safa 1995a) As Samaria once told me of the women who dropped out of the Academy, "Women whose fathers abused them have a harder time. They say, 'my father is dead,' because he did that. They won't contact their families." The nuclear family model promoted at the Academy, exhorting them to honor fathers, husbands, and male pastors as instruments of God, might not resonate with this distrust. The patriarchal nuclear family, historically a privilege of elite men with the political-economic means to enforce female subservience (Safa 1995b), was costly to these women.

The women of Victory Academy revealed one way in which the spiritual capital of Pentecostal ministries mirrored economic capital: reproducing itself by widening social inequalities, such as gender inequalities. Where addicted men invigorated their masculinity with a reinvented patriarchy, this strategy further marginalized addicted women. Furthermore, in its ethos of personal transformation and family reclamation, the ministry celebrated the self-sufficiency and discipline of the individual as steward of the nuclear family unit, which negated and weakened the compensatory power of extended families among people who have historically survived by pooling their resources. And, ironically, as I later learned, the long-term success of ministry converts hinged on the resources that these extended families provided, even as those resources were misrecognized as individual gifts and personal resolve.

6

Family Values

The premise of street ministry conversions dovetailed with a familiar claim of American social policy at the turn of the twenty-first century: good societies are the cumulative product of sound personal choices, and sound choices stem from solid personal values. That is to say, individuals with responsible characters build strong social networks, rather than the other way around; strong social networks enable people to live up to their responsibilities. The popular appeal of this claim—that individual character is primary—led to faith-based initiatives as the lynchpin of millennial U.S. social welfare policy. It also iconized narcotics addiction as the embodiment of personal irresponsibility as the root of social decay. Policy makers spun this into a punitive politics against unnamed racial and ethnic others, targeting poor Latino and black city neighborhoods, as well as Puerto Rico and the Mexican border, for supply-side narcotics interdiction and mass incarceration.

As I followed the arc of Pentecostal ex-addicts' process of change over time, however, the connections between personal and community responsibility turned out to be more complex. Personal transformation did not always lead to strong families and communities. Family and community rejection could unravel the new selves that converts had carefully crafted in the ministries. Missing from the discourse of conversion as a way to take personal responsibility for addiction was an appreciation of conversion as an uncertain negotiation: the remaking of relatedness, authority, and identity all became projects over which the possibility of defeat always loomed. Although converts wanted to be thrust into new networks and roles, their long-term success required reworking relationships with pre-conversion families and lives. Pentecostal rupture with the unconverted world in practice was not ever complete, as each encounter that converts described to me often showed. Converts' success hinged on the uncertain prospect of exchanging spiritual capital gained in the ministry for the local currency of their fragile families. Ironically, those converts who had more resources before conversion were often those who could best capitalize on their new Christian relationships, their identities and authority both inside and outside of the ministries. Thus, the radical egalitarianism of each saved soul's worth was continually undercut by differential access in the present material world.

Gabriel was one convert who had more pre-conversion resources than others. I reconnected with him two years after my return to the mainland, after he had become co-pastor of Victory Academy's new center in Humacao. Gabriel and I exchanged letters and, in honor of the birth of my son, he sent me a Mother's Day card. When I returned to Ponce for a visit, Gabriel asked to see me.

Gabriel appeared at my door in a carefully pressed shirt. He kissed my cheek and fawned over my three-month-old son, walked us to the plaza and bought my three-year-old daughter strawberry ice cream. Then he announced that he was taking us to a birthday party for his niece.

He led me to his car and fastened my son in an infant seat. After praying for safe passage, he deftly rode the curves up the neighboring mountain. As we climbed, our view of the valley below expanded; by dusk we looked over the entire metropolis. The peak of this mountain was lined by cars, and by people seated in lawn chairs or standing on the road. Gabriel pointed out a ninety-year-old matriarch clutching her cane with one hand and cradling a newborn infant in a pink monogrammed blanket with the other.

Gabriel's brother's wife organized these parties. Once a month the party rotated from house to house, through the extended family. Gabriel told me they were good people, and said, "Some of them drink, and they are not Christian, they are Catholic, but I am here every month because I think family is good. I am very close to my nieces, they talk to me about anything.

Gabriel introduced me to his niece's husband, a wide-shouldered young man in a football shirt who was sitting in a lawn chair sipping beer, and to his youngest nieces, dressed in bell-bottom jeans. He then brought me to their mother, the organizer of the event, a well-built brown-skinned woman who spoke casually of cooking for the sixty people in attendance. She set a plate of spiced rice, red beans, chicken, and boiled root vegetables in front of me, telling me "My father used to say, no one leaves my house unless they've eaten."

My son became the centerpiece of the living room; Gabriel's nieces-in-law held him in standing position to test his legs, offered him candies, and tried to teach him Spanish. He was rivaled only by the newborn, a girl with a pink feather clipped to her wisp of hair.

Members of the clan arrived in waves and made their way to pots of beans, rice, and chicken; Gabriel's sister-in-law motioned the group into a circle and led a prayer: "Thank God for our family, because our family is our strength. Without it we are nothing." She called up her sister, also a sturdy woman dressed in a tropical-print blouse, to lead the group in signing the cross and quiet prayer. Lastly, she called Gabriel to lead a prayer. Gabriel walked to the center of the group, straightened his back, and folded his hands, saying it was God's glory that brought us together. He was the only man to offer a prayer.

Gabriel's sister-in-law announced that this month they had certain people to recognize: "Many of our children had graduations." Naming them off one by one, she identified them as grammar school or junior high school graduates. Last, she called her granddaughter. "Monica, where are you?" A thin pre-teen girl in an orange halter top walked shyly to the center of the circle. "Monica got the trophy for excellence in her sixth-grade class!" Monica's mother emerged from the house with Monica's three-foot tall trophy into a round of loud applause. Next the mother of the newborn girl brought her baby to the center. In silence a cluster of women lit candles and brought forth a silver bowl of water. They formed a tight circle around the newborn, signed the cross, and in unison recited the Lord's prayer as Gabriel's sister-in-law poured water on the newborn's forehead.

I sat next to Gabriel's sister-in-law in a lawn chair and watched grade-schoolers dance to salsa on the radio. She told me that these days, Gabriel came to these reunions every month, not like before when he was *en vicio* ("in vice": taking drugs). We always loved him, she said. We always recognized him as family, but when he was *en vicio* he avoided us.

Gabriel confirmed this as we drove home that night.

> I didn't want to go, to have them see [that I was using drugs]. But now I see how important these parties are. I tried to start a tradition of reunions on my side of the family, at my mother's house, but after the first one it fell apart. There were so many disagreements, and people are scattered, living on the mainland [United States] and in other parts of the island. It was too difficult. My sister-in-law's family, on the other hand, has always lived in this neighborhood, and if they ever move they always come back. My brother married into this family after meeting my sister-in-law at a dance club. Her family owned the place. He and I used to ride a horse up here on Saturday nights, before the roads were paved. After he married he moved into her family's house and never came back.

I sensed longing in Gabriel's voice. We had just witnessed the idealized Puerto Rican family: widely extended, inclusive, nourished by a powerful matriarch. The men in the family were present, but ceremonies were a feminine domain. Women marked the passage of family members from school to school, and from birth to membership in the family. Gabriel had found a niche in his sister-in-law's family; as the austere, self-ordained Pentecostal in a family of lay Catholics, he led prayers and counseled his nieces in a way that other men in the family could not. In his view, his family was too scattered and disorganized to rally for these events, or to rally for him, but his sister-in-law's family provided a forum for recognizing his transformation. The fact that he was Pentecostal freed him from the ordinarily gendered domains of his sister-in-law's Marianist lay Catholicism, in which women were the keepers of the family's spiritual well-being within the home.

Gabriel aspired to a hybrid of the extended family and patriarchy. Ironically, Puerto Rican social policies and economic trends have undermined both of these models in the past several decades; the economy of unemployment could not sustain male providers, at the same time that U.S. social welfare programs disqualified common-law spouses and extended kin from housing and food benefits.

Not everyone found a way to make Christian and family ties work in concert as Gabriel had. I asked Yeyo how life was for him, now that he had been named director of the Academy. Yeyo, who was named after his father, had been through hard times:

> My father died two weeks ago. There were only thirteen people at the funeral; my sister couldn't stand [our father] and didn't come. I learned a lot from the funeral. I have the same name as my father, so it was creepy seeing the casket, hearing people call my name as they passed by. I realized I don't have much time; I'm 43, I only have twenty years left to work.
>
> You ever had a relationship you knew you wanted to leave, but you wanted to end it good, you were afraid to sever the relationship. . . ? It's that my kids need me. I want to be there for them, to teach them basketball. I also want a wife, and to work. I know I have touched the lives of a lot of people here. It's been four years—that's a long time! But it's time to go. I don't have plans yet, and I'll stay until they find someone else, probably two or three months. If I didn't that would be ungrateful. The pastor says Christ can make me stay but I'm ready to go.

In Yeyo's case, fatherhood and ministry duties conflicted with one another. Pastor Mendoza had labeled Yeyo's children, as well as Yeyo's longing for married life, as satanic temptations to leave the ministry. At the time that Yeyo was promoted to director of the Academy, the ministry was expanding to new locations and needed leaders. I noticed a mismatch between the timing and course of Yeyo's family events—his father's death and the young age of his children—and the timing and course of the ministry's expansion as well as the longer, salvation-and-eternity view that the pastor had of the consequences of Yeyo's decision. The pastor saw Yeyo's desire for reconnection with his biological family only as temptation, not as a developmental moment in a man's life.

A few months later, Yeyo did leave the ministry against Pastor Mendoza's wishes, and when he did, he lost contact with the ministry altogether. I lost contact with him as well, and never found out what this meant for Yeyo's Christianity, or his drug use.

Juan, who was not a father and had not been married, nonetheless had difficulty reintegrating himself into his family. During my return visit with my new son, I passed by Juan's mother's house several times hoping to get news of Juan. Her house was as I remembered it; with a freshly white-washed iron grate fence, and pruned mango trees. The only change was that someone had removed the handmade placard that Juan's mother normally hung on her front door, which had read "*Somos CATOLICOS. No soliciten Testigos de Jehova, ni Mormones, ni nadie.*" ("We are CATHOLIC. No solicitation by Jehovah's Witnesses, or Mormons, or anyone else").

No one was at home, but later Juan wrote to tell me that he'd had a relapse lasting half a year, had gone back to Restoration House for a few months and then enrolled in a seminary in San Juan. I was not surprised. The year before I had happened to pass by his mother's house at the moment that his mother evicted him. Juan emerged looking serious; his face was thin and drawn. He avoided my eyes: "I have to see a friend because I don't have a place to stay." He got into a dented car and drove off.

His mother's eyes were bloodshot, her hair was thinning; she told me that she had threatened to kick Juan out because he was back to *lo mismo* ("the same thing"). His knowledge of the Bible was tremendous, she said, holding back tears. "He could easily be a pastor. But he stopped going to church. He got around the wrong people. I keep telling him, if you turn off your sisters, your brothers, and then me, where will you go? You will have no one left."

Juan's mother allowed Juan to come home that night, saying that he could stay there as long as he followed the rules. He insisted that he was fine, but he missed two dates for dinner with my family, and he asked me for money, saying that a friend's car broke down on the way to pay his university tuition.

Juan finally admitted that he had not been registered at school for some time. According to Juan, his troubles began when he tried to transfer to the University of Puerto Rico campus in San Juan. His brother lived in San Juan and had offered Juan a place to stay in his house. But just after Juan arranged to transfer to the San Juan campus, his brother withdrew his offer of housing. His brother's wife still saw Juan as an addict, and worried that he would be a bad influence on their two small daughters.

It pained me to hear of Juan, who loved to bounce children on his knee, and who begged for photos of my infant son, being judged unfit for contact with his nieces. Juan's eyes moistened as he recounted his brother's words. They hit him hard, despite Juan's declaration the year before that "When you know the Bible, you look up instead of side to side. For example, [if] I wanna study, I don't ask Mami. I ask God. I turn my life to [the] hands of God." But exclusive reliance on God was hard to sustain. As imbedded in church life as Juan was when he left Restoration House, he still looked to his family for affirmation of his progress. And his family looked at his past unreliability and drug use as a guide to his future risks. They did not share the optimism of Pentecostal converts, among whom a person's future potential is judged based on his or her current spiritual practices, rather than a disavowed past to which the convert "died" during baptism.

Shortly after visiting Juan I returned to Restoration House to find that Padín had been hired as a security guard. He was dressed in a crisp white shirt with a photo ID badge clipped to his collar, and I complimented him on his professional look. He chuckled that he had to look good since he was on the payroll. He pointed proudly to the new Toyota parked in front of the office and told me that he was borrowing it from his daughter, who had just graduated from pharmacology school.

Padín mentioned that when he was last downtown he had seen Jorge, a gentle young man who had once excelled at making picture frames in the ministry workshop. Jorge was back on the street and *Bien flaco, bien flaco* (extremely skinny) Padín said, shaking his head from side to side. Some people relapse because when they get to the community, people put them down because they're evangelical. I asked him why people don't see their conversion as a positive thing.

> Not everyone believes they've changed. They caused a lot of damage as an addict, their family doesn't trust them. When I got out of prison, I asked every member of my family for forgiveness. Luckily they gave it to me; my daughter, my wife, they knew that when I was using drugs I was not myself. They gave me their support. But not everyone gets that, and that's where faith comes in. Faith is not just belief, it is what you do. You have to take responsibility, and that is what God sees and what your family sees.

Padín's reasoning was circular: if you have faith, you take responsibility even if your family does not acknowledge it. But your family will acknowledge your transformation if you take responsibility. His reasoning called to mind two tensions between the orientation of Pentecostals and that of unconverted family members. Pentecostalism calls on followers to believe—and to act as if—a convert has permanently changed, although non-Pentecostal family members have been disappointed by past promises and might not see conversion as different. Second, in Pentecostalism, salvation operates on a transcendental timescale, and refers to final judgment, whereas families operate on day-to-day timescales of family well-being in which pragmatic short-term decisions must be made. Padín thus raised the question: what happens to your faith if your family never acknowledges you?

· · ·

Two years after he left Restoration House, Wilson struggled both with family responsibilities and with his church. His parents were disabled by heart disease, but Wilson could not move in to care for them because he had to maintain the house that he bought for his new wife. He did not have enough to buy a stucco house in his parents' stable, working-class neighborhood, so he bought a wooden bungalow in a part of town whose abandoned lots were drug markets. As he explained it, if he did not live full-time on his new property, his neighbors would deal from it. His wife, struggling with cocaine, enrolled in the only long-term residential drug-treatment program for women they could find, located almost two hours north. Wilson was left alone in their wooden shack, shuttling back and forth from his parents' house to feed them and take them to doctor's appointments. He continued to attend the Pentecostal church in his parents' neighborhood, but many of his friends had left the church because they suspected the pastor of sexual liaisons with parishioners.

When I showed up at his bungalow, Wilson helped me to climb the splintering boards on the staircase to the second floor. From his balcony we saw a panorama of littered lots and gutted buildings. He apologized for the broken hinges on the refrigerator, and the garden hose that he had strung up his stairs as his makeshift shower. The southeast corner of his apartment was stacked to the ceiling with the bottled water that he sold on the street to pay his mortgage. I asked about the empty beer cans below the staircase: Wilson pointed to two men pacing nervously in front of the house. He allowed them to stay downstairs in exchange for their protection of the property. They were into crack, he said, but he was giving them the word of God daily.

I worried about Wilson, because he seemed so isolated. There was a desperate quality to the success story he told me of becoming a husband, a homeowner, entrepreneur, and Christian. He was working hard to hold all of the threads of male responsibility. Remaining a homeowner required him to live in a part of town that exposed him daily to drug dealing and violence. To maintain the property, he had to invite two crack users to live on the first floor of his home. To care for his parents, he had to commute to their house daily, easily a one hour walk on foot, and his ten-year-old Jeep was unreliable. His wife was working on her sobriety, but visiting her each weekend required four hours of mountain driving in his aging car, and he had already had a breakdown on the way. When his wife returned home, after a year of treatment, she and Wilson would both be trying to avoid relapse in an apartment that gave them a balcony view of drug deals. And Wilson had to contend with his ministry, which was disintegrating over his pastor's sex scandal.

RESPONSIBLE FAMILIES

The struggles of Yeyo, Juan, and Wilson to find a place in their families as ex-addicted Christians took place within a broader societal discourse of addiction and families in crisis. Images of the ideal family held up by mainstream Puerto Rican media often conflicted with the everyday realities that Yeyo, Juan, and Wilson (and their wives and family members) faced. To repatriate the respectability and social mobility they had gained through the ministries into secular life, converts had to rework the received knowledge of family and addiction.

One metanarrative that dominated the Puerto Rican press was of the disintegration of the Puerto Rican family. It is a metanarrative with longstanding counterparts on the mainland United States, including that of the pathological black family which underpinned War on Poverty policies of the 1960s and '70s. The narrative asserted that family relations determined societal well-being. For instance, the major San Juan daily newspaper, *El Nuevo Día*, reported on an island-wide conference to address the role of social agencies in Puerto Rico in "Urging Reform of Family Values" (Ortiz 1998). In the article, university presidents and governmental cabinet members asserted that individualism and materialism—as well as electronic media and teenaged sex leading to pregnancy—were eroding the Puerto Rican family. Although social-service agencies were the slated topic of discussion, speakers focused on the role of parents instead. If parents could resist the unsound trends of modern society and cultivate social virtues, serving as role models and unifying the family, the logic ran, then social problems such as abuse, school dropout rates, and teenage pregnancy would resolve themselves.

An opinion piece in *El Nuevo Día*, entitled "The Deterioration of the Family," asserted that families should unite because the family's disintegration marks the beginning of Babylonian societal collapse. "When civilizations reach their highest levels of splendor their customs deteriorate. Men become effeminate. Prostitution flourishes . . . the family—which is the vital nucleus of society, starts to waver" (Martinez 1998, 49).

The author, a male university professor, cited the ease of divorce as the source of modern decadence and delinquency, called on women to invest in homemaking, and called on both parents to spend more time with their children. An article in *Nuevo Día*, entitled "The Family and Crime," reinforced this theme of the Biblical centrality of the family and its relation to societal corruption. It concluded that "If God doesn't enter into the school and the family, sources of principles of good and evil . . . success in the struggle against crime is highly improbable" (Mateo 1993, 65).

A third opinion piece in *El Nuevo Día*, "New Start for the Family," asserted that "The family is society in miniature . . . it is the base, the bridge, the road and the ship to bring us to a secure port in a world in which it appears about to sink" (Rodríguez de Rivera 1995, 71).

The author recommended that the society improve the self-esteem of parents in crisis, showing a man how to "feel proud of gaining his subsistence with his own hands" (Rodríguez de Rivera 1995, 71) and reducing his welfare dependency. These pieces advanced a theory of the family as moral agent that was echoed in evangelist sermons and Puerto Rican popular culture alike. Good families—those in which the roles of members were fixed, in which men provided, women nurtured, and parents shepherded children away from delinquency—these were the cause of a harmonious society, not its result. This is a model of virtue from the bottom up, not from the top down.

This metanarrative of the disintegration of the Puerto Rican family overlooked important realities of Puerto Rican life. The first was that the nuclear family headed by a married couple was never the norm for the Puerto Rican working class that composed the majority of the population. Civil and church marriage were historically privileges reserved for the middle to upper classes who were able to afford marriage fees, and for whom the social capital to be gained by formal marriage into a given family was worth the trouble (Martinez-Fernandez 2000, Potthast-Jutkeit 1997). This pattern held across Latin America from colonization to the present (Castro Martin 2002). The low marriage rate was not a sign of a woman's liberation but rather a sign of her low social standing; as Castro Martin points out,

> [I]n developed countries, cohabitation is usually portrayed as a sign of women's emancipation . . . [but in Latin America] the higher prevalence of consensual unions among lower educated strata suggests that the type of marital arrangement women end up living in may not always be a matter of choice, but rather the outcome of social constraints (Castro Martin 2002, 50).

Some argue that, given their circumstances, working-class women might have judged marriage to be contrary to their interests, as "legal marriage strengthened a man's authority as head of household" (Safa 2003). Regardless of the decision making which led to them, however, consensual unions within extended families have for centuries been the units of cohabitation and mutual aid of most Puerto Ricans.

Second, this contemporary metanarrative harkens to an idealized past of parental control and youthful restraint that is contradicted by the widespread adolescent pregnancy and heavy alcohol consumption described among the Puerto Rican working class in the early twentieth century (Mintz 1960; Steward et al. 1956).

Third, given that infusions of funds from U.S. federal assistance programs after World War Two helped to build Puerto Rico's current system of public housing, modern highways, universal electricity and water supply, and public education (Dietz 1986, Safa 1974), it is only in the past forty years that the North American middle-class ideal—of nuclear families with independent dwellings and children who reproduce after they graduate from high school and are legally wed—has been a possibility for ordinary Puerto Ricans. That a minority of Puerto Ricans fulfill this ideal does not pose a new crisis; it is a continuation of—not a reversal of—the historical social order.

The newspapers' call to arms to defend the family drew explicit and implicit connections between families and addiction. Not only did articles sounding the alarm for family disintegration list drug addiction as a primary sign of the societal collapse caused by broken families, but these articles were published alongside a series of features describing an explosion of drug use and drug trade in Puerto Rico.[1] Articles with headlines such as "Heroin: Drug of Choice and Death"; "The use of cocaine increasing in Puerto Rico"; "Losing the Battle Against Addiction"; "DEA Says Island Cocaine, Heroin Consumption on the Rise"; "Consumption of Heroin Rising"; "Drug Addiction Grips Island, Becomes Way of Life for the Poor"; "More than 30 Thousand Initiate Drug Use in 2000" (Ponti 1993, Bauza 1986, Millan 1993, Hopgood 1990, Suarez 1995, Pares 2001) fanned the flame of public fear of the decadence, crime, violence, impulsivity, and amorality symbolically associated with drug use. Articles claiming that drug use was at an all-time high often contradicted each other, such as "Census at 50 Thousand Addicts" (Associated Press 1999), which was published seven years after "Around 72 Thousand Addicts in Puerto Rico" (Varela 1992). They sustained an impression of constant siege by, and rampant multiplication of, drug users.

Such headlines were accompanied by graphic close-ups of arms with syringes hanging from their veins; the front page of a Sunday edition of *El Nuevo Día* featured an illustration of a skull over two marijuana cigarettes folded into crossbones, over a syringe, needle, and cocaine razor. The cover of another paper featured a close-up of a young man, face down on the ground, found dead of overdose in a housing project. Articles about drug use on the island appealed to their readers' voyeurism; "A Visit to the Nightmare World of Addiction" (Ponti 1994) described a journalist's evening among prostitutes and heroin injectors in a shooting gallery, and "Creating Under-Cover Pipes" (Colombani 2001) elaborated the ways that drug paraphernalia such as pipes for smoking crack cocaine had been crafted to resemble everyday objects such as lipstick cases and tennis balls. The overall effect was to heighten paranoia; a reader could be led to see drugs hidden in every magic marker, to see violent addicts among passersby.

addict stigma

Readers might also be led to see a violent addict in their own homes. As Jessica told me at Victory Academy, her brother refused contact with her when he found out she was an addict because he thought addicts robbed their families. Juan's brother would not allow Juan contact with his daughters because he thought Juan would be a bad influence on them. Their ideas about addiction might have been reinforced by authoritative articles such as one which quoted psychiatrist Efrain Ramirez, founder of the first biomedical addiction treatment program in Puerto Rico, as saying that addicts themselves helped to spread addiction through their families. "[Addicts] will steal from their friend and families and when there is nothing to steal they will hook the working members of their family on drugs so that when they buy, they buy for them too" (Suarez 1995).

Another article published by the same paper and entitled, "Father, Daughter Fight to Kick Heroin" brings this family connection home with a story about a father in addiction treatment who enrolled his nineteen-year-old daughter in his methadone maintenance program after learning that his daughter was buying

heroin from his former dealer. The daughter was quoted as saying "[W]hen I
learned about my father taking drugs, I felt that if he does it, it is all right for me to
do it too" (Friedman n.d., 21). The story closes a loop: Just as bad families cause
addiction, addiction causes bad families.

A series of public service announcements, aired on Puerto Rican television in
2000–2001, further cemented the common knowledge that families were responsible for addiction. The announcements were produced by the anti-drug organization Alianza Para Un Puerto Rico Sin Drogas (Partnership for a Drug Free Puerto
Rico), the island counterpart of the U.S.-based campaign Partnership for a Drug
Free America, and featured thirty- to sixty-second ads depicting scenes such as a
mother engrossed in a telephone conversation, and ignoring the attempts of her
school-aged child to ask her questions about drugs. Some ads were testimonials
from recovering addicts about the ways that their drug use had destroyed their
family lives. These images reflected popular wisdom about addiction and families
to which ex-addicts, and their families, were not immune. They also romanticized
the power of family bonds in a way that, for a growing number of Puerto Ricans,
did not reflect their domestic realities.

Newspaper articles and public service announcements suggested that if families would simply pull together, by a collective act of moral resolve, then the problems of addiction would solve themselves. None of the complexities of sustaining
family unity and family support in the face of unemployment, dangerous neighborhoods, gendered role displacement, and geographic dispersion of family members came to light in these media assertions of family responsibility for addiction.
The assertions provide a window on the popular discourses with which Gabriel,
Yeyo, Juan, and Wilson and their families had to engage—discourses that were
hegemonic, shaping the ways that large segments of the Puerto Rican public made
sense of their lived realities. They helped to forestall a structural analysis of the
impact of U.S. policies on Puerto Rico's infrastructure and ability to foster local
economic reinvestments. As in any hegemonic system, there are counter-hegemonic thought leaders that challenge the status quo. For example, the pro-independence paper, *Claridad*, with a highly educated readership, published an article entitled, "The Puerto Rican Family and Political Change" which argued that U.S.
federal policies imposed on the Puerto Rican state were destructive of the family.
The article cited limitations on public assistance required by U.S. welfare reform
law, and the "One Strike Out" law requiring eviction of families with members
convicted of serious crime from public-housing complexes. It concluded by alluding to a "neoliberal hurricane more barbaric than any that have lashed our institution of the family" (Reyes 2001, 37). Among working-class people, Pentecostalism
only superficially reproduced the popular discourse on addiction and family. In
practical terms, it gave addicted people a way to redeem themselves within ministries that did not rely on their reunification with their often-alienated families.

FRAGMENTED FAMILIES

Historical, demographic, and ethnographic studies of the family in Puerto Rico provide a narrative of industrialization, urbanization, and North Americanization that eroded the extended families that traditionally had been a safety net for poor people. In this narrative, once-dense networks of extended agrarian families were replaced by smaller, often female-headed families that struggled to survive while approximating a North American nuclear ideal. Although this might simplify and romanticize the complex realities of agrarian and urban life within the symbolic dichotomy of (moral) country and (immoral) city critiqued by Raymond Williams (1975), demographers of Puerto Rico do report that multiple generations co-residing in the same home is not as prevalent in Puerto Rico as in other parts of Latin America, and is becoming less common. This is most visible among the elderly: according to the 1990 U.S. Census, only 12.8% of all Puerto Ricans age 65 and older were living in a multigenerational household (Zsembik and Bonilla 2000). As anthropologist Helen Safa points out, U.S. federal policies requiring marriage for a partner's receipt of state insurance, social security, and veteran's benefits, worked in tandem with American-model social policy in housing, health, education, and social work, to promote the nuclear family ideal in Puerto Rico. In fact, extended families were deliberately dismantled as part of U.S. sponsored post-World War II housing policies: kin and neighborhood networks in shantytowns were broken and families—defined as mothers with children, with the father only if legally married to the mother—were dispersed to various housing projects in an effort to reduce crime and promote upward mobility, an effort that has more than backfired (Safa 2003).

Ironically, U.S.-model public-housing policies designed to promote nuclear families instead created an environment conducive to single generation, female-headed households and, as of the 1970s, welfare eligibility requirements have also meant that most Puerto Rican female heads of households live only with their children rather than in extended families, and that 70% have incomes below the poverty line (Safa 2003, 30). This pattern is being replicated throughout Latin America as an increasing percentage of families are headed by women, most of them low income and on average poorer than male-headed households (Arias and Palloni 1999:2). In the Americas, family poverty is women's poverty, and in Puerto Rico these women are increasingly isolated from their extended families.

These policies literally also have left men out in the cold. As Joanne Pessaro's study of gender and homelessness on the U.S. mainland suggests, policies prohibiting male cohabitants for mothers to qualify for family benefits have led to male dislocation—both physically from their households, and socially from their roles in their communities (Pessaro 1996).

Yet extended families are still useful for Puerto Ricans in post-industrial cities. As the author of a study of Puerto Ricans in Boston wrote, "Close ties between family members and the extended family serve to maintain strong family bonds and unity—a key Puerto Rican value. Busy working parents can use their limited time more efficiently with the help of the extended family" (Hidalgo 1997).

One study of New York Puerto Ricans defined this ethos as "Familism, [which] as a belief system, refers to feelings of loyalty, reciprocity, and solidarity toward members of the family, as well as to the notion of the family as an extension of self" (Cortes 1995, 1).

Yet another research team saw familism as the foundation for a natural support system, a primary survival strategy. Even in U.S. urban centers with a high density of public services, the Puerto Ricans they studied sought help for financial and emotional problems exclusively from their families, and always sought family help in combination with public services in the case of school- or health-related needs (Delgado and Rivera 1997).

Many of the resources that people need to survive in post-industrial environments are located outside of the family, however. As a research team that investigated homelessness in Puerto Rico suggested, Puerto Ricans need to be

> psychologically prepared for the likelihood that as time goes on, they may need [more] formal, non-familial sources of social support. . . . The current reality is that fewer intergenerational (extended) families, elderly family members, and women are all living under the same roof . . . and the capacity of families to deal with the needs of the extended family members are increasingly limited. . . . In financial terms, nuclear families have fewer human resources to meet the needs of their members than did traditional, extended families (Julia and Hartnett 1999).

Throughout the Americas, in the wake of its economic crises of the 1980s and reduced public services, extended families have taken on increasing importance as buffers for urban workers in "mediating poverty and cushioning the effects of the crisis" (Gonzalez de la Rocha and Gantt 1995, 18). The global economic crisis of 2008 only exacerbated the importance of family resources as buffers, and family instability as a risk factor for downward mobility (Edin and Kissane 2010). With Puerto Rican extended families in decline, the corporate structure of street ministries as metaphorical families takes on increasing relevance. Ex-addict men struggle to fit themselves into family structures that look increasingly feminine and contracted. The blend of patriarchal and extended family metaphors employed by the ministries holds up the possibility of a niche outside of the drug economy that men strive to escape.

THE MONASTIC MARKETPLACE

Addiction ministries argue that families are fragmented because they lack what ex-addicted converts gain though their spiritual odyssey of descent, suffering, and triumph over addiction. In this version of the story, the converts' renewed authority and sense of purpose realigns the family unit. Family members can put away resentments in the service of a larger goal: serving the Holy Spirit.

For many, however, the tensions between evangelism, the demands of their families, and the resources they brought to both family and church life proved too great. The ministries' bid for a reinvented patriarchy also limited the utility of the model for women leaders such as Samaria and Carmen.

Men who succeeded in addiction ministries had forms of pre-conversion cultural or social capital to draw upon as evangelists. Gabriel, for instance, was not an educated man but he had a strong support network in his mother and his brother's extended family. Mama Tita and Pastor Mendoza opened five Victory centers for addicts across the island in seven years *por fe* (on faith; here, meaning without government funds), using management and bookkeeping skills from their previous careers in the army.[2] The director of Restoration House had graduated from a seminary before founding the House, and formed a network of community churches and politicians to fund the House. Juan, who went to a university and then a theological seminary, was a history teacher's son.

In contrast, Wilson launched his new life as a Christian with less than a high-school education, no work experience outside of the drug trade, and ailing parents who demanded a lot of care. In the end, he was not embedded in the leadership structure of a thriving ministry, but rather, marginally involved in a faltering local church. Raúl's family support network was rather sparse; in fact, Raúl, just after graduating from Restoration House, was called into service as the main support for his wife's family. These obligations deprived him of a certificate from his night school training in refrigeration technology, and ultimately prevented him from attending church at all.

Their movement from the drug life to the ministry tracked the findings of American welfare researchers Edin and Lein (1997), that it is paradoxically the better-off segment of the poor which can afford to leave welfare for low-wage work, because they have transportation, childcare, and the ability to pursue additional job training. Additionally, following Carol Stack (1975), the extended family networks of poor people that might appear to be sources of social capital can just as easily be sources of social debt, as scarce resources of individuals in the family are claimed by needy members. An ethic of reciprocity within a gendered division of responsibility for care-giving both sustain and enmesh families in poverty, as Stack's and other classical studies have shown.

Ministries speak of personal morality as the engine of social change, but in practice they provide a social and institutional milieu to produce this morality. It is their collective bodily and emotional practices that cultivate personal encounters with God. Pentecostal individualism, which puts a premium on personal, mystical experience, is enabled by family recognition of spiritual authority. This spiritual authority is discursively gendered, with practical consequences that are as likely to tear families apart as to unite them. The variable outcomes encountered by Pentecostal converts are patterned by converts' family supports, resources, and skills, suggesting that spiritual transcendence of addiction is intimately tied to the material, worldly structures of spiritual practice, a point that has implications not only for street ministries but also for biomedical clinical practice, a theme explored in Chapter 7.

7

Bringing It Home

Three years after I left Puerto Rico, *Hogar Restauracion*, and *Academia La Fe*, I met Ruben in the New York City clinic where I worked as a psychiatry resident. He was a Puerto Rican who had struggled with addiction since his twenties, when he drove disabled children and seniors for an accessible van company. His boss rewarded him for his long hours by giving him cocaine, then heroin. Eventually his boss became his dealer. Ruben stopped working and entered the circuit of homeless shelters in the City.

This downward spiral of addiction was a familiar story, but when he was fifty-four, Ruben underwent an unexpected transformation. It happened in the clinic, not a ministry, yet his change was as complete as any Pentecostal conversion. Ruben's transformation helped me to see parallels between what biomedical clinics and addiction ministries try to accomplish. Both reinterpret the meaning of addiction through mutual aid. Both reveal injuries of displacement (from homes, families, communities, and economies) that are common antecedents to addiction, and provide a renewed sense of belonging, altering their identities as addicts.

On the surface, Ruben's existence was worlds apart from that of the ministries I'd studied. For one, he had never been to Puerto Rico. Although his parents migrated from the island, he was born in the same New York City hospital that was now treating him for addiction. He'd learned Spanish in the *bodegas* of the Lower East Side of Manhattan, and had never left New York.

Neither was he overtly spiritual. His turnaround began with a cocktail of prescribed opioids, antidepressants, sedatives, and antipsychotics, not with the Holy Spirit. He opened each day at dawn not with prayer, but with methadone taken in front of a nurse. He then went not to Bible study, but to therapy groups with names

149

like "Anger Management" and "Recognizing Your Triggers." Anger management was apt: he was a notorious crank. He took up an entire group meeting complaining about subway delays caused by a "jumper," a teenager who took his own life in front of an oncoming train. "I hate it when that happens!" Ruben spewed. "They spend hours cleaning up after those idiots."

None of us anticipated the other side of Ruben. When he was handed a paint brush in his first art-therapy group, he could not put it down. Ruben stayed until the janitor came to sweep for the night. His mixed media collage-paintings were intricate, and filled with brick walls. Over time the walls expanded, the paint got thicker and more textured to resemble bricks erupting from the canvass.

After the art room, the clinic's sobriety garden was his favorite place. He worked there on the weekends, planting seeds in the spring weeding; harvesting tomatoes, beans, and corn through the summer; cutting sunflowers; and planting tulip bulbs in the fall. He barbecued at garden parties for the clinic's patients, and when the grill broke, he used his social security check to replace it.

Ruben did so well, staying on his medications and winning art competitions, that he was told it was time for him to "graduate" from the program. His social security payments paid for a room in a recovery house for men in Brownsville, Brooklyn. He had a workspace in an art studio for "outsider artists"—people without formal art training who had diagnoses of mental illness and addictions. He volunteered to organize events in the clinic and to work in the garden.

When Ruben posted photos from clinic events on Facebook, a counselor told him he had violated patient confidentiality. Ruben was surprised. He told her "I just wanted to show my family's Halloween party."

It took me a moment to realize that Ruben was speaking of clinic staff and patients as his family. They insulated him against his biological family. As a child, Ruben had seen his father, a veteran who returned from the Korean war with one arm, injecting heroin into his remaining arm with the help of a war buddy. His mother was alcoholic. After years of reproducing brick walls in the clinic art room, Ruben recovered a memory of his mother, screaming profanities at him from the third-story window of their housing project while blood ran down his chin and onto the snow. He was six, and had ridden a sled into a brick wall.

The oldest of twelve children, Ruben was left in charge of his siblings. He was often told to keep them quiet inside a van in a parking lot. One day his parents did not return for eight hours. Only after his mother's death did he discover the reason for his parents' disappearances. Looking through an old chest, he found props and footage from sadomasochist scenes that his parents had filmed in the pornography studio next to the parking lot.

At eighteen, he left his eleven brothers and sisters to have his own life. Forty years later, they had still not forgiven him. In Ruben's words, they "acted out" when he abandoned them. His brothers had all been involved with drug trade and most had been incarcerated, although his second oldest brother had later used his inside knowledge to get a job as a DEA agent. His sisters had also been involved in drugs and the corrections system. Liza, now in her forties, was arrested for sex work. Tina had been elected to City Council after local newspapers covered her rise from crack dens to public housing advocacy. A relapse in her second term led to charges of embezzlement of City funds that had been earmarked for Thanksgiving turkeys for the homeless.

I accompanied Ruben to Tina's house on Mother's Day. She invited him because their brother David was visiting from Miami. Ruben had not seen Tina or David for almost a decade. Ruben was nervous; Tina had texted him at 3 a.m. the day of their meeting to say that she wasn't sure if he should come.

The day of the meeting, Ruben waited outside of Tina's house. After a few minutes, David sauntered up with a cane that he used because of diabetic nerve damage to his feet. He told Ruben to prepare himself, that their sister had lost a lot of weight to AIDS, and that she was "not right in the head." Ruben paced and cursed in front of her house as David went in to ask if Ruben should enter.

Ruben got inside, and gave his sister a postcard announcing an outsider art show with a photo of his brick montage on the front (fig 13). "I'm an artist now" he told her. "My art was chosen in Recovery Arts as the best in the State."

She waived the card away without looking at it. "You still homeless?"

There was something familiar about Ruben's attempt to get his sister's recognition. Despite her own struggles with crack cocaine, Tina made Ruben feel like the black sheep. When their mother was alive, Tina referred to Ruben as "the heroin addict," the one from whom her nieces and nephews had to be protected. It brought to mind Juan's foiled attempts to be seen by his brother and mother as a university student and pastor-in-training, rather than a crack addict.

For a while, Ruben had been thriving in the clinic art studio and in the sobriety garden. What he did not realize, and I did not realize, was that it was a tenuous form of life made possible by a fragile alignment of public and private institutions. His best years were those after he qualified for Social Security benefits based on comorbid mental illness—for his mood swings, later diagnosed as bipolar disorder, since addiction alone does not make one eligible for benefits. He could not find legal housing for the amount that his benefit check afforded him, but he did find a room in an overcrowded, unlicensed recovery group home in Brownsville, Brooklyn, an isolated outer borough neighborhood with little public transportation. A sea of tenements, Brownsville had the highest concentration of public housing in the United States. For $500 a month taken directly out of his Social Security check, the landlord rented him a closet-sized room with three padlocks on the door, next to a bathroom shared by ten other men. It was the kind of housing that has cropped up in low-income neighborhoods across the

FIGURE 13. Anxiety. Reprinted courtesy of Ruben Lopez.

United States as rent continues to increase. Cities make little provision for low-income housing, even though people recovering from addiction are desperate for a place to sleep, and street-level entrepreneurs repurpose abandoned buildings to house them in exchange for direct payments from public benefit checks (Fairbanks 2009).

Ruben complained that his padlocks were repeatedly broken by hall-mates looking for something to sell for crack, and that the ex-convict in his house who had served time for murder was now fixated on him. But he did have a place to stay. Until one night the fire marshal came unannounced to shut down the house, which violated occupancy laws. Ruben and his housemates were thrust to the curb with only what they could carry.

For a time, Ruben slept in the outsider art studio that had adopted him. When the studio director discovered he was living there, she evicted him. Stubborn, and worried about what he would encounter in homeless shelters, Ruben attempted to live on the subways, but only made it four days before the sleep deprivation, irregular meals, and missed doses of diabetes medication got to him. After his emergency room visit for headache and dizziness, Ruben was sent to a Bronx shelter.

In his first three months there, Ruben witnessed two murders, one of them in the bathroom next to his bed. He texted me photos of the blood streaked floor tiles after the police removed the body, with the message "They're not even cleaning it. How am I gonna sleep next to this?"

While at the shelter, Ruben volunteered in one of the clinic's creative arts groups, and he came to the garden on Sundays. But after a few weeks watching shelter roommates smoking crack and synthetic marijuana in the bed next to him, he began to miss days at the clinic. He said he had migraine headaches, and he stopped taking his medications—for blood pressure, diabetes, and mood stability. The only medication that he still took was buprenorphine, the methadone analog used to prevent symptoms of opiate withdrawal.

It seemed to me that Ruben's odyssey had been a spiritual one. He had learned new bodily practices involving rituals of medication, morning testimony in group therapy, and the discipline of labor in the kitchen and garden, all in the service of a new, chosen family. He had become a disciple to the art therapist, with whom his time in the art studio had been guided meditation. He had reworked his painful memories with his fingers and his paintbrush, containing them and molding them into his bricks, where they were fixed on the page rather than spinning in his *art* mind. Angry, swirling lines coalesced into faces, and shadows of bodies against forests of high-rise buildings conveyed the menacing figures and emotional states that haunted him (fig. 13, fig. 14), along with the dry sarcasm he used to shrug them off (fig. 15, fig. 16), and his political commentary (fig. 17). It was a practice through which he could imagine and enact his "sacred self:" a self capable of transcending its limitations and, thereby, of embodying aspects of the holy (Csordas 1994).

Like the addiction ministry converts that I had known, however, Ruben was brought back to earth by mundane constraints. He was a casualty of a housing crisis precipitated by decades of city politics that incentivized upper-income taxpayers' return from the suburbs, and displaced low-income residents through racially segregating mortgage lending and developer-driven policies that cleared poor people from their neighborhoods through urban renewal and planned shrinkage, followed by gentrification (Fullilove 2004). Ruben had grown on the trellis of the clinic: the therapy groups, the studio, the garden. But after a short period of allowing him to thrive, the crumbling macro-structures of housing policy and disability payments left him out in the cold.

FIGURE 14. Worried. Reprinted courtesy of Ruben Lopez.

FROM REFORMATION TO CLINICAL "RECOVERY"

Ruben's clinical recovery was not the same as Pentecostal conversion. Although Ruben's clinic prescribed him opioids (methadone and buprenorphine) indefinitely, possibly for life, to compensate for his permanent neurophysiological deficits, Pentecostals reject all substances in the service of ritual cleansing and renewal. Additionally, though biomedicine offers addicted people some measure of absolution by categorizing them as permanently disabled, Pentecostals provide ex-addicted converts a heroic narrative of self-discipline and rebirth as a spiritual authority. Yet, the puzzling familiarity of Ruben's transformation forced me to reconsider whether the ministries I'd known in Puerto Rico and the biomedicine which I was now licensed to practice were the polar opposites that they appeared

FIGURE 15. Life Goes On. Reprinted courtesy of Ruben Lopez.

to be. Their metaphors and methods diverged, but ultimately both drew from Occidental mysticism, and attempted to stem the effects of post-industrial social disintegration and displacement.

Years before meeting Ruben, as a medical student, I was assigned to a famous psychiatrist who had me observe his interviews. One interviewee was a young Puerto Rican who had been raised as a sex slave in a notorious gang, the Latin Kings. Pixie-cut curls framed her carefully penciled almond eyes. We scanned her face for emotion, having read in her chart that she had been serially raped as a child. She had been on the unit several times before, in psychotic crises precipitated by cocaine. The psychiatrist asked her what she wanted to accomplish during this admission. "I want to stay off crack" she said flatly. He nodded. "We'll see what

FIGURE 16. Days Numbered. Reprinted courtesy of Ruben Lopez.

we can do." He shut the door after her and turned to me. "This is someone who our treatments will not touch." His look was somber. "The only thing that would work for her is evangelical conversion. I've seen it happen. She has to leave her life behind and get absorbed into something that will take her over completely." I was caught off guard that a psychiatry professor saw a use for evangelism.

What I did not realize at the time was that our clinical goals for addiction treatment shared a kinship with those of evangelists. Ruben, for instance, not only stayed on his pharmaceuticals, he also shifted his identity on a corporeal level through his everyday practices: he changed his *habitus* (Mauss 1934, Bourdieu 1984)—his embodied sense of place in the world, of social relationships and "feel for the game" of daily living, culturally learned and shaped by historically specific social structures but made to feel natural and universal.[1] These he retrained with

habitus

FIGURE 17. Non-Affordable NYC Housing. Reprinted courtesy of Ruben Lopez.

his intricate paintings, by teaching new patients to use art materials, and by cultivating the Sobriety Garden.

Formerly the addict who had abandoned his brothers and sisters, he was now
the artist who donated his time and meager income to the clinic. In the language of
Martin Luther's Protestant Reformation, Ruben had found his *calling*. It was a democ-
ratizing event that placed Ruben, as ex-addict, on equal moral footing with clinical
professionals. As Max Weber wrote of the Protestant idea of the calling: "It and it
alone is the will of God, and hence every legitimate calling has exactly the same worth
in the sight of God" (Weber 1930, 41). A clinician hopes that histories of addiction will
take on meaning when sufferers find a redemptive purpose. He or she attempts to
guide recovering addicts toward this end, in a crypto-Protestant version of "therapeutic emplotment"—the clinical script for progression of recovery (Mattingly 1994).[2]

Even within the logic of biomedicine, addiction is not only a neurophysiological deficiency, it is also a deficiency of purpose and social value, a deficiency that

requires re-identification through disciplinary practice. Although maintenance medications such as methadone and buprenorphine are stop-gap measures to keep people from craving their drugs of choice, the ultimate goal of treatment is a "higher-functioning" self that sees limits, controls impulses, and defers gratification in pursuit of larger goals. This higher functioning—referred to as "insight" and "sublimation" in the psychological language of the clinic—is a biomedical version of transcendence and salvation. Addicted patients are saved when they recognize their self-destruction and redirect their energies toward helping others.

Clinicians also see addictions as the sequelae of toxic external assaults on the self that lead people to self-medicate with substances. This is reflected in the pervasive clinical discourse of trauma. With origins in late-nineteenth century debates among psychoanalysts about the developmental cause of neuroses, and in forensic and military psychiatry around compensation for work- and war-related psychological injury, trauma re-emerged an organizing principle in late twentieth-century psychiatry following the coinage of "post-traumatic stress disorder" among Vietnam veterans, which feminists extended to include survivors of childhood abuse and interpersonal violence (Fassin and Rechtman 2009; Andreasen 2010). Socially minded clinicians highlighted the systemic causes of trauma, such as the injuries and dislocation of major disasters, war, and political repression, signaled with the term "collective trauma" (Saul 2013). Government regulators direct addiction clinics to acknowledge trauma in the form of "trauma-informed care," based on principles of safety, trust, support, and empowerment of the patient to avoid "retraumatization" by the health care system itself (Substance Abuse and Mental Health Services Administration 2014). Trauma-informed care also involves recognition of primal trauma: early assaults to the integrity of the self that are especially damaging to children and adolescents who have a tenuous and developing sense of self. In this formulation, if the assault is not neutralized with corrective affirmations of the self, it is likely to fester in self-medication with drugs of abuse. Ruben's art therapist used his paintings as a portal to his memories of primal traumas, traumas that she encouraged him to discuss in therapy group confessionals.

 Clinical ideas about the heritability of trauma and addiction resemble Christian concepts of original sin and genealogies of guilt. One biomedical version of heritability of trauma is that genetic traits predispose carriers to substance abuse. Another version is the "intergenerational transmission" of trauma, in which traumatized parents convey the effects of their own trauma to their children through abuse, neglect, and addiction. A family history like Ruben's—his father's heroin use, his mother's alcoholism, the cocaine addiction of his sisters and brothers—is common in psychiatric narratives of addiction. And the idea that external rupture is necessary to break the chain of family transmission is reminiscent of evangelical conversion. Ruben's discovery of art, for example, separated him from his pathogenic family and bound him to the fictive kin of clinic patients and staff.

With the bodily discipline of kitchen and cleaning duty, planting, and harvesting in the sobriety garden, the clinic created a version of the moral therapy that has been central to Euro-American mental hospitals, asylums, and sanatoria for more than a century. Building on the image of eighteenth-century psychiatrist Philippe Pinel breaking the chains that bound patients to the walls of the Parisian Hospital Bicetre in an effort to establish humane treatment for the insane, the Narcotic Farm in Lexington, Kentucky—a U.S. Public Health Service Hospital—was founded in 1935 as the first federally funded inpatient hospital for addiction. Its research unit later became the National Institute on Drug Abuse. From the beginning, it blended state-of-the-art pharmaceutical and neuroscientific knowledge of addiction (hosting early studies of tolerance and withdrawal, craving, and methadone detox) with music, dance, art therapies, and farming on 1,000 acres of hospital grounds. The Narcotic Farm was the largest U.S. federal addiction hospital and ran until 1975. Widespread theories and methods of addiction treatment, including the use of methadone and the psychology of addiction-related reward, triggers, and withdrawal, were established by its clinicians and researchers (Campbell, Olson and Walden 2008). Yet, its goals for treatment went beyond biochemical correction and behavioral control. Its animal husbandry, horticulture, and creative arts therapies drew on organic, pastoral images of growth and harmony with seasonal cycles, rather than the mechanical image of chemical replacement promised by medications. In this pastoral frame, the self is strengthened by adversity and by labor, which gives it a purpose greater than itself. The addict thereby finds not just sobriety, but a calling in life, reminiscent of Protestant redemption through good works.[3]

The pastoral imagery of New York City's public clinics and of Puerto Rico's ministries highlight the centrality of place and belonging in addiction. Ruben had been homeless, as had many Puerto Rican ministry leaders before their conversion. A majority of ministry converts could not find employment in the formal economy, or sustain their families before conversion. It is no accident that their moral therapies center on the re-creation of home, work, and domestic life. In Puerto Rico and on the U.S. mainland, concentrated drug deaths and AIDS in poor city neighborhoods occur in the wake of raced-based relocation and exclusion created by urban renewal, planned shrinkage, and discriminatory housing and lending practices (Fullilove 2004). The pathogenic ingredient of contemporary poverty is racialized residential instability that disrupts neighborhoods and their support and kinship networks, something that social analysts came to name "precarity" following the 2008 financial crisis, to indicate chronic instability as a condition of poverty and growing dispossession in the form of evicted people and refugees on a global scale (Muehlebach 2013, Das and Randeria 2015).

The systemic response to displacement in the United States is an "institutional circuit" (Hopper et al. 1997) of homeless people with psychiatric diagnoses who travel from the street to inpatient hospitalizations, to shelters, to transitional housing, then back to the street. A parallel process occurs in Latin America, including in Brazil, where poor people with addiction, HIV, or psychiatric diagnoses are consigned to "zones of abandonment," trapped between clinics and the streets, in which evangelical residences are a last resort (Biehl 2005). In response, marginalized people might use biomedical language of healthcare rights to secure their bodily place in society—through legal recognition and claims on the state—as genetic citizenship (Heath, Rapp, and Taussig 2008), biological citizenship (Petryna 2006), or pharmaceutical citizenship (Ecks 2005). Ministries, for their part, use pastoral imagery from the Bible—of a resting place with a herd of fellow converts—to answer this crisis of place and citizenship.

The clinic in which I work, in which Ruben found his place, is a pasture. The founder of the clinic is a psychiatrist and visual artist who combined art-therapy groups with mainstream pharmaceutical treatment, and created a Sobriety Garden by breaking the cement of an abandoned hospital parking lot, kneading, and planting the soil alongside her patients. As she put it, psychiatry is "art with found objects: we help people take the shards of their shattered lives and put them together again in new ways." The garden embodies this philosophy: handmade sculptures of rams, lions, and pigs hold up benches and trellises. The eyes, hooves, and paws of the sculptures are accented with fragments from the ceramics and jewelry of patients' deceased friends and relatives. The garden and its totems are tangible markers of the project of selfhood upon which recovering patients[4] are embarked.

The garden's ethos of self-cultivation references a Euro-American mysticism[5] that also can be found in psychoanalytic models of the mind as made up of parts with conflicting motives and functions; the mind as a divided self that in its paralyzing inner conflict alienates itself from other people. Psychoanalyst Carl Jung saw this self-division and conflict as counterbalanced by a universal collective unconscious, expressed in the "archetypal" symbolism of myths and religions, symbolism which is designed to reintegrate conflicted individuals into the collective unconscious. This was the basis for his theory of a "thirst for wholeness" in addiction. He argued that alienated people use substances to feel connected to humanity but ultimately are further isolated by their addiction, and that only a radical spiritual conversion can provide them with a sense of connection.

Jung's thinking about conversion ultimately contributed to the founding of Alcoholics Anonymous when he told his patient, Roland H., that only conversion could cure his alcoholism. Roland migrated to the United States in the 1930s and converted in the evangelical Oxford Group of AA founders Bill W. and Dr. Bob. Jungian thought thus deeply influenced the AA concept of spiritual awakening from addiction. The idea is that recovery involves a collapse of the ego, or old self, in which a sufferer hits "rock bottom" and acknowledges a lack of self-control, followed by an initiation (such as conversion) that marks the rebirth of a new self, and then by transformation into what Jung termed a "wounded healer": someone who experiences personal growth through mutual aid and identification with fellow sufferers (Addenbrook 2015). With this allegory, Jung and Twelve Step founders addressed a paradox of Euro-American individualism: the use of substances to ease the anhedonia and pain of isolation, while further isolating oneself with the stigma and dysregulation of addiction.

The understandings of addiction described in this chapter—as a prelude to a calling, as self-medication for trauma, as something that is overcome through transformation into a healer, are mystical linkages of the individual to the collective. They emerged in the post–World War II era, during U.S. industrial expansion, and came into fruition at the end of the twentieth century when waves of industrial capitalist expansion and contraction led to widespread homelessness, unemployment, and global narcotics trade fed by the racial, ethnic, gender, and class exclusions that provided low-cost labor for industrial enterprise. These exclusions, in turn, were followed by mass incarceration, HIV, and drug homicides—all cloaked in languages of failed personal responsibility. A discourse of nations and nationality sets the terms for industries and their regulation, including narcotics trade, the laws illegalizing it, and the funding to enforce narcotics laws. In this discourse, nation-building has focused on strengthening the borders around which people are defined as non-citizens or threats to the nation—as undocumented immigrants, as black and brown welfare dependents, as migratory Puerto Ricans with ambiguous racial and national loyalties, as irresponsible addicts who neglect their families. Non-citizens are outside of the nation; they are easily discarded when their labor is no longer needed, and easily consumed by multinational drug trade when illegal markets are needed. Addiction thus is produced by weakened social accountability and heightened human disposability. *Connect to Marx!*

For Puerto Rican men, living in a stateless zone without sovereignty, without federal representation, and without local control of investments or labor, the lure of citizenship in a global Christian nation is strong. Add to that the racial and ethnic ambiguity of a people who are mixed race, Spanish-speaking, and located in the Latin American Caribbean but who live under Anglo-American rule, in which the nation of the United States has been built on an exclusive whiteness separating those with claims on the state from those without (Garner 2007). Global Pentecostal evangelism promises a nation outside of race, ethnicity, language, geography, or monetary assets, a nation built on a transcendental connection to fellow worshippers, in which (spiritual) investments and labor are controlled by individuals and their congregations.

Puerto Rican evangelical nationhood has precursors in the "cultural nationalism" strategy of post-War Puerto Rican leaders who negotiated the island's commonwealth status with the United States. Commonwealth status continued most U.S. entitlements, but curtailed the island's political privileges of statehood including the federal vote and congressional representation. Cultural nationalism complemented commonwealth status by maintaining Spanish as the official language and high-lighting the Spanish colonial heritage of the island, skirting the issue of political autonomy while, at least in part, extending the cultural nation beyond the spatial boundaries of the island to include Puerto Ricans who had migrated to the mainland (Duany 2002).

Begun as a heritage project of the Puerto Rican state involving the founding of museums and festivals, cultural nationalism later was tapped by multinational corporations as a strategy for marketing consumer goods to island and mainland Puerto Ricans through sponsorship of cultural events and institutions (e.g., festivals, sports teams, exhibits) that aspire to define "Puerto Ricanness" (Davila 1997).

Pentecostal evangelism takes borderless nation-building further, offering membership to anyone who will cultivate their spiritual gifts regardless of their birthplace, current residence, or worldly language. Recall Pastor Mendoza's statement that, after conversion, he no longer saw himself as Puerto Rican, nor as a U.S. veteran, but instead, saw himself simply as a Christian. For poor, addicted people who are excluded from both the Puerto Rican and the American national imaginary, global Pentecostalism offers a citizenship of last resort.

The parallel narrative of biomedical moral therapies is that through self-discovery and cultivation of personal gifts (whether in art, gardening, or inspirational testimony), people recovering from addiction come together as members of clinic-sponsored therapy groups, online self-help groups, or worldwide Twelve-Step fellowships. They create new biosocialities (Rabinow 1996) based on their shared understanding of their addiction as a chronic disease, rather than on shared racial, ethnic, class, gender, or geographical identities. Ruben, for example, gained a network of people recovering from addiction who were African American, white, and Asian; men; and women with origins in a range of cities and countries, and with whom he came to identify more strongly than his biological family or people in his neighborhood. The emotional intensity of these biosocial groups speaks to their power to re-enchant; to give members a heightened sense of their unique place in the world and of their connection to the rest of humanity. Like networks of Pentecostal ministries, biosocial groups also provide forms of capital to which members would otherwise not have access: connections in elite art worlds; studio space; contacts within government agencies; and knowledge of psychological theory, of housing law, and of social security benefits.

In "We Have Never Been Disenchanted," religion scholar Eugene McCarraher challenges "one of the stories that modernity tells itself" about the spirits and deities who, in the past, shaped natural and human worlds: that "with the victories of science, technology, and capitalism, we have discovered that the cosmos of enchantment was unreal, or at best, utterly unverifiable" (McCarraher 2015, 86). He argues that contemporary capitalism itself is the product of enchantment: of the fetishism of monetary currency and commodities.[6] Adam Smith, the eighteenth-century prophet of neoliberal economics, spread enchantment with an "invisible hand" of the (free) market as something that would bring a prosperous and moral social order into being through the self-interested acts of individuals. Global enchantment with money and commodities has reached its culmination in this century's "millennial capitalism . . . messianic, salvific, even magical . . . in shaping selfhood, society, identity, even epistemic reality" (Comaroff and Comaroff 2000, 293), a capitalism that is characterized by a shift from labor and production to consumption and speculation as processes of self-making that "produce desire and expectation . . . [yet] decrease the certainty of work or the security of persons" (Comaroff and Comaroff 2000, 298). This description applies to the international narcotics trade in which Puerto Rico plays a key role. In narcotraffic, the mystical and spiritual are not eclipsed by rationalism; rather, they transmute into monetary form, into an obsession with calculation and maximization that is fed by the uncontrolled consumption of others. Pentecostal addiction ministries attempt to redirect this ethos of maximization from the material to the spiritual realm, to recover addicts from the waste bin of "others."

A number of critical scholars have written about the illusory nature of individualism in U.S. neoliberal ideology, pointing out that it renders invisible the systemic advantages of inherited education, class membership and White race in the form of segregated neighborhoods, schools and employment (Bourdieu 1984, Edin and Lein 1997, Sharkey 2013, Feagin 2013). In this system, achievements are celebrated as due to individual effort, and the role of network-based social, cultural, and financial capital is erased. Pentecostal ministries create alternative networks and capital while preserving a rhetoric of personal discipline as the fountain of success. When Pentecostalism works, it works by usurping individualist ideology to achieve communal ends for people who do not have access to mainstream capital. It is a move that might be seen as quietly subversive from one point of view, but seen from another perspective it provides "evidence" that addiction is a problem of personal morality, because the social infrastructures of ministries remain hidden. The hidden quality of the religious institutional infrastructures driving "individual" success also holds true of broader social projects such as the resettlement of immigrants (Mooney 2009). In this way, ministries can paradoxically reinforce the trap of individual accountability from which they serve as an escape.

Another approach, informed by the longstanding movement of social medicine, is to foreground public policies, institutions, communities, and families as targets of intervention. It is an approach that I have attempted to rebrand with the contemporary language of clinical training as "structural competency" (Hansen and Metzl 2017, Metzl and Hansen 2014). This would require clinicians to begin by analyzing the structural factors driving the phenomenon in question (such as addiction), and then to collaborate with relevant actors and institutions to craft structural solutions. In Ruben's case, this involved his clinical team connecting

enchantment & awe

him with a housing placement program and helping him to get readmitted to his outsider art studio. Samaria, for instance, had room and board at Victory Academy, the support of her pastor and co-leaders to take her HIV medications, and use of the ministry van to get to clinic appointments. Her doctor was thus able to maintain her on antiviral medications and monitor her viral load. What her doctor did not do, however, was to ask Samaria about her living conditions at Victory Academy. Had he done so, he might have learned about Samaria's (gendered) struggles to stay on as a leader, and helped to arrange alternative housing and transportation after her departure from her ministry. In Samaria's case, the ministry mattered as a structure of material support; as a lattice for the affective and bodily transformation that she experienced as enchanted.

Enchantment is critical to addiction recovery. Enchantment is, in fact, a technology, in the sense that anthropologist Alfred Gell famously defined it: a "means by which individuals are persuaded of the necessity and desirability of the social order which encompasses them" (Gell 1992, 44). Gell analogized the awe inspired by art with the awe inspired by religious experience, and, in this century, with the awe inspired by technological advances such as feats of mechanical engineering or biomedicine. He argued that enchantment was the viewer's sense of wonder at the entity that had produced the object (art, creation, high technology), wonder which leads the viewer to desire connection with the artist/creator/inventor of the object, and therefore with the collectivity or society in which they are embedded. Enchantment is therefore a moment of alchemy in which the materials of art, religion, or high technology transmute into shared affective and cognitive states, states of hope and an ability to conceive of greater goals that transcend individuals.

These moments of alchemy are what attract me to grassroots ministries, and to the art and gardens of old city hospitals. They show how the material, the affective, and the cognitive are entwined; how institutions and bodies constitute, and are constituted by, thought styles and motivations. Addiction is biocultural: the social imaginary determines biological outcomes, because what addicted people think of themselves and see as possible drives their risk of overdose, infection, violence, and incarceration. The question is how to cultivate social imaginaries and lattices of relationships that foster therapeutic (or liberatory, or counterhegemonic) ways of living. These imaginaries and their lattices do not have predetermined outcomes. They are potentialities, sources of innovation and adaptation, akin to what Raymond Williams long ago called "structures of feeling" in reference to shifts in cultural style prior to their articulation and institutionalization (Williams 1977), and akin to what Gilles Deleuze later called "becomings," in reference to the dynamic expression of social and biological life through ceaseless differentiation and change over time (Deleuze and Boundas 1993). This dynamic view, in which people make use of the materials and concepts at hand (i.e., street evangelism, art therapy), in ways that are contingent upon the time and location in which they find themselves, is missing from biomedical approaches. As anthropologist Carolyn Rouse argues, "evidenced based" medicine does not account for the uncertainty of clinical trajectories, or for the community-level conditional nature of chronic illness among groups with disparate health outcomes, such as African Americans (Rouse 2009). In addiction, biomedicine attempts to achieve universality by controlling for, and therefore erasing, the very variables (time in history, and social position in communities) that fuel or hamper personal transformation. In contrast, Puerto Rican ministries accent capital and social inequality as key historical and geographical variables.

Pentecostalism is not an escape from capitalism, nor from its inequalities. It has an intimate relationship with capitalism, both lending and borrowing capitalism's logics of individual gifts and the power of the will to make the self. Pentecostalism can loosen the hierarchies that devalue addicted people by legitimating alternative authorities and identifications. At times, Pentecostalism opens spaces for marginal people to create a new order based on narratives of ascetic redemption, domesticity, and universal access to knowledge and gifts. At other times, it draws on elements of the old order—such as patriarchy—empowering some members at the expense of others. It is neither a seamless continuation of neoliberal hegemony, nor a complete break from it. Rather, it is the site of a provincial struggle of neoliberal subjects to renegotiate its terms.[7] The provincial ground of struggle is where lived realities are produced and occasionally transformed. To paraphrase bell hooks: to dismiss the stories of the actors in this struggle is to recolonize them by co-opting their authorship.

In the beginning of my study of addiction in Pentecostal ministries, I'd asked how people make something out of nothing. I now believe the answer is that they don't. Ministries build congregations through practices that reshape relationships. Converts use pre-conversion education, family relationships, and skills to transform themselves. Successful clinics do this as well, leveraging the creativity of patients and institutional resources such as housing and disability programs—however scarce—to help patients build a life. Mysticism and metaphors of rebirth are as crucial to this alchemy in clinics as they are in ministries. They constitute practices of hope that, at times, enable people to become artists with the found objects of their lives.

NOTES

PREFACE

1. Crack houses and shooting galleries are buildings in which cocaine or heroin are smoked or injected.

2. I credit the late Patricia Pessar with helping me to articulate this insight.

INTRODUCTION

1. The names of all study participants, treatment centers, and cities (except Ponce) in this book have been changed to protect the identities of study participants. Human subjects' approval for the study's informed-consent process was obtained from Yale University Faculty of Arts and Sciences, and a Certificate of Confidentiality was obtained from the U.S. Secretary of Health and Human Services to protect the identity of study participants from court subpoena due to the nature of the subject matter of many interviews (i.e., personal histories of illicit drug use and related crimes).

2. All quotes are my own translations from Spanish to English except where I indicate that the interview was conducted in English. In my translations of the interview material from Spanish to English, I preserved a few key drug use–related and evangelical terms in Spanish to convey some of the aesthetic and linguistic nuance of the ways in which my informants talked. In these ways I have drawn on the richness of both interview material and my participant observation data in an effort to recreate some of the social complexity of my informants.

3. Many anthropologists have looked upon evangelism with suspicion. Twentieth-century cultural anthropology, in its effort to shed its nineteenth-century legacy as an instrument of European missionaries and colonists, developed a tradition of salvage ethnography that sought to document and preserve pre-Christian practices and folklore in the non-European

world (Clifford 2008), a tradition that was primarily concerned with preserving cultures that were thought to represent earlier evolutionary stages of human social evolution, and, as a result, cast Christian evangelism as a cultural pollutant. In the twenty-first century, anthropology of Christianity often addresses conservative Christian politics that originate in the U.S. white middle class, critically unpacking their discourses of individual responsibility as they are used against movements for economic, ethnic/racial, and gender equality. Evangelists from marginalized groups, however, might be differently motivated. As a converted informant for a critical ethnography of the neoliberal politics in Guatemalan evangelism told the ethnographer, "I mean, I'm smart too." (O'Neill 2015, 190). I interpret this as his invitation to be seen as a thinking subject, as someone who has used evangelical practices to survive under toxic conditions.

4. Interview with Irene Meléndez, consultant to the Puerto Rican Administration for Addiction and Mental Health Services (AAMSCA), San Juan, Puerto Rico, November 28, 2000.

5. A literature on "spiritual capital" also emerged among sociologists of religion and others who drew on earlier formulations of human and religious capital (Iannaccone 1990), and were responding to political scientist Robert Putnam's (2000) formulation of social capital, which focused on the declining density of social networks as a function of the collapse of U.S. civil society. The Templeton Foundation sponsored an international research program on spiritual capital which led to the publication of a series of scholarly papers (Hansell 2006). Putnam's formulation of social capital advocates strengthening non-governmental organizations as instruments of civil society, including churches, which he deems the largest generator of social capital in the United States. The version of spiritual capital that I use refers to Bourdieu's less normative and more analytical symbolic-economic concept that knowledge and social relationships are forms of capital that are interchangeable in limited ways with financial capital and with each other. I use it because it foregrounds the mechanisms by which ministries can enhance the agency among converts, as well as the way ministries can delimit converts and their access to alternative forms of capital.

CHAPTER 1

1. All interview quotations in this chapter are my translations from Spanish, except of interviews with Juan, which were conducted in English with some Spanish terms, as written.

2. The names of the ministries (and those of the people) I studied have been changed to protect the confidentiality of participants in the study.

3. "*Trigueño*" often is used euphemistically to refer to people whose skin tone is quite a bit darker than wheat; it is a subconscious feature of contemporary Puerto Rican racism to consider dark skin, hair, and eyes as inferior and thus to politely overstate the lightness of a person's features. For instance, light-brown eyes like my daughter's often were called blue or green.

A psychologist in Ponce once gave me her rendering of Puerto Rico's elaborate racial-classification system, including "*Mulatto*," denoting people of mixed African and Spanish heritage, with a prominent buttocks, kinky hair, and wheat-colored skin; "*Trigueño*," for those with "soft" coloring, straight hair, large lips, and a defined nose; "*Negrito*," a term indicating African features usually used affectionately between lovers, presumably because it is an insult in the public sphere; "*Javao*," refers to a black person with blond hair, and "*Indio*," refers to a person with "*Taino*" (Caribbean Native American) features including straight hair, dark skin, and small nose.

4. In keeping with feminist standpoint theory (Harding 1991), I find it important to account for myself in relation to my informants when reporting my findings and offering my analysis. Sandra Harding (1991) proposes that because knowledge is a social construction, researchers from non-dominant social backgrounds (e.g., women, African Americans) work from social locations that lead them challenge dominant assumptions, thereby critically strengthening academic knowledge.

5. I had come "under conviction" as Susan Harding (2000) so aptly describes of herself during her ethnography of the Moral Majority in the United States. With Harding, "I had been inhabited by the fundamentalist . . . tongue I was investigating" (Harding 2000, 34). As she points out, fundamentalists conceive of conversion as a process of entering a conversational relationship with God, and salvation involves appropriating the language of the saved, achieved when "the listener becomes a speaker" (Harding 2000, 34), conferring the narrative authority of the Holy Spirit onto the saved. A similar phenomenon of being inhabited by the spirits under study is described by Jeanne Favret-Saada (1980) in reference to bewitchment during field research.

6. As pointed out by feminist observers, Twelve-Step philosophy assumes that denial is the major barrier to recovery, that addicts hold on to a self-image as omnipotent and in control, an assumption that might not hold for women or other non-dominant groups (Saulnier 1996). This focus on denial could be a product of Alcoholics Anonymous' origins among white middle- to upper-class men: founder Bill W. was a businessman and co-founder Dr. Bob a licensed physician.

CHAPTER 2

1. Men and women at Victory Academy were required to sell chocolates on the streets to raise money for the academy, and to evangelize bystanders. Selling chocolates also was a part of Christian drug treatment: as Samaria told Alexis when Alexis said she was afraid of relapse while selling chocolates near her old drug-dealing haunts, "You need to learn to spread the word of God to them instead of seeing them as a source of drugs."

2. Pain is a part of many forms of addiction treatment, including that of therapeutic communities based on the model of Synanon (Weppner 1983) which sees confrontation and imposition of psychological and physical pain as a way to build character, and the Mexican *anexos* described by Angela Garcia (2015), which use beatings and physical discipline to change the behavior or addicted participants. What is unique about Pentecostal street ministries is that converts voluntarily accept their own pain—even seek out pain—and see suffering through pain as a route to a form of power.

3. Some historians identify Agnes Osman as black (*see* Alexander 2011).

4. Dayton (1987) takes on the complex task of tracing the theological roots of Pentecostalism, a movement that sees itself as unified by experience and narrative tradition rather than formal theology. Furthermore, it is an internally diverse movement encompassing independent churches and international missions, as well as charismatic congregations of Catholics and mainline Protestants. Nonetheless, Dayton is able to define the "Pentecostal

movement [as] that group of sects . . . characterized by belief that the occurrence mentioned in Acts 2 on the Day of the Pentecost not only signaled the birth of the church, but described an experience available to believers [in] all [historical] ages. The experience of enduement with power, called the 'baptism in the Holy Spirit', is believed to be evidenced by the accompanying sign of 'speaking with other tongues as the spirit gives utterance.' " (Dayton 1987, 24). As in the first-century church, the "modern believer becomes a disciple of Jesus Christ and receives the fullness of the Spirit's baptism in separate events or 'experiences' " (Dayton 1987, 26). Pentecostalism tends toward five recurring motifs: three works of grace (conversion, entire sanctification, and further baptism in the Holy Spirit as evidenced by speaking in tongues), divine healing by faith, and Jesus' second coming. Miracles, healing by faith, acts of the Spirit (such as glossolalia) are manifestations of the Holy Spirit's power; Pentecostals use these to argue that the gifts and miracles of Apostolic age, as described in the Book of Acts, are operative in modern times. These signs of the Holy Spirit are crucial because Pentecostal authority derives directly from Jesus and his apostles.

Dayton begins his theological history of Pentecostalism with Wesleyan Methodism, arguing that early nineteenth-century Wesleyan belief in human attainability of moral perfection was a precursor to the Holiness movement in the United States. The optimism of the Christian Perfectionism movement was later hampered by class and denominational conflicts deriving from immigration, urbanization, abolitionism, and the Civil War, however. Many churches turned to private devotion rather than public responsibility, through the experiential and "spiritual" mood of the Holiness movement. Holiness churches appealed to the (black and white) poor and lower middle classes in central cities. Rather than address social ills directly, they searched for the "power" to cope or sustain the self. In this way they sought to recover the balance between divine and human agency that was threatened by the Wesleyan emphasis on free will. The end of the nineteenth century saw a remarkable increase in interest in Holy Spirit; one theologian wrote in 1899 that more had been written and said upon the doctrine of the Holy Spirit than in the preceding 1,800 years.

Some Holiness revivalists began to speak of a doctrine of Pentecostal Spirit baptism after the civil war; they described baptism as "empowerment" through . . . 'a positive, specific, conscious instantaneous experience' " (Dayton 1987, 90). Holiness preachers increasingly linked Wesleyan themes of purity and spiritual cleansing to Pentecostal notions of the spiritual power manifest in healing and miracles. The three blessings teaching of late-nineteenth century Holiness preachers included three elements: the first blessing was spiritual cleansing (justification), the second was anointing as a priest mighty through God (sanctification), and the third was baptism in the Holy Spirit, which could manifest itself through prostration, ecstasy, and immediate laughter. In fact, by the time of Charles Parnham's New Year's Eve Bible school prayer meeting in 1899, accounts of glossolalia and prostration in Holiness churches had already generated years of controversy among Holiness followers. Pentecostal congregations eventually splintered from turn-of-the-century Holiness groups who suspected tongues as a sign of demonic possession rather than baptism.

5. The growth of Pentecostalism in industrial Puerto Rico was rivaled only by that in Central and South America. As of 1986, 20% of Guatemalans and 22% of Chileans were Pentecostal (Stoll 1990). Of the many competing explanations for this growth is that Pentecostalism appealed to a collectivist cultural ethos among recently urbanized low-income Latin Americans. The doctrine that any believer can become a minister, and the apprentice

system of pastoral training not requiring high levels of literacy or resources for ordination both contributed to the appeal and multiplication of Pentecostal groups (Matviuk 2002). Others argue that Pentecostalism appeals to Latin Americans because it preserves a not overly-rationalized Catholic worldview that accepts workings of the supernatural, while resisting the legalism and ritualism of the Catholic Church (Alvarez 2002). Chavan de Matviuk (2002) argues that Pentecostalism re-injected sacredness and transcendence of the religious experience among groups of people for whom experience and events were primary, faith and life were inseparable, but for whom Catholicism was emotionally remote. In fact, the Catholic Church found itself in competition with Pentecostals for Latin American souls and responded in at least two ways. First, politically progressive Catholic leaders espousing liberation theology have engaged Pentecostals in dialogue with the hope of fomenting an ecumenical movement for social change (Bergunder 2002). Second, Latin American Catholics, by undertaking charismatic renewal, have adopted a worship style which resembles that of Pentecostals (Chestnut 2003).

CHAPTER 3

1. At that moment in Puerto Rico, services accounted for 77% of the employment, less than 20% of the legally employed worked in manufacturing and only 3% worked in agriculture (CIA 2002).

2. In its testimony, the DEA also reported that "Puerto Rico has a local distribution market that is highly profitable. . . . The per kilogram price for cocaine in Puerto Rico is lower than anywhere else in the United States. . . . It is estimated that 20 percent of the drugs that transit the island stay there and are consumed by Puerto Ricans," leaving listeners to assume that those figures explained why "70 percent of all documented homicides in Puerto Rico are drug-related" and that "Puerto Rico also leads the nation in the number of car-jacking incidents" (U.S. DEA 1997). This testimony prompted Congress to allot $20 million for advanced equipment and special agents to coordinate operations in Puerto Rico, such as Operation SOS and Operation SOS II, which led to mass arrests of violent drug traffickers, mostly in the Ponce metropolitan area (Washington Office on Latin America 2002, U.S. DEA 2002).

3. I thank Rayna Rapp for pointing out that Oscar Lewis' views of the causes of were complex and not reflected in the uses that were later made of his culture of poverty theory. Lewis and his students, who edited *Peoples of Puerto Rico*, including Julian Steward, debated the effects that colonialism and neocolonialism had wrought on the inhabitants and the culture of the island (Roseberry 1978). His theory of the culture of poverty evolved over three books: in *5 families*, culture of poverty was seen as an effect of the social isolation into which rural-to-urban working-class migrants had been driven; it was only self-perpetuating because these families had no access to education, jobs, or social integration. By La Vida, it's an internalized discourse. He was Marxist in his belief in the causation of material conditions as these constructed culture, and in his later formulations of culture of poverty advanced a home-grown theory of "false consciousness."

4. Such images were reinforced by further social science studies of families, gender, and reproduction in Puerto Rico. Morris (1979) argued that in Puerto Rico male unemployment combined with the availability of welfare for single mothers had discouraged stable unions.

She also argued that welfare in particular had eliminated the need for wider kin networks and three-generation households that once compensated for absent fathers. Gurak and Falcón (1990) argue that common-law marriage and out-of-wedlock births were historically normative in Puerto Rico, explaining the disproportionate number of migrants to New York from Puerto Rico were single mothers, and thus the persistence of poverty among urban mainland Puerto Ricans.

5. Lemann (1991) called New York Puerto Ricans of the 1980s and '90s the true underclass, pointing out that they were even less likely to move out of poverty, and had worse social indicators (high school dropout and out-of-wedlock birth rates, high unemployment) than African Americans.

6. In 1978, among those corporations with the most plants in Puerto Rico were: Westinghouse, General Electric, Gulf & Western, Johnson and Johnson, Motorola, Squibb, Bell & Howell, Bristol-Myers, Du Pont, General Mills, Ralston Purina, RCA, and Colgate-Palmolive (Dietz 1986, 267).

7. Interview with Salvador Santiago, President of Carlos Albizu University, San Juan, Puerto Rico, January 12, 2002.

8. *Hogar Crea*, an international self-help group for addiction that was founded in Puerto Rico, based on the model of Synanon, is not considered an evangelical Christian or faith-based movement for purposes of this article. Its curriculum includes modules on spirituality but evangelism is not its central objective.

9. Most of the thirteen Christian addiction-rehabilitation programs I visited in my research either prohibited the use of medication for pain and withdrawal symptoms, or minimized the use of medication with the goal of teaching recruits to rely on prayer and other spiritual techniques for controlling their symptoms. There were some exceptions: a few programs with enough government funding to hire a staff physician used medications more liberally.

10. All interviews quoted in this chapter were translated from Spanish by the author.

11. Interview with Olga Rodríguez, Administrator, Hospital San Lucas, Ponce, Puerto Rico, January 12, 2001.

12. Radio Revelacion. Guayama, Puerto Rico. September 11, 2000.

CHAPTER 4

1. Brusco's findings were consistent with classic historiography of nineteenth-century North American evangelical strategies of male domestication through temperance.

2. I take this phrase from Pierre Bourdieu in his discussion of habitus: the ways that cultural capital, or socially conveyed knowledge, is embodied and structures the way that people interpret and interact with their environment from birth. In this way, habitus is the product of prior experiences, from which people navigate social fields, using their bodily, almost automatic ("natural") sense of how to react to social scenarios (Bourdieu 1977, Bourdieu 1998).

3. From "shooting gallery" in English.

4. In the past, scholars have defined machismo as "culturally sanctioned displays of hypermasculinity" (Gilmore and Gilmore, 1979, 281) and identified its two central elements as physical aggression toward other males, and sexual aggression toward females (Ingoldsby 1991). The first element, that of physical strength and courage, is referred to in Spain as

"*hombría.*" Blok's (1981) symbolic analysis of the Mediterranean code of male honor under-
lying machismo ties together class, criminal subcultures, and industrial-state formation in
explaining the southern and rural European regional distribution of *hombría*. Blok argues
that in bureaucratized western Europe, as people became more dependent on state appara-
tuses for their protection and security, machismo subsided in mainstream society but
thrived in "peripheral subcultures" including bars, prisons, and organized crime—where
"rank and esteem are largely matters of sheer physical force" (Blok 1981, 435). Gilmore and
Gilmore (1979) focus on sexual aggressiveness in Andalucía and, in a parallel examination,
point to the socioeconomic and political marginality of the chronically unemployed male
farm workers in their study. Using psychoanalytic concepts of sex-role conflicts, they argue
that men's sexual aggressiveness toward women is a manifestation of their lack of an ideo-
logically consonant gender role in Andalusian society. Women, the major breadwinners,
control the domestic sphere, and only upper-class men hold power in the public political-
economic sphere. They point out that in this environment, fathers flee the matrifocal home
for male congregation points such as bars, deserting young sons who struggle with identity
separation from domineering female relatives by displaying sexual aggressiveness toward
and emotional detachment from women.

   Contemporary critics of these classical formulations of machismo in Iberian and Latin
American societies have pointed to their one-dimensional portrayal of men in these societies, and to the fact that they fail to consider the extent to which images of machismo are
generated in varying times and places to support specific national, class-based or racial
ideologies. Gutmann, for example, cites the role of Mexican cowboy cinema of the 1940s, as
well as the post-revolutionary Mexican State's search for a national icon, in popularizing
machismo as the image of Mexican masculinity. As evidence of the contextually varying
quality of machismo, Gutmann points out that macho has been "considered brutish, gallant
or cowardly" for various sectors of Mexican society over time (Gutmann 2000). He argues
that although post-war nationalists emphasized the personal valor of Mexican "manliness,"
the negative connotations of Mexican macho as being vulgar or misogynist have been
emphasized by upper-class Mexicans and by North Americans. Gutmann offers ethnographic evidence that Mexican men fall into a broad range of behaviors in family and public
life, all of which they portray as masculine.

   Ramirez (1999), who criticizes the use of the term "*machismo*" as applied to Puerto Rican
men, points out that scholars using the term confound *machismo* with general ideologies of
male supremacy, attribute to lower-class Latin American men negative traits which can be
found in other societies and classes, and confuse ideology with practice. He also argues that
they fail to consider empirical evidence that Puerto Rican men associate masculinity mainly
with a man's responsibility to his family as father and breadwinner. His own characterization
of Puerto Rican masculine ideology nonetheless emphasizes sexual domination of women,
competition with and demonstration of invulnerability to other men, and the fact that men
who are unable to fulfill the role of breadwinner keep their sense of masculinity intact by
exaggerating other traits, such as sexuality. As Ramirez states, "Sexuality, competition, and
power are elements that constitute the masculine ideologies . . . in all the societies through
time and space in which we men have imposed our hegemony" (Ramirez 1999, 42).

   5. A clinical version of this theory is "gender role stress," which refers to "men who fail to
live up to the traditional demands of masculinity [and who] can experience conflict-related

dissonance . . . and a strong propensity to engage in high-risk behaviors like high consumption of drugs. . . ." (Casas and Wagenheim 1994, 2). Another clinical formulation is "protest masculinity," which has been proposed to stem from the absence of male authority figures in pre-adolescent boys' upbringing, leading to a low degree of correction for aggressive male behavior in childhood (Broude 1990).

6. Scholar of masculinity Matthew Gutmann paraphrases Puerto Rican anthropologist Rafael Ramirez as saying "Risky behavior on the part of men is linked to unequal gender relations between men . . . and not to genetic, primordial features of masculinity" (Gutmann 2000, 545).

7. Scholars of kinship working outside of Latin America, such as Carol Stack (1974), have argued that such webs of obligation to and dependence on extended families represent a strategy for surviving poverty, and not an essentially ethnic mode of relating. DeVos (1993) points out that, even within Latin America, extended household composition is associated with socioeconomic status.

8. In contrast, Puerto Rican women's gender and family roles are bound together more rigidly. Women's substance use, multiple sex partners, and abandonment of their children exclude them from Puerto Rican mainstream female respectability in more permanent way. Women in treatment for addiction often highlight the role of the men in their lives in leading them into these behaviors, presenting themselves as marginalized by male domination rather than their own choices. As shown in Chapter 5, treatment for substance abuse also can bring into focus the problems of performing femininity.

9. Linda-Anne Rebhun describes a similar phenomenon in Brazil where working class people uphold an ideal of the male breadwinner despite higher levels of female employment: as she points out, working class men attempt to confine women to the home "where tension between the men's actual and expected economic power is greatest" (Rebhun 2005, 16).

10. Scholarship of such authors points to the role of religious institutions, private industry, and the State in defining gender and family roles and using such definitions for their purposes. Safa (1995a), for instance, argues that employers have leveraged the image of female workers as supplemental wage earners to justify paying them low wages and resisting demands to improve their working conditions. Martinez-Fernandez (2000) points to the historical role of Protestant churches and the State in promoting marriage among the poor in Puerto Rico. In the nineteenth century, the Catholic Church required such high sacramental fees and extensive documentation for marriage ceremonies that only the wealthy—who had much at stake in the form of the social and economic capital to be gained through legal marriage—pursued legal marriage. The early Protestant missionaries, with in interest in gaining converts, made marriage ceremonies affordable and accessible. They were supported of the Puerto Rican State, which gained social control through the documentation of married citizens who became less geographically mobile after marriage. Thus, in the nineteenth and early twentieth century, the Protestants and the State collaborated to promote the legally recognized nuclear family unit among the lower classes.

11. Salles and Tuiran (1997) contend that conjugal ties and normative gender roles in the Latin American extended family have been weakened in the course of industrial modernization by high divorce and separation rates, increased rates of premarital sex among women, a large variety of family types (reconstituted, single-parent), increases in women's wage labor, and increases in the number of families living in poverty. Others argue that the claims and

buffers of the extended family (often female headed, often reconstituted with fictive or distant kin) always have been important tools of survival for the poor among whom the
patriarchal ideal is unattainable, although under these circumstances women must "manipu-
late concepts of domestic virtue to justify and lend moral weight to their political and
economic activities outside the family home" because this is where the "tension between
men's actual and expected economic power is greatest" (Rebhun 2005, 16). Historical exami-
nations of family life in Latin America and the Caribbean have pointed to the "high rates
of illegitimacy, concubinage, and female-headed households" that were ubiquitous among
mestizos, Indians, and blacks, and are a result of economic necessity, heritage of non-
European family practices, and the incomplete colonial imposition of the European patriarchal ideal (Potthast-Jukheit 1997).

12. As an indication of how central family membership is to Puerto Rican social identity, a study of homeless men and women in San Juan found that initially none of the
respondents admitted to having any family whatsoever. Further questioning revealed that
the majority of respondents said they were homeless because of family neglect (Julia and
Harnett 1999). The authors attributed the homeless respondents' denial that they had a family to their desire to save the family name from shame by absolving the family from responsibility for neglect (Julia and Harnett 1999). Another possible interpretation is that the
responses of homeless Puerto Ricans hinged on the meaning of "family" itself. For them, is
"family" defined by biology, or by behavior? Perhaps they saw themselves as without family
because no biological relative fulfilled the obligations of a family member.

13. Literature on Latin American evangelists' models of the family is scarce, but contemporary North American evangelicals openly debate the role of patriarchy and the nature of
authority in the family. For example, studies of evangelicals' best-selling manuals on the
family reveal disagreement among authors regarding the interpretation of biblical scripture
on gender and the family, and the conflicting models of spousal authority that result despite
uniform belief in biblical inerrancy. The more authoritarian manuals cite Ephesians 5,
which in effect says that men are the head of women as Christ is the head of the Church. The
fateful and independent actions of Eve in Genesis 3 is interpreted as a "confirmation of
the pitfalls of feminine leadership in marriage" (Bartowski 1997, 11). Divine commands
for patriarchal household authority rest on sharp distinctions between "masculine" traits
of logic and assertiveness and "feminine" traits of responsiveness, vulnerability, and
desire for relational stability. Other more egalitarian commentators interpret the word
"head" literally to mean a part of a larger body, interdependent with other parts. They argue
that men and women are "joint heirs" of God's grace and must make decisions collabora-
tively. In the process, they appeal either to gender sameness or to the complementarity
of gender qualities (e.g., masculine initiative and feminine intuition) in making decisions.
Other studies of gender roles within evangelical families have concluded that evangelicals
hold onto symbolic traditionalism, espousing male headship as an ideological tool to
maintain their sense of distinctiveness from secular culture, while practicing pragmatic
egalitarianism in the home (i.e., female wage earners, shared decision making) (Gallagher
and Smith 1999). Interview and participant observation data from a study of conservative
Protestant families in Texas found that gender relations in these families combined elements of traditional and progressive practices, revealing wage-earning, child-rearing, and
household chores to be topics of negotiation between spouses that—although mediated by

conservative religious ideologies—led couples to a wide array of arrangements with regard to sharing and responsibility. Study participants invoked individual preference, personal needs, and notions of fairness distinctive to their domestic arrangement to explain their arrangements, rather than the dominant evangelical discourse of biblical gender essentialism (Bartowski 1999).

Gender roles within the family have been the organizing force for recent popular movements among U.S. evangelical Christians. The best known of these, the Promise Keepers, is organization established in 1990 in Boulder, Colorado, grew to a membership of 280,000 men by 1995. They have held mass rallies in many major U.S. cities and inspired the publication of Christian men's journals, centering on each man's promise to practice spiritual, moral, ethical, and sexual purity; to build strong marriages, support their local church and pastor; and work for ecumenical and interracial unity. At the core of the Promise Keepers' platform, however, is that the (traditional nuclear) family is the only viable foundation for a successful society, and that this calls upon men to act as responsible fathers and husbands (Parker 1995). In fact, data from the National Survey of Families and Households indicates that, counter to stereotypes of stern patriarchal authoritarianism, conservative Protestant men are more likely than their non-evangelical counterparts to engage in paternal supervision and emotionally expressive parenting (Bartowski and Xu 2000).

Conversely, corresponding evangelical women's groups, such as Chosen Women, urge women "to be focused on the family and complement, not compete, with men" (Goodale 1997). Ironically, turn-of-the-century Pentecostal denominations demonstrated far more leadership by women than seen at the end of the century. Early Pentecostal Bible schools, such as the Bethel Bible College in Kansas, ordained women pastors; the Church of God granted women ministerial licenses starting in 1909; and the Assemblies of God ordained women at its first General Council in 1914. Women also founded several Pentecostal denominations, such as Florence Crawford, founder of the Apostolic Faith Mission, and Amie Semple McPherson founder of the International Church of the Foursquare Gospel. It was not until the post–World War II era that Pentecostals allied themselves with male-led evangelicalism, and in their aspiration to middle-class status embraced the symbol of the stay-at-home mother (Roebuck 1998).

14. As historian Margaret Lamberts Bendroth (1999) points out, ironically, turn-of-the-century fundamentalist U.S. Christians from whom later evangelical movements developed avoided the issue of family life except as a way to draw lines separating them from the surrounding culture. Indeed, concerns about family life, and in particular the responsibility of fathers to guide and nurture their children as contemporary evangelicals articulate it, were considered by early fundamentalists as "a worldly metaphor of personal compromise and secular burdens" (49). The Victorian domestic ideal and veneration of the home against which early fundamentalists were reacting was to the fundamentalists a form of idolatry, full of sentimentality which enshrined women as mothers and saintly protectors, all but absolving them of original sin. This fundamentalism defined itself within the conventions of masculine individualism, adopting "Christ's lonely example as a model of holiness," and rejecting "the conflation of godliness with the middle-class family, and along with it the pious notion that the outside world was an extension of the home, waiting to be 'domesticated' by middle-class, white women" (40). What little literature early fundamentalists produced on the family emphasized order and discipline, the rejection of psychological experts

and their nurturant, relational language, as well as the "foolish theory that love can rule adequately without punishment for sin" (Rice as cited in Lamberts Bendroth 41).

The story of how an expressive ideal of family life came to dominate the descendants of these fundamentalists, the neo-evangelicals, involves a cultural shift in postwar America from the Victorian language of order and duty to the "new ethic of individual self-expression" (42). As television and radio invaded even fundamentalist homes, rising middle-class divorce rates starting in the 1950s, followed by debates about contraception, abortion, and homosexuality, and the growing neo-evangelical movement's discovery that family matters resonated with churchgoers, led neo-evangelicals who emerged from the fundamentalist tradition to adopt the pro-family movement as a way to distinguish themselves from the surrounding culture and the unrighteous. Pro-family neo-evangelicals such as James Dobson and Bill Gothard negotiated between older fundamentalist authoritarianism and the new relational language of childrearing. Yet, the politicization of fundamentalism represented by Jerry Falwell's Moral Majority was quite controversial among fundamentalists, who expressed distaste for worldly, political engagement even in the name of evangelism. Even so, neo-evangelical preachers found that they could "evoke a separatist fundamentalist past and speak a prophetic word to present-day American culture" (48) by advancing a pro-family agenda (Lamberts Bendroth 1999).

CHAPTER 5

1. Early twentieth-century Pentecostal Bible schools such as Bethel Bible College in Kansas ordained women pastors, the Church of God granted women ministerial licenses starting in 1909, and the Assemblies of God ordained women at its first General Council in 1914. Women also founded several Pentecostal denominations, such as Florence Crawford, founder of the Apostolic Faith Mission, and Amiee Semple McPherson of the international Church of the Foursquare Gospel. It was not until after World War II that Pentecostals allied themselves with male-dominated evangelical denominations, and in their aspiration to middle-class status embraced the symbol of the stay-at-home mother (Roebuck 1998).

2. Other reports on Pentecostalism in the Caribbean have reached opposite conclusions about the effects of anti-Marionism on Pentecostal gender ideology: Boudewijnse's (1998) study of Pentecostal Catholics in the Antilles found that women prayer leaders refused to pray the Hail Mary, because they rejected the double standards of womanhood promoted by the image of Mary for an alternative, gender-neutral ideal of "personhood" promoted by a focus on the Holy Spirit.

3. Summarizing her review of a second generation of scholarship on women in Latin America, Susan Tiano points to the recurrent theme that, "Traditional gender roles have resisted the potentially transformative effect of women's employment" (Tiano 2001). That is to say that, despite male unemployment and female breadwinning patterns in industrial and post-industrial Latin America, men have maintained the image of household head and key provider as their female partners subscribed to subordinate positions despite their economic power as wage-earning women.

4. Take enough drugs to prevent the onset of withdrawal symptoms.

5. Stevens (1973a, 1973b) observed that in Mexico and other parts of Latin America, women exercised moral authority in the domestic sphere, and their children and husbands

nearly worshiped them as mothers, making themselves dependent on women for suste-nance and approval. Stevens theorized that this stemmed from the icon of the Virgin Mary in popular Catholicism, and coined the term "*marianismo*" to denote the sexual naivete, self-sacrificial suffering, and confinement to the domestic sphere that was the source of moral authority for many women in Latin America. In her model, women earn respect and influence to the extent that they conform to the *marianismo* ideal. Critiques of *marianismo* include that of Ehlers (1991) who argues that Stevens based her theory on observations of middle-class Mexican women, while working-class Latin American women report they are subservient in the public sphere only because of their economic need for support from men.

6. Joanne Pessaro (1996) traces the institutional effects of the trope of women-as-victims in her ethnography of male homelessness in New York City: Women and their chil-dren were seen by policy makers as appropriate recipients of social services (conditional on their submission to bureaucratic authority), and men were not.

7. Helen Safa (1995a) describes the extension of the welfare to support for single moth-ers with children in the wake of male unemployment as a symbolic and economic replace-ment of male breadwinner by the state.

CHAPTER 6

1. A more in-depth study of trends in the Puerto Rican media would investigate the motivations and intended target of the media decision makers responsible for this recurrent theme of addiction. One suggestive observation, however, is that these stories ran contem-poraneously with the 1990s peak in U.S. and Puerto Rican narcotics law enforcement efforts on the island, a time during which politicians sought public support for increased funding for the War on Drugs.

2. I credit Linda-Anne Rebhun with helping me to articulate this point.

CHAPTER 7

1. Pierre Bourdieu's concept of habitus goes beyond individual habituation; in his ver-sion, embodied, everyday senses of self are deeply rooted in the societal structures and in the historical moment in which an individual develops in interaction with his or her social milieu. Such structural elements of the embodied self cannot be changed through individ-ual practices alone.

2. Ironically, psychiatrists rate themselves as less spiritual than other professionals of other medical specialties (Galanter 2010, Galanter et al. 2007), possibly because psychiatry is close to actual pastoral care. It is, in fact, in competition with it.

3. Post-modern theorist Michel Foucault famously critiqued the moral therapies of eighteenth-century asylums as technologies of social control that subjugated bodies to pre-viously unknown levels of institutional surveillance by doctors and custodians (Foucault 1965). Contemporary ministries and addiction clinics are less centered on surveillance than on self-regulation, however; they are more legible in terms of Foucault's theory of biopower, in which individuals internalize self-discipline as a route to health and citizenship (Foucault 1998). Foucaultian theorists have argued that contemporary psychotherapy replaced the

asylum as a technology that, over time, operates within the individual, without the surveillance of doctors and other custodians (Rose 1998). Yet street ministries and Ruben's clinic demonstrate that institutional moral therapies endure, and that these institutions not only delimit and control selves, they also produce selves through ritual bodily practices, as well as through alternative homes, kin, and vocations.

4. The idea that people in psychic distress should rebuild themselves through communal acts is not new. In fact, it is central to two major recovery movements in the United States. One of them is focused addiction and is rooted in the chronic disease concept of Twelve-Step programs such as Alcoholics Anonymous—that addiction is incurable and lifelong—making recovery a process of abstinence maintenance that is never complete, that requires constant vigilance through group ritual and self-improvement (Watson 2012). The other version of recovery involves people living with diagnoses of severe mental illness and is simultaneously a clinical outcome, an adaptation to disability, and a politics of recognition. The clinical outcome concept of recovery stems from epidemiological evidence that people diagnosed with schizophrenia—a condition thought to be biological and unremitting—improve over time, even without medication, when living in community settings. This concept of recovery as adaptation to disability stems from the field of psychiatric rehabilitation that focuses on overcoming limitations and living in society through interventions such as transitional housing and sheltered employment. The identity politics concept of recovery emerged from former and current patients calling themselves consumers and survivors of psychiatric treatment who had experienced violence in psychiatric facilities—physical restraints, heavy sedation, and abusive hospital staff (Jacobson 2004). They organized to reclaim their personhood and political citizenship as "mad pride," modeled on gay pride and black pride movements of the civil rights era, which challenges the ethic of normality and social conformity implied by the disease model of mental distress (B. Lewis 2013). Following decades of reducing the number of available mental hospital beds and increasing reliance on psychotropic medication ushered in by second-generation antipsychotics and antidepressants (Prozak and other serotonin reuptake inhibitors), in the 1990s mental-health policy makers and the federal Substance Abuse and Mental Health Services Administration adopted the language of recovery. They were reacting to the narrowness of psychiatry's attempt to control symptoms with medication, asserting that a sense of meaning, purpose, and community, and the cultivation of hope are crucial elements of treatment (SAMHSA 2012). Like Twelve-Step programs, mental health recovery revives the pastoral ethos of self-cultivation.

5. Biomedicine has incorporated socially mediated approaches to mental health that draw on religious traditions other than Christianity. Buddhist mindfulness, for example, is now making an appearance in U.S. addiction psychiatry (Dermatis and Egelko 2014), and in dialectical behavioral treatment for "borderline personality," a disorder that is associated with addiction, in which people experience a thin sense of self and conflict in intimate relationships (Linehan et al. 2006). In contrast with Christian prescriptions for self-cultivation, dharma portrays the individual self as a delusion, as something to be overcome that is a barrier to compassion, rather than something to be discovered and developed. Rather than establishing a new metaphorical home and family in Christ, Buddhist practice aims to help people to see their emotional need for environmental constancy and markers of self-hood as illusory, and, in their stead, to build a sense of connection to all living beings and

places. Traumatic displacement, therefore, is addressed by overcoming one's attachment to place and to self (S. Lewis 2013). Yet, as in the Christian pastoral, the end goal is still securing one's relationship to a greater whole.

6. This has been underscored by anthropologists such as Michael Taussig in his classic ethnography of indigenous Central Americans who, in their transition from barter to cash-based economies, circulated rumors of people who made living sacrifices to the Devil to multiply their money (Taussig 1980).

7. Marx wrote about the limits of such struggle in the Eighteenth Brumaire: "Men make their own history, but they do not make it as they please . . . but under circumstances existing already, given and transmitted from the past" (Marx 1937).

BIBLIOGRAPHY

Abel, David. 1998. "Puerto Rico: Back Door for Drug Trafficking in the U.S." *Christian Science Monitor* 90(245): 3.

Acosta-Belén, Edna. 1986. "Puerto Rican Women in Culture, History, and Society." In *The Puerto Rican Woman: Perspectives on Culture, History and Society*, edited by Edna Acosta-Belén. New York: Praeger.

Addenbrooke, Mary. 2015. "Jung and the Labyrinth of Addiction." *AA Agnostica.* http://aaagnostica.org/2015/07/01/jung-and-the-labyrinth-of-addiction/. Accessed December 4, 2017.

Agar, Michael. 2003. "The Story of Crack: Towards a Theory of Illicit Drug Trends." *Addiction Research and Theory* 11(1): 3–29.

Agar, Michael and Heather Schacht Reisinger. 2002. "A Heroin Epidemic at the Intersection of Histories: The 1960's Epidemic Among African Americans in Baltimore." *Medical Anthropology* 21: 115–156.

Alaniz, Maria Louisa. 2002. "Migration, Acculturation, Displacement: Migratory Workers and 'Substance Abuse'." *Substance Use & Misuse* 37(8–10): 1253–1257.

Alcoholics Anonymous. 2004. "The Twelve Steps of Alcoholics Anonymous." March 11, 2004. www.alcoholics-anonymous.org.

Alegría, M., T. McGuire, M. Vera, G. Canino, D. Freeman, L. Matías, C. Albizu, H. Marín, and J. Calderón. 2001/2002. "The Impact of Managed Care on the Use of Outpatient Mental Health and Substance Abuse Services in Puerto Rico." *Inquiry* 38: 381–395.

Alexander, Bobby. 1991. *Victor Turner Revisited: Ritual As Social Change.* Atlanta, GA: Scholar's Press.

Alexander, Estrelda. 2011. *Black Fire: One Hundred Years of African American Pentecostalism.* Wheaton, IL: InterVarsity Press.

Alexander, Michelle. 2012. *The New Jim Crow: Mass Incarceration in the Age of Colorblindness.* New York: The New Press.

Alvarez, Miguel. 2002. "The South and the Latin American Paradigm of the Pentecostal Movement." *Asian Journal of Pentecostal Studies* 5(1): 135–153.

American Psychiatric Association (APA). 1994. *Diagnostic and Statistical Manual of Psychiatric Disorders: DSM IV.* Washington, DC: APA.

Anderson, Elijah. 1990. *Streetwise: Race, Class and Change in an Urban Community.* Chicago: University of Chicago Press.

Andreasen, Nancy. 2010. "Posttraumatic Stress Disorder: A History and a Critique." *Annals of the New York Academy of Sciences* 1208(1): 67–71.

Arias, Elizabeth and Alberto Palloni. 1999. "Prevalence and Patterns of Female Headed Households in Latin America: 1970–1990." *Journal of Comparative Family Studies* 30(2): 257–279.

Asad, Talal. 1993. *Genealogies of Religion: Discipline and Reasons of Power in Christianity and Islam.* Baltimore, MD: Johns Hopkins University Press.

Ashley, Olivia Silber, Mary Ellen Marsden, and Thomas M. Brady. 2003. "Effectiveness of Substance Abuse Treatment Programming for Women: A Review." *The American Journal of Drug and Alcohol Abuse* 29(1): 19–53.

Associated Press. 1999. "Censan en 50 mil los Adictos." *El Nuevo Día,* January 24.

Badger, Emily. 2015. "How Mass Incarceration Creates 'Million Dollar Blocks' in Poor Neighborhoods." *Washington Post,* July 30. https://www.washingtonpost.com/news/wonk/wp/2015/07/30/how-mass-incarceration-creates-million-dollar-blocks-in-poor-neighborhoods/?utm_term=.327b286fa205.

Bartowski, John. 1997. "Debating Patriarchy: Discursive Disputes Over Spousal Authority Among Evangelical Family Commentators." *Journal for the Scientific Study of Religion* 36(3): 393–401.

Bartowski, John. 1999. "One Step Forward, One Step Back: 'Progressive Traditionalism' and the Negotiation of Domestic Labor in Evangelical Families." *Gender Issues* 17(4): 37–61.

Bartowski, John and Xiaohe Xu. 2000. "Distant Patriarchs or Expressive Dads? The Discourse and Practice of Fathering in Conservative Protestant Families." *Sociological Quarterly* 41(3): 465–485.

Baum, Dan. 1997. *Smoke and Mirrors: The War on Drugs and the Politics of Failure.* Boston: Little and Brown.

Bauza, N. 1986. "Aumenta el Uso de 'Coca' en P.R." *El Reportero,* February 27, p. 14.

Baxter, Megan. 2011. " 'Would You Sell Yourself for a Drink, Boy?' Masculinity and Christianity in the Ontario Temperance Movement." *Historical Papers.*

Becker, Howard. 1963. *Outsiders: Studies in the Sociology of Deviance.* New York: The Free Press.

Becker, Howard, Blanche Geer, Everett Hughes, and Anslem Straus. 1961. *Boys in White: Student Culture in Medical School.* Chicago: University of Chicago Press.

Bergunder, Michael. 2002. "America: Sociological Theories and Theological Debates." *International Review of the Pentecostal Movement and Basic Ecclesiastical Communities in Latin Mission* 91(361): 163–186.

Berkley Fletcher, Holly. 2007. *Gender and the American Temperance Movement in the Nineteenth Century.* NY: Routledge.

Biehl, João and Peter Locke. 2010. "Deleuze and the Anthropology of Becoming." *Current Anthropology* 50(3): 317–351.

Biehl, João with Torben Eskerod. 2005. *Vita: Life in a Zone of Social Abandonment*. Berkeley: University of California Press.

Blasor, Lorraine. 1998. "Deficiente Atención a Salud Mental." *El Star*. December 30, n.p.

Blok, Anton. 1981. "Rams and Billy-Goats: A Key to the Mediterranean Code of Honour." *Man* 16(3):427–440.

Boddy, Janice. 1989. *Wombs and Alien Spirits: Women, Men, and the Zar Cult in Northern Sudan*. Madison: University of Wisconsin Press.

Bomann, Rebecca Pierce. 1999. *Faith in the Barrios: The Pentecostal Poor in Bogota*. Boulder, CO: Lynn Rienner Publishers.

Booth, Cathy and Tammerlin Drummond. 1996. "Caribbean Blizzard." *Time* 147(9): 46.

Borges, Guilherme, Maria Elena Medina-Mora, Joshua Breslau, and Sergio Aguilar-Gaxiola. 2007. "The Effect of Migration to the United States on Substance Use Disorders Among Returned Mexican Migrants and Families of Migrants." *American Journal of Public Health* 97(10): 1847–1851.

Boudewijnse, Barbara. 1998. "A Farewell to Mary? Women, Pentecostal Faith, and the Roman Catholic Church on Curacao, N.A." In *More Than Opium: An Anthropological Approach to Latin American and Caribbean Pentecostal Praxis*, edited by Barbara Boudewijnse, Andre Droogers, and Frans Kamsteeg. Lanham, MD: The Scarecrow Press.

Bourdieu, Pierre. 1977. *Outline of a Theory of Practice*. New York: Cambridge University Press.

Bourdieu, Pierre. 1984. *Distinction: A Social Critique of the Judgement of Taste*. London: Routledge.

Bourdieu, Pierre. 1986. "The Forms of Capital." In *Handbook of Theory and Research for the Sociology of Education*, edited by John Richardson. Westport, CT: Greenwood Press.

Bourdieu, Pierre. 1998. *Practical Reason: On the Theory of Action*. Stanford: Stanford University Press.

Bourgois, Philippe. 1995. *In Search of Respect: Dealing Crack in El Barrio*. New York: Cambridge University Press.

Bourgois, Philippe. 1998a. "Just Another Night in the Shooting Gallery." *Theory Culture and Society* 15(2): 37–66.

Bourgois, Philippe 1998b. "The Moral Economy of Homeless Heroin Addicts: Confronting Ethnography, HIV Risk, and Everyday Violence in San Francisco Shooting Encampments." *Substance Use and Misuse* 33(11): 2323–2351.

Bourgois, Philippe. 2000. "Disciplining Addictions: The Bio-Politics of Methadone and Heroin in the United States." *Culture, Medicine and Psychiatry* 24(2): 165–195.

Bourgois, Philippe. 2002. "Resistance and Self-Destruction Under U.S. Apartheid." In *Anthropology for the World*, edited by MacClancy. New Haven: Yale University Press.

Bourgois, Phillipe. 2001. "The Power of Violence in War and Peace: Post-Cold War Lessons from El Salvador." *Ethnography* 2(1): 5–37.

Bourgois, Philippe and Jeffrey Schonberg. 2009. *Righteous Dopefiend*. Berkeley: University of California Press.

Bowler, Kate. 2013. *Blessed: A History of the American Prosperity Gospel*. New York: Oxford University Press.

Brenneman, Robert. 2011. *Homies and Hermanos: God and Gangs in Central America*. New York: Oxford University Press.

Briggs, Laura. 2002. "La Vida, Moynihan, and Other Libels: Migration, Social Science, and the Making of the Puerto Rican Welfare Queen." *Centro Journal* 14(1): 75–101.

Broude, Gwen. 1990. "Protest Masculinity: A Further Look at the Causes and the Concept." *Ethos* 18(1): 103–122.

Brusco, Elizabeth. 1995. *The Reformation of Machismo*. Austin: University of Texas Press.

Buckley, William 1998. "Misfire on Puerto Rico." *National Review* (April 6): 62–63.

Burrus, Virginia. 2004. *The Sex Lives of Saints: An Erotics of Ancient Hagiography*. Philadelphia: University of Pennsylvania Press.

Campbell, Nancy, J. P. Olsen, and Luke Walden. 2008. *The Narcotic Farm: The Rise and Fall of America's First Prison for Drug Addicts*. New York: Abrams.

Carr, E. Summerson. 2010. *Scripting Addiction: The Politics of Therapeutic Talk and American Sobriety*. Princeton: Princeton University Press.

CASA (National Center on Addiction and Substance Abuse at Columbia University) (2009). "Shoveling Up II: The Impact of Substance Abuse on Federal, State and Local Budgets." www.casacolumbia.org/templates/publications_reports.aspx.

Casas, Manuel and Burl Wagenheim. 1994. "Hispanic Masculinity: Myth or Psychological Schema Meriting Clinical Consideration." *Hispanic Journal of Behavioral Sciences* 16(3): 315–332.

Casriel, Daniel and Grover Amen. 1971. *Daytop: Three Addicts and Their Cure*. New York: Hill and Wang.

Casselberry, Judith. 2017. *The Labor of Faith: Gender and Power in Black Apostolic Pentecostalism*. Durham: Duke University Press.

Castaneda, X., V. Ortiz, B. Allen, C. Garcia, and M. Hernandez-Avila. 1996. "Sex Masks: The Double Life of Female Commercial Sex Workers in Mexico City." *Culture, Medicine and Psychiatry* 20: 228–247.

Castro Martin, Teresa. 2002. "Consensual Unions in Latin America: Persistence of a Dual Nuptiality System." *Journal of Comparative Family Studies* 33(1): 35–55.

Centers for Disease Control (CDC). 2001. "Basic Statistics—Ten States/Territories and Cities Reporting the Highest Number of AIDS Cases." Electronic document. www.cdc.gov /hiv/stats/topten.htm. Accessed June 6, 2003.

Central Intelligence Agency (CIA). 2002. "The World Factbook 2002—Puerto Rico." Electronic document. www.cia.gov/cia/publications/factbook/geos/rq.html. Accessed February 11, 2005.

Centro de Estudios en Adicción. 1997. *Directorio de Recursos y Servicios Sobre Adicción, VIH y SIDA*. Bayamón, Puerto Rico: Universidad Central del Caribe.

Chalk, Peter. 2011. *The Latin American Drug Trade: Scope, Dimensions, Impact, and Response*. Santa Monica, CA: Rand Corporation.

Chavan de Matviuk, Marcela. 2002. "Latin American Pentecostal Growth: Culture, Orality and the Power of Testimonies." *Asian Journal of Pentecostal Studies* 5(2): 205–222.

Chavez, Linda. 1998. "No to Puerto Rican Statehood." *Human Events* 54(9): 1.

Chestnut, R. Andrew. 2003. "A Preferential Option for the Spirit: The Catholic Charismatic Renewal in Latin America's New Religious Economy." *Latin American Politics and Society* 45(1): 55–85.

Chitando, Ezra. 2013. " 'Faithful Men of a Faithful God'? Masculinities in the Zimbabwe Assemblies of God Africa." *Exchange* 42.1: 34–50.

Christensen, Edward. 1979. "The Puerto Rican Woman: A Profile." In *The Puerto Rican Woman*, edited by Edna Acosta-Belén and Elia Hidalgo Christensen. New York: Praeger Press.

Christie, Edward. 2004. "Self-Mastery and Submission: Holiness and Masculinity in the Lives of Anglo-Saxon Martyr Kings." In *Holiness and Masculinity in the Middle Ages* edited by P. H. Cullum and Katherine J. Lewis. Cardiff: University of Wales Press.

Clark, T. 1995. "Prohibition in Puerto Rico, 1917–1933." *Journal of Latin American Studies* 27: 77–97.

Cleary, Edward and Hannah Stewart-Gambino. 1997. *Power, Politics and Pentecostals in Latin America*. Boulder: Westview Press.

Clifford, James. 2008. "The Others: Beyond the 'Salvage' Paradigm." *Third Text* 3(6): 73–78.

Cockburn, Andrew. 2003. "True Colors." *National Geographic* 203(3): 34–56.

Colombani, J. 2001. "Crean Pipas Para 'el Tape'." *El Nuevo Día*, June 4, p. 36.

Comaroff, Jean. 1985. *Body of Power, Spirit of Resistance: The Culture and History of a South African People*. Chicago: University of Chicago Press.

Comaroff, Jean, and John L. Comaroff. 2000. "Millennial Capitalism: First Thoughts on a Second Coming." *Public Culture* 12(2): 291–343.

Connor, Michael. 2013. "Analysis: Puerto Rico's Population Drops as Economy Wobbles." Reuters. September 10. https://www.reuters.com/article/us-puertorico-population-analysis/analysis-puerto-ricos-population-drops-as-economy-wobbles-idUSBRE9890JZ20130910.

Conroy, Bill. 2012. "Drug War-Related Homicides in the US Average at Least 1.100 a Year." Narconews.com. *The Narcosphere*. March 10. https://narcosphere.narconews.com/notebook/bill-conroy/2012/03/drug-war-related-homicides-us-average-least-1100-year.

Copeland, Jan, and Wayne Hall. 1992. "A Comparison of Women Seeking Drug and Alcohol Treatment in a Specialist Women's and Two Traditional Mixed-Sex Treatment Services." *Addiction* 87(9): 1293–1302.

Cortes, Dharma. 1995. "Variations in Familism in Two Generations of Puerto Ricans." *Hispanic Journal of Behavioral Sciences* 17(2): 249–256.

Courtwright, David, Joseph, Herman, and Don Des Jarlais. 1989. *Addicts Who Survived: An Oral History of Narcotic Use in America, 1923–1965*. Knoxville: University of Tennessee Press.

Covington, Herbert E., Ian Maze, HaoSheng Sun, Howard Bomze, Kristine DeMaio, Emma Wu, and David M. Dietz. 2011. "A Role for Repressive Histone Methylation in Cocaine-Induced Vulnerability to Stress." *Neuron* 71(4): 656–670.

Covington, Stephanie. 2002. "Helping Women Recover: Creating Gender-Responsive Treatment." In *The Handbook of Addiction Treatment for Women: Theory and Practice*, edited by S. L. A. Straussner & S. Browns. Indianapolis, IN: Jossey-Bass.

Cox, Harvey. 1994. *Fire from Heaven: The Rise of Pentecostal Spirituality and the Reshaping of Religion in the Twenty-First Century*. Boston, MA: Addison-Wesley Publishing Company.

Craun, Christopher. 2004. "Matronly Monks: Theodore of Cyrrhus' Sexual Imagery in the Historia Religiosa." In *Holiness and Masculinity in the Middle Ages,* edited by P. H. Cullum and Katherine J. Lewis. Cardiff: University of Wales Press.

Cruz, Nicky and Jamie Buckingham. 1968. *Run Baby Run*. Plainfield, NJ: Logos Books.

Csordas, Thomas. 1994. *The Sacred Self: A Cultural Phenomenology of Charismatic Healing.* Berkeley: University of California Press.

Csordas, Thomas. 2009. *Transnational Transcendence: Essays on Religion and Globalization.* Berkeley: University of California Press.

Damphousse, Kelly and Howard Kaplan. 1998. "Intervening Processes Between Adolescent Drug Use and Psychological Distress: An Examination of the Self-Medication Hypothesis." *Social Behavior and Personality: An International Journal* 26(2): 115–131.

Das, Veena, and Shalini Randeria. 2015. "Politics of the Urban Poor: Aesthetics, Ethics, Volatility, Precarity: An Introduction to Supplement 11." *Current Anthropology* 56(S11): S3–S14.

Davila, Arlene. 1997. *Sponsored Identities: Cultural Politics in Puerto Rico.* Philadelphia: Temple University Press.

Davis, Kenneth. 1994. *Primero Dios: Alcoholics Anonymous and the Hispanic Community.* Selinsgrove: Susquehanna University Press.

Dayton, Donald. 1987. *Theological Roots of Pentecostalism.* Metuchen, NJ: The Scarecrow Press.

de Certeau, Michel. 1984. *The Practice of Everyday Life,* translated by Steven Rendall. Berkeley: University of California Press.

Dei, Kojo. 2002. *Ties that Bind: Youth and Drugs in a Black Community.* Prospect Heights, IL: Waveland Press.

Deleuze, Gilles. 1988. *Foucault.* New York: Athlone Press.

Deleuze, Gilles, and Constantin V. Boundas. 1993. *The Deleuze Reader.* New York: Columbia University Press.

Delgado, Melvin and Hilda Rivera. 1997. "Puerto Rican Natural Support Systems." *Urban Education* 32(1): 81–98.

Delvecchio Good, Mary-Jo. 2001. "The Biotechnical Embrace." *Culture, Medicine and Psychiatry* 25(4): 395–410.

Dermatis, Helen, and Susan Egelko. 2014. "Buddhist Mindfulness As an Influence in Recent Empirical CBT Approaches to Addiction: Convergence with the Alcoholics Anonymous Model." *Alcoholism Treatment Quarterly* 32(2–3): 194–213.

DeVos, Susan. 1993. "Is There a Socioeconomic Dimension to Household Extension in Latin America?" *Journal of Comparative Family Studies* 24(1): 21–35.

Dick B. 2005. "Alcoholics Anonymous History." Electronic document. www.dickb.com /index.shtml. Accessed April 20, 2005.

Dietz, James 1986. *Economic History of Puerto Rico: Institutional Change and Capitalist Development.* Princeton, NJ: Princeton University Press.

Dietz, James. 2003. *Puerto Rico: Negotiating Development and Change.* Boulder, CO: Lynne Rienner Publishers.

Du Bois, William E. B. 1969. *Souls of Black Folk.* New York: New American Library.

Duany, Jorge. 2002. *Puerto Rican Nation on the Move: Identities on the Island and in the United States.* Chapel Hill: University of North Carolina Press.

Duneier, Mitchell. 1999. *Sidewalk.* New York: Farrar, Straus & Giroux.

Durkheim, Émile. 1965. *The Elementary Forms of the Religious Life.* The Free Press.

Eber, Christine. 1995. *Women and Alcohol in a Highland Maya Town: Water of Hope, Water of Sorrow.* Austin: University of Texas Press.

Ecks, Stefan. 2005. "Pharmaceutical Citizenship: Antidepressant Marketing and the Promise of Demarginalization in India." *Anthropology & Medicine* 12(3): 239–254.

Edin, Kathryn, and Laura Lein. 1997. *Making Ends Meet: How Single Mothers Survive Welfare and Low-Wage Work.* New York: Russell Sage.

Edin, Kathryn, and Rebecca Kissane. 2010. "Poverty and the American Family: A Decade in Review." *Journal of Marriage and Family* 72(3): 460–479.

Edmondson, Jolee. 1994. "An Elegant City in Puerto Rico that Time Almost Forgot." *Smithsonian* 25(5): 64–72.

Ehlers, T. 1991. "Debunking Marianismo: Economic Vulnerability and Survival Strategies Among Guatemalan Wives." *Ethnology* 30: 1–14.

Engel, George. 1977. "Need for a New Medical Model: Challenge for Biomedicine." *Science* 196 (4286): 129–136.

Engle Merry, Sally. 2001. "Rights, Religion and Community: Approaches to Violence Against Women in the Context of Globalization." *Law & Society Review* 35(1): 39–88.

Epele, M. E. 2002. "Gender, Violence and HIV: Women's Survival in the Streets." *Cult. Med. Psychiatry* 26(1): 33–54.

Erikson, Kai. 1976. *Everything in Its Path: Destruction of Community in the Buffalo Creek Flood.* New York: Simon & Schuster.

Espinosa, G. 1999. "El Azteca: Francisco Olazabal and Latino Pentecostal Charisma, Power, and Faith Healing in the Borderlands." *Journal of the American Academy of Religion* 67(3): 597–616.

Estrada Resto, Nilka. 2000. "Rosselló Firma el Nuevo Codigo de Salud Mental." *El Nuevo Dia,* October 3, p. 8.

Fairbanks, Robert. 2009. *How It Works: Recovering Citizens in Post-Welfare Philadelphia.* Chicago: University of Chicago Press.

Farmer, Paul. 1999. *Infections and Inequalities: The Modern Plagues.* Berkeley: University of California.

Fassin, Didier, and Richard Rechtman. 2009. *Empire of Trauma: An Inquiry into the Condition of Victimhood.* Princeton, NJ: Princeton University Press.

Favret-Saada, Jeanne. 1980. *Deadly Words: Witchcraft in the Bocage.* Cambridge: Cambridge University Press.

Feagin, Joe. 2013. *Systemic Racism: A Theory of Oppression.* New York: Routledge.

Findlay, Eileen Suarez. 1999. *Imposing Decency: The Politics of Sexuality and Race in Puerto Rico, 1870–1920.* Durham: Duke University Press.

Flores, Edward. 2013. *God's Gangs: Barrio Ministry, Masculinity, and Gang Recovery.* New York: NYU Press.

Foucault, Michel. 1965. *A History of Insanity in the Age of Reason.* New York: Vintage.

Foucault, Michel. 1976. "17 March 1976." *Society Must Be Defended: Lectures at the College de France 1975–1976,* translated by David Macey. New York: Picador, 239–263.

Foucault, Michel. 1998. *The History of Sexuality: The Will to Knowledge.* London: Penguin.

Frank, Arthur W. 2013. *The Wounded Storyteller: Body, Illness, and Ethics.* Chicago: University of Chicago Press.

Frederick, Marla. 2003. *Between Sundays: Black Women and Everyday Struggles of Faith.* Berkeley: University of California Press.

Freeman, Carla. 2000. *High Tech and High Heels in the Global Economy: Women, Work and Pink-Collar Identities in the Caribbean.* Durham: Duke University Press.

Friedman, M. [n.d.]. "Father, Daughter Fight to Kick Heroin." *El Nuevo Dia*, p. 21.

Fullilove, Mindy. 2004. *Root Shock: How Tearing Up City Neighborhoods Hurts America, and What We Can Do About It.* One World/Ballantine.

Fullilove, Mindy Thompson. 2013. *Urban Alchemy: Restoring Joy in America's Sorted-Out Cities.* NY: New Village Press.

Galanter, Marc. 2005. *Spirituality and the Healthy Mind: Science, Therapy and the Need for Personal Meaning.* NY: Oxford University Press.

Galanter, Marc. 2010. "Spirituality in Psychiatry: A Biopsychosocial Perspective." *Psychiatry: Interpersonal and Biological Processes* 73(2): 145–157.

Galanter, Marc, and Sepehr Hafizi. 2007. "Spirituality and the Healthy Mind." *Psychological Medicine* 37(2): 296–297.

Gallagher, Sally and Christian Smith. 1999. "Contemporary Evangelicals, Families, and Gender." *Gender & Society* 13(2): 211–233.

Garcia, Angela. 2010. *The Pastoral Clinic: Addiction and Dispossession Along the Rio Grande.* Berkeley: University of California Press.

Garcia, Angela. 2015. "Serenity: Violence, Inequality, and Recovery on the Edge of Mexico City." *Medical Anthropology Quarterly* 29(4): 455–472.

García, Freddie, and Ninfa García. 1988. *Outcry in the Barrio.* San Antonio, TX: Freddie Garcia Ministries.

Garcia Rios, Juan Jose. 2000. "El Nuevo Codigo de Salud Mental." *El Vocero* (September) 4: 28.

Garner, Steve. 2007. *Whiteness: An Introduction.* New York: Routledge.

Gell, Alfred. 1992. "The Technology of Enchantment and the Enchantment of Technology." *Anthropology, Art and Aesthetics*, edited by J. Coote and A. Sheldon. Oxford: Clarendon Press.

Gilmore, Margaret and David Gilmore. 1979. " 'Machismo': A Psychodynamic Approach (Spain)." *Journal of Psychological Anthropology* 2(3): 281–299.

Goffman, Erving. 1973. *The Presentation of Self in Everyday Life.* Woodstock, NY: Overlook Press.

Goldsmith, Peter 1989/90. "A Women's Place Is in the Church: Black Pentecostalism on the Georgia Coast." *Journal of Religious Thought* 46(2): 53–69.

Gonzalez de la Rocha, Mercedes and Barbara Gantt. 1995. "The Urban Family and Poverty in Latin America." *Latin American Perspectives* 22(2): 12–31.

González-Wippler, Migene. 1996. *Santería: The Religion, Faith, Rites, Magic.* St. Paul: Llewellyn Publications.

Goodale, Gloria. 1997. "Faith and Family Are Chosen Track for 'Chosen Women.'" *Christian Science Monitor* 89(127): 10.

Goodnough, Abby. 2003. "Two-Front Battle in Puerto Rico; Crime and Apathy." *New York Times* (December 28) 153(52711): 20.

Greenfield, Shelly. 2005. "The Council on Addiction Psychiatry." *American Journal of Psychiatry* 162(2): 416.

Grella, Christine E., and Vandana Joshi. 1999. "Gender Differences in Drug Treatment Careers Among Clients in the National Drug Abuse Treatment Outcome Study." *American Journal of Drug and Alcohol Abuse* 25(3): 385–406.

Gurak, Douglas, and Luis Falcón. 1990. "The Puerto Rican Family and Poverty: Complex Paths to Poor Outcomes." *Breaking Out of the Cycle of Poverty*, edited by the National Puerto Rican Coalition. Washington, DC: National Puerto Rican Coalition.

Gutmann, Matthew. 1996. *The Meanings of Macho: Being a Man in Mexico City.* Berkeley: University of California Press.

Gutmann, Matthew. 2000. "Book Reviews." *Journal of the Royal Anthropological Institute* 6(3): 545.

Hacking, Ian. 1995. "The Looping Effect of Human Kinds." In *Causal Cognition: A Multi-Disciplinary Debate*, edited by Dan Sperber, David Premack, and Ann James Premack. New York: Oxford University Press.

Hamid, Ansley, Richard Curtis, Kate McCoy, Judy McGuire, Alix Conde, William Bushell, and Rose Lindenmayer. 1997. "The Heroin Epidemic in New York City: Current Status and Prognoses." *Journal of Psychoactive Drugs* 29(4): 375–391.

Handman, Courtney. 2015. *Critical Christianity: Translation and Denominational Conflict in Papua New Guinea.* Berkeley: University of California Press.

Hansell, Gregory. 2006. "What is Spiritual Capital?" Economics, Religion, and Conference 2006. August 6. http://www.metanexus.net/essay/what-spiritual-capital-economics-religion-and-conference-2006.

Hansen, Helena. 2005. "Isla Evangelista—A Story of Church and State: Puerto Rico's Faith-Based Initiatives." *Culture, Medicine and Psychiatry* 29(4): 433–456.

Hansen, Helena, and Jonathan M. Metzl. 2017. "New Medicine for the US Health Care System: Training Physicians for Structural Interventions." *Academic Medicine* 92(2): 279–281.

Hanson, Bill, George Beschner, James Walters, and Elliott Bovelle. 1985. *Life with Heroin: Voices from the Inner City.* Lexington, MA: Lexington Books.

Hardesty, M. and T. Black. 1999. "Mothering Through Addiction: A Survival Strategy Among Puerto Rican Addicts." *Qualitative Health Research* 9: 602–620.

Harding, Sandra. 1991. *Whose Science? Whose Knowledge? Thinking from Women's Lives.* Buckingham: Open University Press.

Harding, Susan. 2000. *The Book of Jerry Falwell.* Princeton, NJ: Princeton University Press.

Heath, Deborah, Rayna Rapp, and Karen-Sue Taussig. 2008. "Genetic Citizenship." *A Companion to the Anthropology of Politics*, edited by D. Nugent and J. Vincent. New York: John Wiley and Sons.

Heinonen, Meri. 2004. "Henry Suso and the Divine Knighthood." In *Holiness and Masculinity in the Middle Ages*, edited by P. H. Cullum and Katherine J. Lewis. Cardiff: University of Wales Press.

Hidalgo, Nitza. 1997. "A Layering of Family and Friends." *Education and Urban Society* 30(1): 20–41.

Hooks, Bell. 1990. "Marginality As a Site of Resistance." *Out There: Marginalization and Contemporary Cultures*, edited by R. Ferguson. Cambridge, MA: MIT Press.

Hopgood, E. 1990. "DEA Says Island Cocaine, Heroin Consumption on Rise." *San Juan Star.* December 30.

Hopper, Kim, John Jost, Terri Hay, Susan Welber, and Gary Haugland. 1997. "Homelessness, Severe Mental Illness, and the Institutional Circuit." *Psychiatric Services* 48(5): 659–665.

Hyman, Steven E. 2005. "Addiction: A Disease of Learning and Memory." *American Journal of Psychiatry* 162(8): 1414–1422.

Iannaccone, Laurence. 1990. "Religious Practice: A Human Capital Approach." *Journal for the Scientific Study of Religion* 29(3): 297–314.

IMS. 2012. "IMS Health Market Prognosis: Total Unaudited and Audited Global Pharmaceutical Market by Region." http://www.imshealth.com/deployedfiles/ims/Global/Content /Corporate/Press%20Room/Top-Line%20Market%20Data%20&%20Trends/2011%20 Top-line%20Market%20Data/Regional_Pharma_Market_by_Spending_2011-2016.pdf Accessed January 12, 2014..

Inciardi, James, Dorothy Lockwood, and Anne Pottieger. 1993. *Women and Crack Cocaine.* New York: Macmillan Publishing Company.

Ingoldsby, Bron. 1991. "The Latin American Family: Familism vs. Machismo." *Journal of Comparative Family Studies* 22(1): 57–62.

Isaacson, J. H., M. Fleming, M. Kraus, R. Kahn, and M. Mundt. 2000. "A National Survey of Training in Substance Use Disorders in Residency Programs." *Journal of Studies in Alcohol* 61(6): 912–915.

Jackson, Bruce. 1978. "Deviance As Success: The Double Inversion of Stigmatized Roles." In *The Reversible World: Symbolic Inversion in Art and Society,* edited by Barbara Babcock. Ithaca: Cornell University Press.

Jacobs, Claude and Andrew Kaslow. 1991. *The Spiritualist Churches of New Orleans: Origins, Beliefs, and Rituals of an African-American Religion.* Knoxville: University of Tennessee Press.

Jacobson, Nora. 2004. *In Recovery: The Making of Mental Health Policy.* Nashville: Vanderbilt University Press.

Jenkins, Janis. 2010. *Pharmaceutical Self: The Global Shaping of Experience in Age of Psychopharmacology.* Santa Fe, NM: School of Advanced Research Press.

Johnson, Kevin. 2004. "Puerto Rico Is Dangerous Ground for Police." *USA Today,* November 23.

Julia, Maria and Helen Hartnett. 1999. "Exploring Cultural Issues in Puerto Rican Homelessness." *Cross-Cultural Research* 33(4): 318–341.

Jung, Carl. 1966. *Collected Works of C. G. Jung,* 2nd ed. Vol. 16. Princeton, NJ: Princeton University Press.

Kilmer, Beau, Susan Sohler Everingham, Jonathan Caulkins, Greg Midgette, Rosalie Liccardo Pacula, Peter Reuter, Rachel Burns, Bing Han, and Russell Lundberg. 2014. "What America's Users Spend on Illegal Drugs." *Rand Corporation Research Reports.* https:// www.rand.org/pubs/research_reports/RR534.html.

Kleinman, Arthur. 1988. *The Illness Narratives: Suffering, Healing and the Human Condition.* New York: Basic Books.

Kleinman, Arthur. 2007. *What Really Matters: Living a Moral Life Amidst Uncertainty and Danger.* Oxford: Oxford University Press.

Knight, Franklin. 1990. *The Caribbean: The Genesis of a Fragmented Nationalism.* New York: Oxford University Press.

Lakoff, Andrew. 2005. *Pharmaceutical reason: Knowledge and value in global psychiatry.* Cambridge: Cambridge University Press.

Lalive D'Epinay, Christian. 1969. *"Haven of the Masses." A study of the pentecostal movement in Chile.* London: Lutterworth.

Lamberts Bendroth, Margaret. 1999. "Fundamentalism and the Family: Gender, Culture, and the American Pro-Family Movement." *Journal of Women's History* 10(4): 36–54.

Latin American Herald Tribune. 2012. "Violence Continues in Puerto Rico After Close of Deadliest Year." http://www.laht.com/article.asp?ArticleId=458247&CategoryId=14092. Accessed January 16, 2018.

Lavrin, Ascuncion. 1987. "Women, the Family and Social Change in Latin America." *World Affairs* 150(2): 109–128.

Lawless, Elaine J. 1991. "Rescripting Their Lives and Narratives: Spiritual Life Stories of Pentecostal Women Preachers." *Journal of Feminist Studies in Religion* 7.1: 53–71.

Lawless, Elaine. 2003. "Transforming the Master Narrative: How Women Shift the Religious Subject." *Frontiers* 24(1): 61–75.

Leland, John. 2004 (June 10). "Offering Ministry, and Early Release, to Prisoners." *The New York Times Online.* www.nytimes.com/2004/06/10/national/10CHUR.html. Accessed April 7, 2005.

Lemann, Nicholas. 1991. "The Other Underclass." *Atlantic* 268(6): 96–110.

Lewis, Bradley. 2011. *Narrative Psychiatry: How Stories Can Shape Clinical Practice.* Baltimore: Johns Hopkins University Press.

Lewis, Bradley. 2013. "Mad Fight: Psychiatry and Disability Activism." *The Disability Studies Reader* 4th edition, edited by Lennie Davis. New York: Routledge.

Lewis, Sarah. 2013. "Trauma and the Making of Flexible Minds in the Tibetan Exile Community." *Ethos* 41(3): 313–336.

Lewis, Oscar 1966. *Vida: A Puerto Rican Family in the Culture of Poverty.* New York: Random House.

Leyser, C. 1999. "Masculinity in Flux: Nocturnal Emission and the Limits of Celibacy in the Early Middle Ages." *In Masculinity in Medieval Europe,* edited by D. M. Hadley. London: Addison Wesley Longman Press.

Lindhardt, Martin. 2015. "Men of God: Neo-Pentecostalism and Masculinities in Urban Tanzania." *Religion* 45: 252–272.

Linehan, Marsha, Comtois, Katherine Anne, Murray, Angela, Brown, Milton, Gallop, Robert J., Heard, Heidi L., Korslund, Kathryn E., Tutek, Darren A., Reynolds, Sarah K. and Noam Lindenboim. 2006. "Two-Year Randomized Controlled Trial and Follow-Up of Dialectical Behavior Therapy vs Therapy by Experts for Suicidal Behaviors and Borderline Personality Disorder." *Archives of General Psychiatry* 63(7): 757–766.

Link, Bruce G., and Jo Phelan. 2010. "Social Conditions As Fundamental Causes of Health Inequalities." *Handbook of Medical Sociology* 6: 3–17, edited by C. Bird, P. Conrad, A. Fremont and S. Timmermans. Nashville: Vanderbilt University Press.

Lock, Margaret. 2001. "The Tempering of Medical Anthropology: Troubling Natural Categories." *Medical Anthropology Quarterly* 15(4): 478–492.

Lopez, M. Lisette and Carol Stack. 2002. "Social Capital and the Culture of Power: Lessons from the Field." *In Building Social Capital to Combat Poverty,* edited by Susan Saegert, J. Phillip Thompson, and Mark R. Warren. New York: Russell Sage Foundation Press.

Loreto Mariz, Cecilia. 1998. "Deliverance Ethics: An Analysis of the Discourse of Pentecostals Who Have Recovered from Alcoholism." *In More Than Opium: An Anthropological*

Approach to Latin American and Caribbean Pentecostal Praxis, edited by Barbara Boudewijnse, Andre Droogers, and Frans Kamsteeg. Lanham, MD: The Scarecrow Press.

Luhrmann, Tanya. 2004. "Metakinesis: How God Becomes Intimate in Contemporary U.S. Christianity." *American Anthropologist* 106(3): 518–528.

Luhrmann, Tanya. 2012. *When God Talks Back: Understanding the American Evangelical Relationship with God.* New York: Random House.

Lurie, Peter and Ernest Drucker 1997. "An Opportunity Lost: HIV Infections Associated with Lack of a Needle-Exchange Programme in the USA." *Lancet* 349: 604–608.

MacAndrew, Craig and Robert Edgerton. 1969. *Drunken Comportment: A Social Explanation.* Chicago: Aldine Publishers.

MacRobert, I. 1988. *Black Roots and White Racism of Early Pentecostals in the USA.* London: MacMillan Press.

Mahler, Sarah, Anna Pagano, Yves Labissiere, and Michelle Hamann. Unpublished Manuscript. "Treating Substance Abuse Rehabilitation Programs As 'Cultures': Looking Back to the Future."

Mahmood, Saba. 2004. *Politics of Piety: The Islamic Revival and the Feminist Subject.* Princeton: Princeton University Press.

Makela, Klaus. 1991. "Social and Cultural Preconditions of Alcoholics Anonymous (AA) and Factors Associated with the Strength of AA." *British Journal of Addiction* 86: 1405–1413.

Marsh, Jeanne C., Thomas A. D'Aunno, and Brenda D. Smith. 2000. "Increasing Access and Providing Social Services to Improve Drug Abuse Treatment for Women with Children." *Addiction* 95(8): 1237–1247.

Martin, Bernice. 2001. "The Pentecostal Gender Paradox: A Cautionary Tale for the Sociology of Religion." In *The Blackwell Companion to Sociology of Religion*, edited by Richard Fenn. Malden, MA: Wiley Blackwell.

Martin, David. 1990. *Tongues of Fire: The Pentecostal Revolution in Latin America.* Oxford: Blackwell Publishers.

Martin, Emily. 2006. "The Pharmaceutical Person." *Biosocieties* 1(3): 273–287.

Martin, Luther, Huck Gutman, and Patrick Hutton eds. 1988. *Technologies of the Self: A Seminar with Michel Foucault.* Amherst: University of Massachusetts Press.

Martinez, L. 1998. "El Deterioro de la Familia." *El Nuevo Día*, June 15, p. 49.

Martinez-Fernandez, L. 2000. "Marriage, Protestantism and Religious Conflict in Nineteenth Century Puerto Rico." *Journal of Religious History* 24(3): 263–278.

Marx, Karl. 1937. *The Eighteenth Brumaire of Louis Napoleon. Translated by Saul K. Padover from the German Edition. Prepared by Engels* (1869). Moscow: Progress Publishers.

Maskens, Maïté. 2015. "The Pentecostal Reworking of Male Identities in Brussels: Producing Moral Masculinities." *Etnográfica. Revista do Centro em Rede de Investigação em Antropologia* 19(2): 323–345.

Mateo, M. 1993. "La Familia y el Crimen." *El Nuevo Día*, May 22, p. 65.

Mattingly, Cheryl. 1994. "The Concept of Therapeutic 'Emplotment'." *Social Science & Medicine* 38(6): 811–822.

Mattingly, Cheryl. 2010. *Paradox of Hope: Journeys Through a Clinical Borderland.* Berkeley: University of California Press.

Matviuk, Sergio. 2002. "Pentecostal Leadership Development and Church Growth in Latin America." *Asian Journal of Pentecostal Studies* 5(1): 155–172.

Maurer, Marc and Ryan King. 2007. *Uneven Justice: State Rates of Incarceration by Race and Ethnicity.* Washington, DC: The Sentencing Project.

Mauss, Marcel. 1934. *Techniques of the Body.* New York: Pantheon Books.

McCarraher, Eugene. 2015. "We Have Never Been Disenchanted." *Hedgehog Review* 17(3). http://iasc-culture.org/THR/THR_article_2015_Fall_McCarraher.php.

McLellan, A. T., D. C. Lewis, C. P. O'Brien, H. D. Kleber. 2000. "Drug Dependence: A Chronic Medical Illness." *JAMA* 284: 1689–1694.

Mead, Margaret. 1973. "American Ambivalence Toward Drugs." In *The Politics of Moral Behavior: Prohibition and Drug Abuse,* edited by K. A. Kerr. Reading, MA: Addison-Wesley Publishing Co.

Melendez, I., H. Colon, R. Robles, and J. Pulliza. 1998. "Puerto Rico Substance Abuse Needs Assessment Program: Treatment Capacity Survey Final Results." Mental Health and Anti-Addiction Services Administration, Commonwealth of Puerto Rico.

Merrill, Joseph, Lorna Rhodes, Richard Deyo, Alan Marlatt, and Katharine Bradley. 2002. "Mutual Mistrust in the Medical Care of Drug Users." *Journal of General Internal Medicine* 17: 327–333.

Merry, Sally Engle 2001. "Rights, Religion and Community: Approaches to Violence Against Women in the Context of Globalization." *Law & Society Review* 35(1): 39–88.

Merton, Robert, George Reader, and Patricia Kendall. 1957. *The Student-Physician: Introductory Studies in the Sociology of Medical Education.* Cambridge: Harvard University Press.

Metzl, Jonathan M. 2010. *The Protest Psychosis: How Schizophrenia Became a Black Disease.* New York: Beacon Press.

Metzl, Jonathan and Helena Hansen. 2014. "Structural Competency: Theorizing a New Medical Engagement with Stigma and Inequality." *Social Science and Medicine* 103:76-83.

Mieczkowski, Tom. 1994. "The Experiences of Women Who Sell Crack: Some Descriptive Data from the Detroit Crack Ethnography Project." *Journal of Drug Issues* 24: 227–249.

Milham, W. 1951. *Latin America: Expanding Horizons. The Movement for World Evangelization.* Mildmay Centre, London: Founder's Loge.

Millan Pabon, C. 1993. "Pierden la Carrera Contra la Adiccion." *El Nuevo Día,* October 31, p. 4.

Miller, Norman S., Lorinda Sheppard, Christopher Colenda, and Jed Magen. 2001. "Why Physicians Are Unprepared to Treat Patients Who Have Alcohol and Drug-Related Disorders." *Academic Medicine* 7: 410–418.

Miller, William, and Stephen Rollnick. 1992. *Motivational Interviewing: Preparing People to Change Addictive Behavior.* New York: The Guilford Press.

Mills, Robert. 2004. "The Significance of the Tonsure." In *Holiness and Masculinity in the Middle Ages,* edited by P. H. Cullum and Katherine J. Lewis. Cardiff: University of Wales Press.

Mintz, Sidney. 1960. *Worker in the Cane: A Puerto Rican Life History.* New Haven: Yale University Press.

Mokdad, Ali, James Marks, Donna Stroup, and Julie Gerberding. 2004. "Actual Causes of Death in the United States, 2000." *JAMA* 291(10): 1238–1245.

Mooney, Margarita. 2009. *Faith Makes Us Live: Surviving and Thriving in the Haitian Diaspora.* Berkeley: University of California Press.

Moore, Donald. 1969. *Puerto Rico Para Cristo: A History of the Progress of the Evangelical Missions on the Island of Puerto Rico.* Cuenravaca, Mexico: Sondeos No. 43, Centro Intercultural de Documentacion.

Moore, Donald. 1998. "Religion." In *The American Presence in Puerto Rico*. Hato Rey, Puerto Rico: Institute of Puerto Rican Culture.

Morales, Edmundo. 1989. *Cocaine: White Gold Rush in Peru*. Tucson: University of Arizona Press.

Morjaria, Asesha and Jim Orford. 2002. "The Role of Religion and Spirituality in Recovery from Drink Problems: A Qualitative Study of Alcoholics Anonymous Members and South Asian Men." *Addiction Research and Theory* 10(3): 225–256.

Morris, Lydia. 1979. "Women Without Men: Domestic Organization and the Welfare State As Seen in a Coastal Community of Puerto Rico." *British Journal of Sociology* 30(3): 322–340.

Morse, J. 1989. *Qualitative Nursing Research: A Contemporary Dialogue*. Rockville, MD: Aspen Publishers.

Muehlebach, Andrea. 2013. "On Precariousness and the Ethical Imagination: The Year 2012 in Sociocultural Anthropology." *American Anthropologist* 115(2): 297–311.

Mulligan, Jessica M. 2014. *Unmanageable Care: An Ethnography of Health Care Privatization in Puerto Rico*. New York: NYU Press.

Murphy, Sheigla. 1987. "Intravenous Drug Use and AIDS: Notes on the Social Economy of Needle Sharing." *Contemp. Drug Problems* 14: 373.

Murray, Jacqueline. 2004. "Masculinizing Religious Life: Sexual Prowess, the Battle for Chastity and Monastic Identity." In *Holiness and Masculinity in the Middle Ages*, edited by P. H. Cullum and Katherine J. Lewis. Cardiff: University of Wales Press.

Musto, David. 1973. *The American Disease: Origins of Narcotic Control*. New Haven: Yale University Press.

Navarro, Mireya. 1995. "Puerto Rico Reeling Under Scourge of Drugs and Rising Gang Violence." *New York Times*, July 23, 144(50131): 22.

New York Times. 1996a. "Big Housing Project Is Raided by Troops." March 20, 145(50372): A15.

New York Times. 1996b. "Cocaine Concealed in Candy Boxes." April 2, 145(50385): B3.

Newman, Katherine. 2002. "No Shame: The View from the Left Bank." *American Journal of Sociology* 107(6): 1577–1599.

Nickerson, Peter. 2001. "A Poetics and Politics of Possession: Taiwanese Spirit-Medium Cults and Autonomous Popular Cultural Space." *Positions: East Asia Cultures Critique* 9(1): 187–217.

Niezen, Ronald. 1997. "Health and Conversion: Medical Evangelism in James Bay Cree Society." *Ethnohistory* 44(3): 463–491.

Nuevo Día, El. 1990. "Mayor el Consumo de la Heroina" [front-cover title for a series of articles]. July 29, p. 1.

O'Neill, Kevin Lewis. 2015. *Secure the Soul: Christian Piety and Gang Prevention in Guatemala*. Berkeley: University of California Press.

Olson, Elizabeth. 2003. "Big Puerto Rico Bank Settles Money Laundering Case." *New York Times*. January 17, 152(52366): C6.

Ong, Aiwa. 1987. *Spirits of Resistance and Capitalist Discipline: Women Factory Workers in Malaysia*. Albany: State University of New York.

Ortiz, M. 1998. "Urgen Reformular los Valores de la Familia." *El Nuevo Día*, January 22, p. 26.

Padilla, M. 1992. "Puerto Rico Roofs Cover More People." *San Juan Star*, February 24, p. B15.

Pantojas-Garcia, Emilio. 1990. *Development Strategies As Ideology: Puerto Rico's Export-Led Industrialization Experience.* Boulder, CO: Lynne Rienner Publishers.

Paone, Denise, Wendy Chavkin, Ilene Willets, Patricia Friedmann, and Don Des Jarlais. 1992. "The Impact of Sexual Abuse: Implications for Drug Treatment." *Journal of Women's Health* 1(2): 149–153.

Pares Arroyo, M. 2001. "Mas de 30 Mil se Iniciaron en las Drogas en el 2000." *El Nuevo Día,* November 8, p. 16.

Parker, Shafer. 1995. "Christ's Point Men: The Yuppie Men's Movement Dies, While a Christian One Sweeps North America." *Alberta Report* 22(11): 40.

Peele, Stanton. 1989. *The Diseasing of America.* Lexington, MA: Lexington Books, D.C. Heath and Company.

Pescosolido, Bernice A., Jack K. Martin, J. Scott Long, Tait R. Medina, Jo C. Phelan, and Bruce G. Link. 2010. "A Disease Like Any Other? A Decade of Change in Public Reactions to Schizophrenia, Depression, and Alcohol Dependence." *American Journal of Psychiatry* 167(11): 1321–1330.

Pessar, Patricia. 1996. *A Visa for a Dream: Dominicans in the United States.* Boston: Pearson Allyn and Bacon Publishers.

Pessaro, Joanne. 1993. *The Unequal Homeless: Men on the Streets, Women in Their Place.* New York: Routledge.

Petryna, Adriana. 2013. *Life Exposed: Biological Citizens After Chernobyl.* Princeton: Princeton University Press.

Pew Forum on Religion and Public Life. 2006. "Overview: Pentecostalism in Latin America." Electronic document. http://pewforum.org/surveys/pentecostal/latinamerica/. Accessed January 16, 2018.

Pitts, Walter. 1993. *Old Ship of Zion: The Afro-Baptist Ritual in the African Diaspora.* New York: Oxford University Press.

Poitevin, Rene Francisco. 2000. "Political Surveillance, State Repression, and Class Resistance: The Puerto Rican Experience." *Social Justice* 27(3): 89–100.

Ponti, G. 1993. "Heroin: Drug of Choice and of Death." *San Juan Star,* September 6, p. 6.

Ponti, G. 1994. "A Visit to the Nightmare World of Addiction." *San Juan Star,* November 11, p. 44.

Potthast-Jutkeit, Barbara. 1997. "The History of Family and Colonialism: Examples from Africa, Latin America, and the Caribbean." *History of the Family* 2(2): 115–122.

Prochaska, J. O. and C. C. DiClemente. 2005. "The Transtheoretical Approach." In *Handbook of Psychotherapy Integration,* 2nd ed., edited by J. C. Norcross and M. R. Goldfried. New York: Oxford University Press.

Pullum, Stephen. 1999. *"Foul Demons, Come Out!" The Rhetoric of Twentieth Century American Faith Healing.* Westport, CT: Praeger Press.

Putnam, Robert. 2000. *Bowling Alone: America's Declining Social Capital.* New York: Simon and Schuster.

Rabelo, Miriam C. M., Sueli Ribeiro Mota, and Claudio Roberto Almeida. 2009. "Cultivating the Senses and Giving in to the Sacred: Notes on Body and Experience Among Pentecostal Women in Salvador, Brazil." *Journal of Contemporary Religion* 24.1: 1–18.

Rabinow, Paul. 1996. *Essays on the Anthropology of Reason.* Princeton: Princeton University Press.

Raboteau, Albert. 1978. *Slave Religion: The "Invisible Institution" in the Antebellum South.* New York: Oxford University Press.

Rainwater, L. 1964. "Marital Sexuality in Four Cultures of Poverty." *Journal of Marriage and the Family* 4: 457–466.

Ramirez, Rafael. 1999. *What it Means to Be a Man: Reflections on Puerto Rican Masculinity.* New Brunswick, NJ: Rutgers University Press.

Ramírez Alers, Betzalda. 2000a. "Raschke Detiene Codigo Salud Mental." *El Vocero,* September 13, p. 3.

Ramírez Alers, Betzalda. 2000b. "Voto de Ultima Hora al Polemico Proyecto." *El Vocero,* September 19, p. 2.

Rapp, Rayna. 2011. "Reproductive Entanglements: Body, State and Culture in the Dys/ Regulation of Child-Bearing." *Social Research* 78: 693–718.

Rapping, Elayne. 1997. "There's Self-Help and Then There's Self-Help." *Social Policy* 27(3): 56–62.

Ratner, M. S. (ed.). 1992. *Crack Pipe As Pimp: An Ethnographic Investigation of Crack-for-Sex Exchanges.* New York: MacMillan.

Rebhun, L. A. 2005. "Families in Brazil." In *Families in Global Perspective,* edited by Uwe Gelen and Jaipaul Roopnarine. Boston, MA: Allyn and Bacon.

Reihling, Hanspeter. 2015. *Spirit and Sentiment: Affective Trajectories of Religious Being in Urban Africa.* International Conference of the Research Network on Religion, AIDS and Social Transformation in Africa (RASTA). Berlin: Freie Universität.

Reinarman, Craig. 1979. "Moral Entrepreneurs and Political Economy: Historical and Ethnographic Notes on the Construction of the Cocaine Menace." *Crime, Law and Social Change* 3(3): 225–254.

Rey, Jeanne. 2013. "Mermaids and Spirit Spouses: Rituals As Technologies of Gender in Transnational African Pentecostal Spaces." *Religion and Gender* 3.1: 60–75.

Reyes, J. O. 2001. "La Familia Puertorriqueña y el Cambio Político." *Claridad,* March 16–22, p. 36–37.

Richard, Alan, David Bell, and Jerry Carlson. 2000. "Individual Religiosity, Moral Community, and Drug User Treatment." *Journal for the Scientific Study of Religion* 39(2): 240–246.

Riley, Kevin Jack. 1996. *Snow Job? The War Against International Cocaine Trafficking.* New Brunswick: Transaction Publishers.

Rivera, Marcia. 1986. "The Development of Capitalism in Puerto Rico and the Incorporation of Women into the Labor Force." *The Puerto Rican Woman: Perspectives on Culture, History and Society,* edited by Edna Acosta-Belén. New York: Praeger.

Robbins, Joel. 2004. "The Globalization of Pentecostal and Charismatic Christianity." *Annual Review of Anthropology* 33: 117–143.

Robbins, Joel. 2009. "Is the Trans in Transnational the Trans in Transcendent? On Alterity and the Sacred in the Age of Globalization." In *Transnational Transcendence: Essays on Religion and Globalization,* edited by T. Csordas. Berkeley: University of California Press.

Robbins, Joel. 2013. "Beyond the Suffering Subject: Toward an Anthropology of the Good." *Journal of the Royal Anthropological Institute* (N.S.) 19: 447–462.

Roberts, Dorothy. 2011. *Fatal invention: How science, politics, and big business re-create race in the twenty-first century.* New York: The New Press.

Rodríguez de Rivera. 1995. "Un nuevo comienzo en la familia." *El Nuevo Día* January 26, p.71.

Rodríguez, Jessica, Helena Hansen, Bendek Hansen, George, Defendini Tony, Nilde and Juan Defendini. 2003. "Effectiveness of Faith-Based Treatment for Substance Abuse: Clinical Comparison in a Puerto Rican Sample." Poster presented at the American Public Health Association Meeting, November 19, San Francisco, California.

Rodríguez, Magdalys. 2000. "Fuera la Definición de que el Adicto es un Enfermo." *El Nuevo Dia*, September 20, p. 8.

Roebuck, David. 1998. "Loose the Women." *Christian History* 17(2): 38–40.

Romberg, Raquel. 2003. *Witchcraft and Welfare: Spiritual Capital and the Business of Magic in Modern Puerto Rico.* University of Texas Press, Austin.

Room, Robin, and Thomas Greenfield, 1993. "Alcoholics Anonymous, Other 12-Step Movements and Psychotherapy in the US Population, 1990." *Addiction* 88: 555–562.

Rosario Urrutia, Mayra and Maria de Fatima Barcelo Miller. 1989. *Temperancia y Sufragismo en el Puerto Rico del Siglo XX.* Santurce, Puerto Rico: Centro de Investigacion Academicas, Universidad del Sagrado Corazon.

Rose, Nikolas. 1998. *Inventing Ourselves: Psychology, Power, and Personhood.* Cambridge: Cambridge University Press.

Rose, Nikolas. 2003. "Neurochemical Selves." *Society* November/December: 46–59.

Roseberry, William. 1978. "Historical Materialism and the People of Puerto Rico." *Revista/ Review Interamericana* 8(1): 26–36.

Rosenbaum, Marsha. 1981. *Women on Heroin.* New Brunswick: Rutgers University Press.

Rouse, Carolyn. 2004. *Engaged Surrender: African American Women and Islam.* Berkeley: UC Press.

Rouse, Carolyn. 2009. *Uncertain Suffering: Racial Health Care Disparities and Sickle Cell Disease.* Berkeley: University of California Press.

Safa, Helen. 1974. *The Urban Poor of Puerto Rico.* New York: Holt, Rinehart and Winston.

Safa, Helen. 1986. "Female Unemployment and the Social Reproduction of the Puerto Rican Working Class." In *The Puerto Rican Woman: Perspectives on Culture, History and Society,* edited by Edna Acosta-Belén. New York: Praeger.

Safa, Helen. 1995a. *The Myth of the Male Breadwinner.* Boulder, CO: Westview Press.

Safa, Helen. 1995b. "Economic Restructuring and Gender Subordination." *Latin American Perspectives* 22(2): 32–50.

Safa, Helen. 2003. "Changing Forms of U.S. Hegemony in Puerto Rico: The Impact on the Family and Sexuality." *Urban Anthropology* 32(1): 7–40.

Said, Edward. 1978. *Orientalism.* New York: Vintage.

Salles, Vania and Rodolfo Tuiran. 1997. "The Family in Latin America: A Gender Approach." *Current Sociology* 45(1): 141–152.

Sanchez-Walsh, Arlene. 2003. *Latino Pentecostal Identity: Evangelical Faith, Self, and Society.* New York: Columbia University Press.

Sanders, Cheryl. 1996. *Saints in Exile: The Holiness-Pentecostal Experience in African American Religion and Culture.* New York: Oxford University Press.

Santiago, W. 1993. "Multiplying in Smaller Numbers." *San Juan Star*, October 31, p. F3.

Saul, Jack. 2013. *Collective Trauma, Collective Healing: Promoting Community Resilience in the Aftermath of Disaster.* New York: Routledge.

Saulnier, Christine. 1996. "Images of the Twelve-Step Model, and Sex and Love Addiction in an Alcohol Intervention Group for Black Women." *Journal of Drug Issues* 26(1): 95–124.

Saunders, George. 1995. "The Crisis of Presence in Italian Pentecostal Conversion." *American Ethnologist* 22(2): 324–340.

Scarry, Elaine. 1985. *The Body in Pain: The Making and Unmaking of the World.* New York: Oxford University Press.

Scheper-Hughes, Nancy and Philippe I. Bourgois, eds. 2004. *Violence in War and Peace.* Oxford: Blackwell.

Sedgwick, Eve Kosofsky. 1993. *Tendencies.* Durham: Duke University Press.

Sharkey, Patrick. 2013. *Stuck in Place: Urban Neighborhoods and the End of Progress Toward Racial Equality.* Chicago: University of Chicago Press.

Shoichet, Catherine. 2012. "Puerto Rico: A Forgotten Front in America's Drug War?" CNN. June 10. http://www.cnn.com/2012/06/09/justice/puerto-rico-drug-trafficking/index.html.

Shkilnyk, Anastasia. 1985. *A Poison Stronger Than Love: The Destruction of an Ojibwa Community.* New Haven: Yale University Press.

Singer, Merrill. 1996. "A Dose of Drugs, a Touch of Violence, a Case of AIDS: Conceptualizing the SAVA Syndemic." *Free Inquiry in Creative Sociology* 24(2): 99–110.

Singer, Merrill. 2008. *Drugs and Development: The Global Impact on Sustainable Growth and Human Rights.* Long Grove, IL: Waveland Press.

Singer, Merrill, Freddie Valentin, Hans Baer, and Jia Zhongke. 1992. "Why Does Juan Garcia Have a Drinking Problem? The Perspective of Critical Medical Anthropology." *Medical Anthropology* 14: 77–108.

Southwick, Steven and Sally Satel. 1990. "Exploring the Meanings of Substance Abuse: An Important Dimension of Early Work with Borderline Patients." *American Journal of Psychotherapy* 44(1): 61–68.

Spicer, Paul. 2001. "Culture and the Restoration of Self Among Former American Indian Drinkers." *Social Science and Medicine* 53: 227–240.

Sprinkle, H., C. Parkin, J. Cintron, C. Lokey, E. May, and A. Rice. 1964. *Spanish Doorways: American Methodists and the Evangelical Mission Among Spanish-Speaking Neighbors.* New York: World Outlook Press.

Stack, Carol. 1974. *All Our Kin: Strategies for Survival in a Black Community.* New York: Harper and Row.

Stein, Howard 1990. "In What Systems Do Alcohol and Chemical Addictions Make Sense? Clinical Ideologies and Practices As Cultural Metaphors." *Social Science and Medicine* 30(9): 987–1000.

Stevens, E. 1973a. "The Prospects for a Women's Liberation Movement in Latin America." *Journal of Marriage and the Family* 35: 313–321.

Stevens, E. 1973b. "Machismo and Marianismo." *Society* 10: 57–63.

Steward, Julian, Robert Manners, Eric Wolf, Elena Seda Padilla, Sidney Mintz, and Raymond Scheele. 1956. *The People of Puerto Rico: A Study in Social Anthropology.* Urbana, IL: University of Illinois Press.

Stewart, Kathleen. 1996. *A Space by the Side of the Road: Cultural Poetics in an "Other" America.* Princeton: Princeton University Press.

Stoll, David. 1990. *Is Latin America Turning Protestant? The Politics of Evangelical Growth.* Berkeley: University of California Press.

Strang, John, Jim McCambridge, David Best, Tracy Beswick, Jenny Bearn, Sian Rees, and Michael Gossop. 2003. "Loss of Tolerance and Overdose Mortality After Inpatient Opiate Detoxification: Follow Up Study." *British Medical Journal* 326: 959–960.

Stycos, J. M. 1955. *Family and Fertility in Puerto Rico, A Study of the Lower Income Group.* New York: Columbia University Press.

Stycos, J. M. 1965. "Female Employment and Fertility in Lima, Peru." *Milbank Fund Quarterly* 43: 42–54.

Suarez, M. 1995. "Drug Addiction Grips Island, Becomes Way of Life for the Poor." *San Juan Star,* July 3, p. 3.

Substance Abuse and Mental Health Administration (SAMHSA). 2001. "SAMHSA Grant Awards FY 2000/FY 2001." Electronic document. www.samhsa.gov/funding/funding .html. Accessed June 6, 2003.

Substance Abuse and Mental Health Services Administration (SAMHSA). 2004. "Results from the 2003 National Survey on Drug Use and Health: National Findings" (Office of Applied Studies, NSDUH Series H–25, DHHS Publication No. SMA 04–3964). Rockville, MD.

Substance Abuse and Mental Health Services Administration (SAMHSA). 2012. *SAMHSA's Working Definition of Recovery.* Rockville, MD: United States Department of Health and Human Services. https://store.samhsa.gov/product/SAMHSA-s-Working-Definition-of-Recovery/PEP12-RECDEF.

Substance Abuse and Mental Health Administration (SAMHSA). 2014. *Trauma Informed Care in Behavioral Health Services.* Rockville, MD: United States Department of Health and Human Services.

Swartz, David. 1997. *Culture and Power: The Sociology of Pierre Bourdieu.* Chicago: University of Chicago Press.

Taussig, J. A., Weinstein, B., Burris, S., and T. S. Jones. 2000. "Syringe Laws and Pharmacy Regulations Are Structural Constraints on HIV Prevention in the U.S." *AIDS* 14: S47–S51 Supplement 1.

Taussig, Michael. 1980. *The Devil and Commodity Fetishism in Latin America.* Chapel Hill: University of North Carolina Press.

Taussig, Michael. 1987. *Shamanism, Colonialism and the Wild Man: A Study in Terror and Healing.* University of Chicago Press, Chicago.

Taylor, Avril. 1993. *Women Drug Users: An Ethnography of a Female Injecting Community.* Oxford: Clarendon Press.

Taylor, Charles. 1992. *The Ethics of Authenticity.* Cambridge, MA: Harvard University Press.

Thiher, Allen. 2004. *Revels in Madness: Insanity in Medicine and Literature.* Ann Arbor, MI: University of Michigan Press.

Thornton, Brendan Jamal. 2013. "Residual Masculinity and the Cultivation of Negative-Charisma in a Caribbean Pentecostal Community." *The Anthropology of Religious Charisma.* Palgrave Macmillan US. 117–143.

Tiano, Susan. 2001. "From Victims to Agents: A New Generation of Literature on Women in Latin America." *Latin American Research Review* 36(3): 183–203.

Torregrossa M., P. Corlett, and J. Taylor. 2011. "Aberrant Learning and Memory in Addiction." *Neurobiol. Learn Mem.* 96(4): 609–623.

Torres, Arlene. 1998. "La Gran Familia Puertorriquena 'El Prieta de Belda' (The Great Puerto Rican Family is Really Black)." In Arlene Torres and Norman E. Whitten, Jr. *Blackness in Latin America and the Caribbean*, Volume II. Bloomington, IN: Indiana University Press.

Tuchman, Ellen. 2010. "Women and Addiction: The Importance of Gender Issues in Substance Abuse Research." *Journal of Addictive Diseases* 29(2): 127–138.

Tuten, Michelle and Hendrée E. Jones. 2003. "A Partner's Drug-Using Status Impacts Women's Drug Treatment Outcome. *Drug and Alcohol Dependence* 70(3): 327–330.

U.S. Census Bureau. 2001. "Puerto Rico Population Estimates and Components of Growth: 2000–2001." Electronic document. www.census.gov/ipc/www/pr2001.html. Accessed November 6, 2010.

U.S. Census Bureau. 2003. "The Hispanic Population in the United States: March 2002." Electronic document. www.census.gov/prod/2003pubs/p20-545.pdf. Accessed January 16, 2018.

U.S. Department of Justice. October 2005. "Bureau of Justice Statistics Bulletin."

U.S. Drug Enforcement Administration (U.S. DEA). 1997. "DEA Congressional Testimony before the Subcommittee on National Security, International Affairs and Criminal Justice, July 17, 1997." Electronic document. www.usdoj.gov/dea/pubs/cngrtest/ct970717.htm.

U.S. Drug Enforcement Agency (U.S. DEA). 2002. "Operation SOS II: DEA Dismantles Seven Violent Drug Trafficking Organizations in Ponce, Puerto Rico." Electronic document. https://www.dea.gov/pubs/states/newsrel/2002/carib101502.html. Accessed January 16, 2018.

Vaillant, George 1983. *The Natural History of Alcoholism*. Cambridge: Harvard University Press.

Valdivia, Yadira 1999. "Privatizan la Salud Mental." *El Nuevo Dia*, May 13, p. 25.

Valdivia, Yadira 2000a. "ASSMCA Dice Debe Incluir Adictos." *El Nuevo Dia*, n.d.

Valdivia, Yadira 2000b. "Pobre Estado Mental Para La Ley." *El Nuevo Dia*, n.d.

Valdivia, Yadira 2000c. "Acusan a los Legisladores de Sucumbir Ante Grupos Religiosos." *El Nuevo Dia*, September 20, p. 12.

Valdivia, Yadira 2000d. "A Nivelar Cubiertas Para Males Fisicos y Mentales." *El Nuevo Dia*, August 27, p. 14.

Valverde, Marianna. 1998. *Diseases of the Will: Alcoholism and the Dilemmas of Freedom*. New York: Cambridge University Press.

Van de Kamp, L. J. 2011. "Violent Conversion: Brazilian Pentecostalism and the Urban Pioneering of Women in Mozambique." Dissertation. Amsterdam: Vrije Universiteit.

Varela, L. 1992. "Alrededor de 72 mil Adictos en Puerto Rico." *El Nuevo Día*, July 17 p. 14.

Varela, Luis 2000. "Alegan Reforma Empeoro Servicios Salud Mental." *El Vocero*, November 27: 9.

Vastag, Brian 2003. "Addiction Poorly Understood by Clinicians: Experts Say Attitudes, Lack of Knowledge Hinder Treatment." *JAMA* 290(10): 1299–1304.

Verter, Bradford. 2003. "Spiritual Capital: Theorizing Religion with Bourdieu and Against Bourdieu." *Sociological Theory* 21(2): 150–174.

Victory Outreach Ministries. 2003. *Sonny's Biography*. Electronic Document. www.sonnyarguinzoni.org/biography.asp.

Wacquant, Loïc. 2002. "Scrutinizing the Street: Poverty, Morality, and the Pitfalls of Urban Ethnography." *American Journal of Sociology* 107(6): 1468–1533.

Wallace, Anthony. 1956. "Revitalization Movements: Some Theoretical Considerations for Their Comparative Study." *American Anthropologist* 58(2): 264–281.

Wallace, J. M. 1999. "The Social Ecology of Addiction: Race, Risk, and Resilience." *Pediatrics* 103(5, Pt. 2), 1122–1227.

Walton, Jonathan. 2009. *Watch This! The Ethics and Aesthetics of Black Televangelism.* New York: NYU Press.

Warner, Greg. 2004. "Pentecostals Lead Modest Growth in U.S. Church Membership." Associated Press, March 16.

Washington Office on Latin America. 2002. "Drugs, Democracy and Human Rights Project: U.S. Law Enforcement Overview, Puerto Rico." Electronic document. http://www.wola.org /publications/ddhr_law_enforcement_overview_pr.htm#_ftnref5. Accessed February 12, 2005.

Watson, Dennis. 2012. "The Evolving Understanding of Recovery: What the Sociology of Mental Health Have to Offer?" *Humanity & Society* 36(4):290-308.

Watts, Linda, and Sara Gutierres. 1997. "A Native American-Based Cultural Model of Substance Dependency and Recovery." *Human Organization* 56(1): 9–18.

Weber, Max. 1930. *The Protestant Ethic and the Spirit of Capitalism.* New York: George, Allen & Unwin.

Weber, Max. 1958. *The Protestant Ethic and the Spirit of Capitalism.* New York: Scribner's Press.

Weber, Max. 1978. *Economy and Society: An Outline of Interpretive Sociology.* Berkeley: University of California Press.

Weisskoff, Richard. 1985. *Factories and Food Stamps: The Puerto Rican Model of Development.* Baltimore: Johns Hopkins University Press.

Weppner, Robert. 1983. *The Untherapeutic Community: Organizational Behavior in a Failed Addiction Treatment Program.* Lincoln: University of Nebraska Press.

Westmeier, Karl-Wilhelm. 1999. *Protestant Pentecostalism in Latin America.* Madison, WI: Fairleigh Dickinson University Press.

Whitehead, Harriet. 1987. *Renunciation and Reformulation: A Study of Conversion in an American Sect.* Ithaca: Cornell University Press.

Wilkerson, David, John Sherrill, and Elizabeth Sherrill. 1963. *The Cross and the Switchblade.* New York: Pyramid Publications and Teen Challenge.

Wilkinson, Iain. 2005. *Suffering: A Sociological Introduction.* Cambridge: Polity Press.

Wilkinson, Iain, and Arthur Kleinman. 2016. *A Passion for Society: How We Think About Human Suffering.* Berkeley: University of California Press.

Williams, Grant. 2003. "$1-Bllion Proposed to Train Mentors and Help Drug and Alcohol Addicts." *Chronicle of Philanthropy* 15(8): 31.

Williams, Raymond. 1975. *The Country and the City.* Oxford: Oxford University Press.

Williams, Raymond. 1977. *Marxism and Literature.* Oxford: Oxford University Press.

Williams, Terry. 1989. *Cocaine Kids: The Inside Story of a Teenaged Drug Ring.* Reading, MA: Addison-Wesley Publishing Company.

Wilson, William Julius. 1996. *When Work Disappears: The New World of the Urban Poor.* New York: Knopf Publishers.

Wolseth, Jon. 2011. *Jesus and the Gang: Youth Violence and Christianity in Urban Honduras.* Phoenix: University of Arizona Press.

Zhang, Zhiwei, Friedmann, Peter, Gerstein, Dean. 2003. "Does Retention in Treatment Matter? Treatment Duration and Improvement in Drug Use." *Addiction* 98(5):673–685.

Zsembik, Barbara and Zobeida Bonilla. 2001. "Eldercare and the Changing Family in Puerto Rico." *Journal of Family Issues* 21(5): 653–676.

INDEX